T3-BOD-734

LITERATURE AND THE URBAN EXPERIENCE

Literature
&
the Urban Experience

Essays on the City and Literature
Edited by Michael C. Jaye and
Ann Chalmers Watts

Rutgers University Press
New Brunswick, New Jersey

FERNALD LIBRARY
COLBY-SAWYER COLLEG.
NEW LONDON, N.H. 0325

Permission from the following publishers to use excerpts from selected poems is gratefully acknowledged.

Reprinted by permission of Atheneum Publishers, Inc. From *They Feed They Lion* by Philip Levine. Copyright © 1972 by Philip Levine.

Reprinted by permission of City Lights Booksellers and Publishers. From *Howl and Other Poems* by Allen Ginsberg. Copyright © 1956, 1959 by Allen Ginsberg.

Reprinted by permission of Farrar, Straus and Giroux, Inc., and Faber and Faber Ltd. From *Day by Day* by Robert Lowell. Copyright © 1975, 1976, 1977 by Robert Lowell. From *For the Union Dead* by Robert Lowell. Copyright © 1956, 1960, 1961, 1962, 1963, 1964 by Robert Lowell. From *Life Studies* by Robert Lowell. Copyright © 1956, 1959 by Robert Lowell. From *Notebook*, Third Edition, revised and expanded, by Robert Lowell. Copyright © 1967, 1968, 1969, 1970 by Robert Lowell.

Reprinted by permission of Harcourt Brace Jovanovich, Inc. Excerpts from *Lord Weary's Castle* by Robert Lowell. Copyright © 1946, 1974 by Robert Lowell.

Reprinted by permission of Harcourt Brace Jovanovich, Inc., and Faber and Faber Ltd. From "The Wasteland," in *Collected Poems: 1909–1962* by T. S. Eliot. Copyright © 1964 by Harcourt Brace Jovanovich, publisher.

Reprinted by permission of Jobete Music Company, Inc., and Black Bull Music, Inc. From "Living for the City" by Stevie Wonder. Copyright © 1973 by Jobete Music Company, Inc.

Reprinted by permission of New Directions Publishing Corporation and Faber and Faber Ltd. From *Collected Early Poems of Ezra Pound* by Ezra Pound. Copyright © 1976 by The Trustees of the Ezra Pound Literary Property Trust.

Library of Congress Cataloging in Publication Data

Main entry under title:
    Literature and the urban experience.
    Based on the papers presented at the Conference on Literature and the Urban Experience, held at Rutgers University, Newark, in April 1980.

    1. American literature—History and criticism—Congresses. 2. Cities and towns in literature—Congresses. 3. Literature and society—Congresses. I. Jaye, Michael C., 1941–   . II. Watts, Ann Chalmers. III. Conference on Literature and the Urban Experience (1980: Rutgers University, Newark)

PS169.C57L5   810'.9'321732   81–5857
ISBN 0–8135–0929–7   AACR2
ISBN 0–8135–0930–0 (pbk.)

Copyright © 1981 by Rutgers,
The State University of New Jersey
All rights reserved
Manufactured in the United States of America

The publication of this book was aided by a grant from the New Jersey Committee for the Humanities.

Contents

Acknowledgments

The editors are deeply grateful to numerous individuals and organizations for their generous assistance to the Conference on Literature and the Urban Experience. First and foremost, we are indebted to Dr. Peter J. Ventimiglia, without whom the Conference, and therefore these essays, would never have existed. Among many other individuals, we are grateful to David A. Cayer, Henry A. Christian, Kay Henson, Madelyn R. Hoffman, Mary Lou Motto, Miriam Murphy, Norman Samuels, Nathan Shoehalter, Carl R. Sonn, Donald H. Van Lenten, James E. Young, Sarah Young, and Karen Way.

The support and participation of many agencies, organizations, foundations, and corporations helped make the Conference possible. To all of them we express our gratitude. Rutgers, The State University of New Jersey, The Newark Museum, and The Newark Public Library were co-sponsors of the Conference. The Conference was funded in part by a grant from The National Endowment for the Humanities, a Federal agency established by Congress. It was also funded by a grant from The New Jersey Committee for the Humanities, with contributing support from The New Jersey State Council on the Arts, the American Hoechst Corporation, Automatic Data Processing Company, The Bell System in New Jersey, Geraldine R. Dodge Foundation, The Fund for New Jersey, The Greater Newark Chamber of Commerce, Hoffmann-La Roche, Incorporated, International Telephone and Telegraph Company, Merck & Co., Inc., Mutual Benefit Life Insurance Company, The Prudential Foundation, Public Service Electric & Gas Company of New Jersey, The Rockefeller Foundation, Schering-Plough Corporation, and Victoria Foundation, Incorporated.

Introduction

The poem and essays in this volume were first presented in different sequence and in somewhat different form at the Conference on Literature and the Urban Experience at Rutgers, The State University of New Jersey, in Newark, on April 17–19, 1980. A word about the Conference, therefore, and the order of the essays included here precedes a brief guide to the essays themselves and should illustrate the nature and purposes of the collection.

The Conference brought together in one place for a few days many distinguished poets, novelists, dramatists, essayists, critics, and educators to consider the reciprocal relations of literature and the city. Several participants were asked to present original papers; others, to lead discussion or contribute their ideas orally to public discourse on this topic. All participants knew they would be addressing an audience, for the most part, from occupations outside academia.

Although the participants were not further restricted than by general topic and general audience, they were encouraged to consider the vital complexity characteristic of relations between literature and urban life. Cities have so strongly suggested particular imagery and themes, and so shaped the attitudes and feelings revealed in many great novels, plays, and poems, that the very existence of these works of literature depends on the existence of the city. But these same novels, plays, and poems, have so interfused the experience of reading with the experience of living that they form our understanding of the city: thus they influence what we do and what we want to do with our cities, and how we live and how we want to live in them. The literature of the city yields experiences that become integral parts of our lives through time; we seek to revisit, discover, locate, avoid, or create those imaginative impressions and journeys anew.

The essays in this book, as might have been expected from such gifted and diverse authors, are wide-ranging and quite different in style, aim, content, and approach. Furthermore, the editors judged it best to preserve this diversity—the most formal literary criticism or the most informal autobiography—as distinctive of the individual authors and true to the Conference as an exciting oral occasion for a general audience. The editors hope that this very diversity breeds a richness and gives the volume an amplitude of expression offering something of interest and thought for almost everyone. Not every essay will be read with equal interest by every reader perhaps; but anyone perusing the whole book will see that the essays arise out of an intense concern for human life in the city and in the literature which that life generates and shapes.

The editors' original intention had been to present the essays by topic and genre, following the pattern of presentation at the Conference—the keynote speeches by James Baldwin, Bruno Bettelheim, and Joyce Carol Oates, and the forums on Drama and the Urban Experience, Ethnicity and Urban Literature, The Novel and the City, The Poet in the City, Urban Literature and the Young, and Literature and the Shaping of Society. Although these categories offered convenient demarcations for discussion, the essays seemed to call for a more organic arrangement. For instance, Lawrence Ferlinghetti's paper was a poem composed for presentation at the poetry forum in the Conference. Perhaps for that reason alone it should begin the book; but it also provides introduction and epigraph because it rehearses a history of modern poetry (city poetry), and sounds a hopeful lament over the "still insurgent voice / lost among machines" that, in radically different ways, the other authors sound as well.

The twenty essays are divided into two large categories: the nine in Part I make literature or literary concerns their major subject, and the eleven in Part II relate literature and the city to some other major subject—autobiography, history, sociology, politics, education. The sequence of the essays within each section, however, is not an obvious arrangement, and the order adopted here is but one of several possible organizations that could have served.

The essays in the first part are written in a traditional mode of literary criticism, or, departing from that mode, they nevertheless depend on careful reading of a literary text and on assuming the essential relation of that text to life and time outside it. Beyond these shared points are many differences of precise thesis and procedure.

The first essays by two of America's most brilliant novelists consider ideas and descriptions of the city in twentieth-century fiction. Joyce Carol Oates in "Imaginary Cities: America" succinctly notes the old heavenly and hellish meanings of the city in Western literature and tradition; she then concentrates on American writers for whom the city is both major fictional scene and major figure for society. The full, chronological discussions of Crane, Dreiser, Yezierska, Bellow, Barthelme, and Updike illustrate her argument that the American fictional city changes during the twentieth century from a place where a good fight is fought (and sometimes won) against terrible odds, to a place of "amoral dynamism," and then finally to a place much like the stagnant hell caught in Updike's image with which she ends—"The building, so lovely in air, had tangled mucky roots." Toni Morrison, in "City Limits, Village Values: Concepts of the Neighborhood in Black Fiction," surveys much the same period in American fiction. She examines in detail works by Toni Cade Bambara and Henry Dumas, while drawing more generally from Toomer, Ellison, Baldwin, and many others to identify an important difference between the recent works of black and of white urban authors. Anti-urbanism in white authors, she says, originates less in hatred "of the idea of a city" than in "the mandates of individualism, which, presumably, cities curtail." She relates anti-urbanism in black fiction to the experience of a "marked and poignant absence of some vital element of city life"—namely, the absence of the ancestor, that "advising, benevolent, protective" figure who flourishes more in villages than in cities.

The next two essays focus on poetry. Stephen Spender's "Poetry and the Modern City" moves from the Romantic poets' rejection of urban crowds, urban deprivation, and early industrial squalor, through the Victorian poets' avoidance of the city's reality, to the Decadent poets—the true inheritors of Romantic anti-urbanism. The Decadents "sought to prove the ugly was beautiful" and by this Romantic aesthetic influenced both the idealistic (but doomed) associations between poet and proletariat in the twentieth century and the general expectation that cities could be made new and good. In contrast to Spender's survey of aesthetic movements that shaped modernism, Helen Vendler considers the work of one modern poet. In "The Poet and the City: Robert Lowell," she describes chronologically Lowell's changing use of the urban image as "emblem," as "palimpsest," as "salience," and finally as a journalist's photo seizing an urban particular so that it becomes "liberated to notice."

Certainly for our time, as for the nineteenth century, the novel in its capaciousness is a favored literary form for ordering the multitudinous in city life, for containing, yet seeming to overflow with numberless details, for creating in a single or in several perceptions both chaos and limit of how it feels to be such a character, in such a city, in this time, that street, and what the feeling signifies. The following four essays, though quite different in scope and attack, consider the novel—mainly twentieth-century American novels—and, not surprisingly, some of the same novelists discussed by Oates and Morrison come in for frequent attention: Ellison, Dreiser, Fitzgerald, Baldwin, Bellow, Malamud, and Barthelme. So, too, the city perceived and presented is usually the northern, industrial metropolis—Boston, New York, Detroit, Chicago.

Leo Marx's essay, "The Puzzle of Anti-Urbanism in Classic American Literature," using Hawthorne and Fitzgerald for detailed examples, argues that classic American writers are not realistic—that their images of the city, not to be taken at face value, make a criticism of the emerging or achieved industrial state. In these writers the "distinguishing features of the American city do not reside in its cityness," just as in their words the country is not real country: the ugliness in the one, the "glorious impracticality" in the other arise from the authors' "highly critical conception" of the American "socioeconomic system and its accompanying culture."

New York was the undisputed center of this culture in its nineteenth-century rapacity. In "New York from Melville to Mailer," Alfred Kazin uses that city to locate important changes in fifteen decades of American fiction. Kazin sets the writers associated with New York in the historical particulars of the city: Melville, the last possible "hermit writer"; the expectant celebratory midwesterners, Fitzgerald, Dos Passos, and Bellow among them, who flocked to New York and traced dream-failure in their works; the literary geniuses among the city's "beleaguered" peoples, her "precarious, isolated, and unloved" minorities, "the children of oppression"; and Mailer, who alone loves the ferocity of the place and is not afraid to damn himself in this love for which "pent-up maddened New York is the symbol."

Both Ihab Hassan's "Cities of Mind, Urban Words: The Dematerialization of Metropolis in Contemporary American Fiction" and Leslie Fiedler's "Mythicizing the City" briefly trace the oldest Western ideas of the city as heaven and as hell before presenting contemporary American urban fiction as myths of the city—individual mental constructs imposed with such force upon more ordinarily perceived data of city life as to create new, highly ambiguous, unreal cities. Hassan's emphasis is on language, on the "complicity of language, knowledge, and artifice" to make what he identifies as modern cities of the mind—the utopias, the dystopias, the futuropoli in fiction by Henry Miller, Nathanael West, Ellison, Bellow, Pyncheon, Burroughs, Barthelme, Marge Piercy, and Samuel Delany. Fiedler's emphasis is more particularly on dystopia, the hellish Dantesque images of city life, especially in nineteenth- and twentieth-century writers of science fiction. He concludes with his own vision from one of his own stories.

In the final essay in this section, "Theater and Cities," the critic Richard Eder rapidly surveys intimate connections between plays written for performance in great urban centers, from ancient Athens to the present, and the cities themselves. He stresses what theaters nourish in cities, and finds in drama a genre that uniquely sustains humanity in times of oppression and despair: drama offers writers, producers, actors, and audiences alike the possibility of "participation in visible and finite tasks."

The essays in Part II of this volume are diverse not only in subject matter and approach, but also in mode. Many belong wholly or in part to the venerable tradition of the informal essay, stretching back through Hazlitt and Lamb to Steele and Pascal, with its admixture of autobiography and general observation, personal instance and large application or widening question. A few, by utter contrast, define a subject and treat it formally and objectively. Again, every reader could make alternative sequences of these essays, for, whatever their mode, their subjects often overlap both with each other and with the literary subjects in the first part of the book.

James Baldwin's essay, "The Language of the Streets," is a case in point. Baldwin moves from informal autobiography, a Harlem childhood, to a different mode—in this instance a plea for the brotherhood of American races strengthened by the example of black Americans' endurance and achievement. A different mixture of modes characterizes Amiri Baraka's "Black Literature and the Afro-American Nation: The Urban Voice." Here a history of Afro-American literature is interfused with a history of the black struggle for freedom in this country. Baraka argues that this is a necessary interfusion, and from his strongly held political position locates such major writers as Richard Wright, Claude McKay, Langston Hughes, W. E. B. Dubois, and Ralph Ellison in the history of literature and struggle.

The next three essays dwell autobiographically on ethnic urban experience in this country, and they conclude with different but compatible points. In "Culture Confrontation in Urban America: A Writer's Beginnings," Chaim Potok draws variously upon his New York Jewish childhood and on other times and places to argue that human imagination advances when there is "core to core culture confrontation." Jerre Mangione remarks in "A Double Life: The Fate of the Urban Ethnic" on this same collision between the ethnic subgroup and the larger national group that catches the American child of immigrants. Briefly describing some novels by Italian-Americans, he offers these and other works by ethnic Americans as books of "self-examination and self-redemption" that can help all Americans in their search for identity. Pedro Juan Soto's "The City and I" examines the Puerto Rican experience in New York City in some novels and in Soto's own life. In the double perspective of "hate and love" for New York, Soto feels with a special intensity its political failures and cultural possibilities.

The poet David Ignatow is also the son of immigrants, but his entire essay, "Living with Change," is an autobiography less of ethnic than of racial and economic collision. Ignatow's stories of Sara, Charlie, his black students at York College, and his inability to remain in the city never move from the mode of reflective memory but of themselves form an absorbing literature of city life.

Like the several essays before it, Marge Piercy's "The City as Battleground: The Novelist as Combatant" creates a literature of urban experience in autobiography—in her case, a Detroit childhood which "formed and deformed" her. In addition, she presents a strong argument for the inescapably political and moral meaning of all literature, including urban fiction.

The remaining essays in the book concern education. In much of "A Child's Perception of the City," Bruno Bettelheim recollects his Viennese childhood to exemplify the thesis that a child's perception of his city, based in his earliest associations—literary or personal, oral or written, good or bad—shapes the adult's perception—loving or despairing. The end of Bettelheim's essay is analytical: there he reviews some reading textbooks currently used by urban school children and finds they have "nothing positive to offer."

In formally argumentative and reportorial essays, Joan N. Burstyn and M. Jerry Weiss write about children's books. Burstyn's "Borrowing and Lending: The Young Reader and the Library" includes a description of public libraries, an analysis of their societal shortcomings, and suggestions for their renewed vitality. Weiss presents a selective and highly useful descriptive bibliography of urban children's literature in "Literature for Youth: The City as Heaven and/or Hell." Finally, in "A People's Paper for the Inner City," John Holt proposes inner-city neighborhood newspapers as one way to combat contemporary illiteracy among children and adults in American cities.

Can one conclude anything from the essays' varied approaches and statements about the intertwining of city life and literature? Clearly, the city still influences literary response, and the urban life depicted in books still influences our perceptions of the city. These mutual influences may easily be argued for in other eras and cultures, but these essays, not surprisingly, are rooted in the modern, industrial,

Western experience. In many of them there is an underlying lament for the passing away of an old idea or old reality of the city as golden, as *polis*, as civilization's highest reach. Yet even by expatriates of the metropolis, urban life is still perceived as vital—the place of "amoral dynamism" instanced by Joyce Carol Oates, for example. The old positive view of the city as spiritual, material, or intellectual deliverance no longer commands unqualified belief, nor does the equally old attitude of the city as corruption, the city as Sodom of the Plains.

What strikes the reader of these essays is the writers' significantly modern attitude. For all their diversity of style, approach, and subject, they share an ambiguous attitude toward the city, an uncertainty about positive and negative, an "unresolvable ambivalence," as Leslie Fiedler puts it. The writers' condemnation of modern cities, however patent, thorough, and open-eyed, is often accompanied by cautious hope, as in Ihab Hassan's speculation that, dying, "the city may simply cede the initiative to another organization of human energies," or Lawrence Ferlinghetti's recognition of good human desire, the "still insurgent voice," or James Baldwin's alternative to destruction—"the miracle of our brotherhood."

This ambiguity itself perhaps defines our present cultural assumptions and feelings toward the city. The city—alive, certainly, but with no clear emerging direction, fecund as well, but defying assigned value. Thus we find ourselves somewhere between the two old attitudes expressed in the eighteenth century by William Cowper's "God made the country, and Man made the town" and by Samuel Johnson's "When a man is tired of London, he is tired of life." This indeterminate positioning, this ambiguity we recognize as modern, as ourselves, is to some large degree still shaped in our awareness by literary power—still being shaped by essays and writers such as are collected here.

Newark, New Jersey, 1980

Part One

Third Populist Manifesto:

Modern Poetry is Prose
(But it is Saying Plenty)

Lawrence Ferlinghetti

I

Most modern poetry is prose
as is this poem
and I am thumbing through a great anthology
of contemporary poetry
and 'The Voice That Is Great Within Us'
sounds within us mostly
in a prose voice
in the typography of poetry
which is not to say it is prosaic
which is not to say it has no depths
which is not to say it is dead or dying
or not lovely or not beautiful
or not well written or not witty
It is very much alive
very well written beautifully written
lovely lively prose
prose that stands without crutches
of punctuation
prose whose syntax is so clear
it can be written all over the page
in open forms and open fields
and still be very clear
very dear prose
in the typography of poetry
(the poetic and the prosaic intellect

© 1981 by Lawrence Ferlinghetti.

masquerading in each other's clothes)
Most modern poetry is prose because
it walks across the page
like an old man in a city park
And walking through our prose buildings
in the year three thousand and one
one may look back and wonder
at this strange age
that made poetry walk in prose rhythms
and called it poetry
Most modern poetry is prose because
it has no *duende*
no soul of dark song
no passion musick
Like modern sculpture
it loves the concrete
Like minimal art
it minimizes emotion
in favor of understated irony
and implied intensity—
And how often does poetry today
rise above the mean sea level
of the darkling plain
where educated armies
march by day?
Ezra Pound once decanted his opinion
that only in times of decadence
does poetry separate itself from music
and this is the way the world ends
not with a song but a whimper

II

Eighty or ninety years ago
when all the machines began to hum
almost (as it seemed) in unison
Whitman was still singing
the song of himself
the song of our self
even as the speech of man
began to approach

the absolute staccato of machines
and the hard rock and punk rock
of electronic existence
Whitman was a holdover
(though even Emerson said the *Leaves of Grass*
was a mix of the *Bhagavad Gita*
and the *New York Herald*)
And Sandburg was a holdover
singing his poems
And Vachel Lindsay was a holdover
drumming his chants
And Wallace Stevens was a holdover
with his harmonious 'fictive music'
And Langston Hughes was a holdover
And Allen Ginsberg a holdover
chanting his mantras
singing Blake
And Kerouac a holdover
with his *Mexico City Blues*
which could indeed be sung
as a drunk sings
And there are others everywhere
jazz poets and jism poets
poetic strummers and wailers
in the streets of the world
making poetry of the urgent insurgent Now
of the immediate instant self
the incarnate carnal self
(as D. H. Lawrence called it)
But the speech of most was caught up
in the linotype's hot slug
and now in the so cold type of IBM
(movable type that doesn't move)
while we continue longing for the nightingale
among the pines of Resphigi
I had not known prose
had done-in so many
Lost in the city waste lands of T. S. Eliot
in the prose masturbations of J. Alfred Prufrock
in the *Four Quartets* that can't be played
on any instrument
and yet is the most beautiful prose of our age

Lost in the prose wastes of Ezra Pound's *Cantos*
which aren't *canti*
because they can't be sung by anyone
Lost in the pangolin prose of Marianne Moore
(who called her writing poetry
for lack of anything better to call it)
Lost in the great prose blank verse
of Karl Shapiro's *Essay on Rime*
and in the inner city speech
of William Carlos Williams
in the flat-out speech of his *Paterson*
and in all the poetry critics and crickets
of *The New York Review of Books*
and of *Poetry* (Chicago)
and every other poetry review
none of whom will commit the original sin
of saying some poet's poetry is prose
in the typography of poetry
just as the poet's friends will never say it
just as the poet's editors will never say it
the dumbest conspiracy of silence
in the history of letters

III

And in that 'turning inward'
away from the discredited clichés
of 1930s politics
Freud and Jung replaced Marx
as intellectual deities
among poets and painters
their radical aspiration turned inward
to the 'discovery of the unknown'
within themselves
and the poets turning inward to record
their personal 'graphs of consciousness'
Robert Creeley and Charles Olson began it
the prose-poetry of introspection
and a whole school followed it
and in the beginning was Ginsberg
who almost singlehandedly

took poetry in a new direction
picking up on Whitman's mimetic
'casual spontaneous utterance'
And the San Francisco poets continued it
and the New York poets continued it
and the objectivists continued it
and the projectivists continued it
and the constructivists continued it
and everyone continues it
in the high academies
and in a thousand little reviews
and big anthologies
spoonfed by the National Endowment of the Arts—
And that poetry which recorded
the movement of the mind
became the norm of American poetry
(the mind somehow assumed to be basically poetic)
and it was a wonder in the mouths
of such as Allen Ginsberg
in whose packrat omnivorous mind
was the seismograph of genius
and if the mind be comely
all that it utters is comely
and divinely sings
in moments of ekstasis
But the graph of more pedestrian poets
could only be walking prose
and the boat of love breaks up
on the shores of everyday life
And the Collective Unconscious
remains uncollected
though poetry has many great voices
many modes and many voices
the best of whom cite music
as their ideal
but few do sound the deep refrains
and leit-motifs
of our still mysterious existence—
too many of our best brains
simply not equal to
the mass confusion of our colliding cultures
nor to the confusion

in how to tell poetry from prose
(that most persistent question running through
the literary meditations of this century)
except as William Carlos Williams saw a way
(in reading Marianne Moore)
of getting around this question
by ignoring it
(He too disliked 'poetry')
and so turned his back on it
in favor of the spoken verse
of the great American idiom

IV

Most modern poetry is prose
but it is saying plenty
about our 'soul-less civilization'
and what it has done to our free man
to our Eros man and Eros woman
the anarchist in each of us
who is the poet in each of us—
Most modern poetry is prose
but it is saying plenty
about how the soul has gone out
of our cities
out of our buildings
out of our streets
no song among the typists
no song in our concrete architecture
our concrete music
And Mumford was right of course—
architecture reflects the soul
of civilizations—
(But man reflects it
more than buildings
as women reflect it—
the true temples of flesh)
Modern poetry is prose
but it is saying plenty
by its very form and tone
about the death the self dies every day

the poet in each of us
that's killed a little every day
'You killed him you sonofabitch
in your Brooks Brothers suit!'
So wailed Kenneth Rexroth long ago
with poetry-and-jazz in San Francisco
And so wailed the young Allen Ginsberg
in his *Howl*:
'What sphinx of cement and aluminum bashed open
     their skulls and ate up their brains and
     imagination?
Moloch! Solitude! Filth! Ugliness! Ashcans and
     unobtainable dollars! Children screaming under
     the stairways! Boys sobbing in the armies!
     Old men weeping in the parks!'
And so wails today a still wild voice
inside of us
a still insurgent voice
lost among machines and insane nationalisms
still longing to break out
still longing for the distant nightingale
that stops and begins again
stops
and begins again
stops
and resumes again

It is the bird singing that makes us happy

Imaginary Cities: America

Joyce Carol Oates

If the City is a text, how shall we read it?

The manifold evidence of our American literature of the twentieth century suggests that the City, an archetype of the human imagination that may well have existed for thousands of years, in various manifestations (as the Heavenly City, the Kingdom of the Dead, the City of God, the City of Man, the Cities of the Plains, etc.), has absorbed into itself presumably opposed images of the "sacred" and the "secular." The City of God and the City of Man have conjoined out of psychological necessity in an era of diminished communal religion. A result of this fusion of polar symbols is that the contemporary City, as an expression of human ingenuity and, indeed, a material expression of civilization itself, must always be read as if it were utopian (that is, "sacred")—and consequently a tragic disappointment, a species of hell. A number of our writers have spoken out boldly (if poetically) about the psychological kinship between the individual and the City, interpreting the fate of one in terms of the influence of the other, which is almost always malefic. Saul Bellow's Charley Citrine says, in his meditation upon the miserable life and premature death of the poet Von Humboldt Fleisher (whom we may equate fairly precisely with Delmore Schwartz): "Chicago with its gigantesque outer life contained the whole problem of poetry and the inner life in America."[1]

The more autonomous an archetype in the unconscious, the greater its numinosity in what we might call, echoing Jung, the collective or mass imagination, the more contradictions it displays in consciousness—the greater the range of emotions it arouses. Like Nature (by which I mean of course the *idea* of Nature, in itself an invention of civilization—Nature as the timeless though hardly exact counterpart of the City), this image functions almost exclusively as a symbol. It is

© 1981 by Joyce Carol Oates.

11

the dramatic background against which fictional persons enact their representative struggles with those values the City embodies, which are frequently internalized. In America, emphasis has generally been upon the City as an expression of the marketplace struggle that will yield—*should* yield, this being the New World—individual success in financial and social terms. Utopia may not really exist, but the utopian dream of salvation is still potent. At one extreme, as depicted in the fiction of late nineteenth- and early twentieth-century writers (among them Stephen Crane, Upton Sinclair, Theodore Dreiser, Anzia Yezierska), the struggle is graphic and literal: the City is a place in which human beings die as a consequence of the unspeakable conditions of slum life and actual mistreatment by employers or by one another. "The things which could not kill you," Anzia Yezierska says in the story "My Last Hollywood Script" (1950), "were the making of you"[2]— but very few people were "made" by the exhausting struggle of daily slum life, of which Yezierska writes so powerfully.

At another extreme, in the fiction of the past several decades, and perhaps most eloquently in that of Saul Bellow, the struggle has become internalized, a ceaseless philosophical inquiry. Bellow's masterful novels all address themselves to "the lessons and theories of power" in a great American city. Bellow is obsessed with the riddle of what it means to be an urban man in a secular, mass-market culture that appears to be vertiginously extraverted, without a coherent sense of history or tradition—in which, in fact, "all the ages of history" can be experienced as simultaneous.[3] The industrial landscapes of Detroit evoked in Philip Levine's poetry—notably in *They Feed They Lion* (1972) and *1933* (1974)—are glimpsed in fragments but coalesce, in the reader's imagination, to a hellish city, a city "pouring fire." And the citizens of Donald Barthelme's *City Life* (1970) suspect (probably with justification) that they are suffering brain damage as a result of their polluted environment: "we are locked in the most exquisite mysterious muck. This muck heaves and palpitates. It is multidirectional and has a mayor. To describe it takes many hundreds of thousands of words. Our muck is only a part of a much greater muck—the nation-state—which is itself the creation of that muck of mucks, human consciousness."[4]

Women in Cities

> *No move in this world without money*
> —Anzia Yezierska, "The Miracle"

Students of American literature are all familiar with the hellish City of late nineteenth- and early twentieth-century literature, powerfully presented by writers like Upton Sinclair (whose equation of Chicago with the "jungle" is still, perhaps, a viable image) and Stephen Crane (whose *Maggie: A Girl of the Streets* is set on the Bowery—in Crane's words, "the only interesting place in New York"). In re-examining *Maggie* (1896) one is struck by the reiteration of images and scenes of sub-human violence, and by the young novelist's sardonic "objective" tone. The city is a "dark region" of "gruesome doorways" that surrender babies to the street and the gutter. Dishevelled women gossip with one another in the street or scream "in frantic quarrels." There are aged, withered persons, and ragged children, and derelicts, and pugnacious young men who imagine the world "composed, for the most part, of despicable creatures who were all trying to take advantage" of them. The novel's opening scene depicts a merciless fight between two groups of slum children (Rum Alley vs. Devil's Row) while adults look on indifferently or with mild curiosity. Maggie's brother Jimmie is savagely stoned by children with "small convulsed faces" and the grins of "true assassins." There is a brilliant three-page *tour de force* describing Jimmie's experience, years later, as a truck driver in the city, which is unfortunately too long to quote in its entirety:

He invaded the turmoil and tumble of the downtown streets, and learned to breathe maledictory defiance at the police, who occasionally used to climb up, drag him from his perch, and punch him. In the lower part of the city he daily involved himself in hideous tangles. . . . He fell into the habit, when starting on a long journey, of fixing his eye on a high and distant object, commanding his horses to start, and then going into a trance of oblivion. Multitudes of drivers might howl in his rear, and passengers might load him with opprobrium, but he would not awaken until some blue policeman . . . began . . . to seize bridles and beat the soft noses of the responsible horses. . . . Foot passengers were mere pestering flies with an insane disregard for their legs and his convenience. He could not comprehend their desire to cross the streets. Their madness smote him with eternal amazement. . . . Yet he achieved a respect for a fire-engine. As one charged toward his truck, he would drive fearfully upon a sidewalk, threatening untold people with annihilation. . . . A fire-engine was enshrined in his heart as an appalling thing that he loved with a distant, dog-like devotion. It had been known to overturn a street-car. . . . The clang of the gong pierced his breast like a noise of remembered war.[5]

The tone is set, in such garish, outsized images, for the destruction of the innocent "girl of the streets" by less physical but equally malicious social forces. Maggie is "ruined"—she has "gone to the devil"—and finally commits suicide by throwing herself in the river.

Theodore Dreiser is a far more meticulous observer of city life than Stephen Crane (who was only twenty-one when he wrote *Maggie*), but in *Sister Carrie* (1900) he could not speak more didactically or explicitly:

When a girl leaves her home at eighteen, she does one of two things. Either she falls into saving hands and becomes better, or she rapidly assumes the cosmopolitan standard of virtue and becomes worse. Of an intermediate balance, under the circumstances [Chicago, 1889] there is no possibility. The city has its cunning wiles, no less than the infinitely smaller and more human tempter. There are large forces which allure with all the soulfulness of expression possible in the most cultured human. The gleam of a thousand lights is often as effective as the persuasive light in a wooing and fascinating eye. Half the undoing of the unsophisticated and natural mind is accomplished by forces wholly superhuman. A blare of sound, a roar of life, a vast array of human hives, appeal to the astonished senses in equivocal terms. . . . Unrecognized for what they are, their beauty, like music, too often relaxes, then weakens, then perverts the simpler human perceptions.[6]

But Carrie is far more resourceful, and more intelligent, than her creator seems to think; despite the leaden moralizing of his prose, he allows his heroine to survive the "ruin" of her innocence, unlike Crane's Maggie. She is even fortunate enough to leave sombre Chicago for the far more seductive city of New York where, along Broadway, she observes the "sprinkling of goodness and the heavy percentage of vice" parading in the latest, most costly fashions—and is quite dazzled by this "indescribable atmosphere" which has the power to make her forget the old Carrie, her past, and her obligations. (*Sister Carrie* is, it must be said, not really a "naturalistic" work at all, despite the fact that it deals with ostensibly naturalistic themes. On the contrary, it is a sort of fairy tale—in relation to which Crane's far cruder *Maggie* is the dark and far more convincing cautionary fable.)

Dreiser's pessimism is strongly and provocatively qualified by what might be called his visionary belief that the City, however immediately corrupting, is nevertheless a symbol of the issuant progress of our species. Beyond the individual Maggie and what she presumably represents, Dreiser sees evidence of growth and evolution, even in a determined cosmos: "Among the forces which sweep and play throughout the universe, untutored man is but a wisp in the wind. Our civilization is still in a middle stage, scarcely beast; . . . scarcely human. . . . We have the consolation of knowing [however] that evolution is ever in action, that the ideal is a light that cannot fail."[7] This is a sentiment that seems but slenderly connected to Carrie's story.

Though nearly unknown at the present time, the novelist and short story writer Anzia Yezierska (1885?–1970) is probably a more realistic portrayer of certain aspects of city life in the early years of the twentieth century than her famous male contemporaries. Her writing is autobiographical and emotional. The City of her fiction—New York's Lower East Side, a Jewish ghetto—is complex and ambiguous, by no means simply a marketplace or jungle in which the individual is suffocated. "The things which could not kill you were the making of you," Yezierska said in an interview, speaking frankly of her own experience.

Between 1920 and 1932 Yezierska published six books, among them her best-known novel, *Bread Givers*. (This novel, long out of print, has been reissued [1979], and *The Open Cage: An Anzia Yezierska Collection* has been published [1979] by Persea Books in New York City with introductions by Alice Kessler Harris.) In fast-moving and relatively unsophisticated prose, Yezierska dramatizes the struggle of a strong-willed young woman to free herself of both the immigrant slums of the New World and the religiously enjoined subservience and chatteldom of the Old World. Along with her mother and sisters she is tyrannized by her father, a completely self-absorbed Talmudic scholar who believes that his family exists only to support him.

Bread Givers evokes an almost Dickensian sense of oppression and injustice: it is shamelessly melodramatic, and yet thoroughly convincing as a document of Yezierska's own emotional experience as the daughter of an extremely religious man. Its picture of the dailyness of life in the Lower East Side, its presentation of the community of Jewish immigrants, has an authenticity lacking in the fiction of most "naturalistic" writers because it is imagined, as theirs is not, from the inside. Slum life is "real life" to Yezierska, however difficult; in escaping from it one risks losing the connection with life altogether.

Anzia Yezierska was born in a *shtetl* in Russian Poland and emigrated with her family in the 1890s to the New World—to the crowded Lower East Side of Manhattan. In this "new" world Jewish immigrants tried with varying degrees of success and failure to reconstruct the "old" world, and the harrowing conflict between Yezierska's heroines and their conservatively pious fathers must stand as a paradigm of this larger cultural conflict. The Old World makes its claim in this typical outburst of the father in *Bread Givers*: "My books, my holy books always were, and always will be, the light of the world. You'll see yet how all America will come to my feet to learn."[8] Yezierska observes: "The prayers of his daughters didn't count because God didn't listen to women. Heaven and the next world were only for men. Women could get into heaven because they were wives and daughters of men. Women had no brains for the study of God's Torah, but they could be the servants of men who studied the Torah." Her heroine Sara breaks with her family at the age of seventeen—an extraordinarily courageous act considering her circumstances, and the fact that she has nowhere to live. Her father is outraged and curses her but she replies: "My will is as strong as yours. I'm going to live my own life. Nobody can stop me. I'm American!"[9]

Sara is bold and impetuous and, in her desperation, exactly right. If she is to save herself from suffocating in her ghetto-bound family she must become *American*. She understands as a very young child that there is "no move in this world without money," and her reasoning leads her to the conclusion that by studying English in night school she will have the means of freeing herself from poverty. And more: "Only to make myself somebody great—and have them [her family] come begging favors at my feet."[10] If the romantically American rags-to-riches plot seems excessive to contemporary readers, one should be reminded that Anzia Yezierska underwent approximately the same experience. Her writing is autobiographical in outline if not always in detail.

Where Crane, Dreiser, Henry James, and, indeed, most serious writers of the epoch severely criticized the very basis of "Americanization" in these terms, Anzia Yezierska takes everything on faith, knowing only that the future—"America"—is infinitely preferable to the past. She is characterized as a pioneer; her heroine Sara exclaims, as a college girl, "Why is it that when a nobody wants to get to be somebody she's got to make herself terribly hard?"[11] No one has written with more tenderness and authority of the almost physical yearning for knowledge a certain kind of young person possesses. (Is this young person inevitably the child of very poor parents? Or is the struggle for education and self-realization simply more vividly italicized, in a context of poverty?) Sara wants to raise herself, she wants power, she wants—everything. "Like a starved thing in the dark" she reaches out blindly, sometimes confusing her longing with men and bringing about humiliation. But in the end she does triumph, like

Yezierska, though she realizes that the shadow of the past, her religious heritage, and her elderly father's expectations still exert their pull: "It wasn't just my father," Sara thinks at the novel's conclusion, "but the generations who made my father whose weight was still upon me."

The City is, ironically, a kind of hell—yet the only possible place for the liberation of a certain kind of independent and courageous woman. The relatively egalitarian nature of the bitter struggle for money allows girls like Yezierska's heroines to break away from the world of their fathers, and if their goals, their triumphs—acquiring a teaching certificate, for instance—seem to us modest enough, we must remember out of what stifling poverty, beneath what appallingly low ceilings, they were dreamt. To become a schoolteacher *and* to return to one's old neighborhood in triumph and yet in a kind of servitude— this is Sara Smolinsky's achievement. Yezierska herself sold a book of short stories, *Hungry Hearts*, to Sam Goldwyn for $10,000 in 1920, and went to work in Hollywood for a while at a salary of $200 a week. There were sensational "rags-to-riches" stories in the Sunday papers, and her dreams of greatness were almost alarmingly fulfilled. Interestingly enough, however, she found herself cut off from the source of both her fictional material and her energy—she felt "without a country, without a people." The congestion and poverty of the Lower East Side, the work she had done in sweatshops and laundries, perhaps even the bitter struggle with her family itself, were so deeply imprinted in this remarkable woman that once freed of them she yearned for them again, recognizing in herself (as Saul Bellow's far more articulate Augie March recognizes in himself) the need to be opposed, to be in opposition, to suffer privation, to *struggle*.

The City, for all its horrors, is the very fountain of emotion: where else can one experience so much, such a cacophonous variety of sensation? And if one has acquired the City's language—in this case American English—surely this language has not the power of moving one's soul as Yiddish does? (Yezierska's prose style reads as if it were translated from Yiddish—hardly as if it were self-consciously written at all. Her voice fairly springs out at you from the page.) At the peak of her success, Yezierska found herself unable to write because, in her words, she had gone "too far away from life" and did not know how to return. One of her heroines exclaims: "I don't believe that I shall ever write again unless I can get back to the real life I once lived when I worked in the factory."

Yezierska writes without irony, however; she is never critical of the lure of "Americanization" itself. And unlike fellow contemporaries (unlike Henry Roth, for instance, whose *Call It Sleep* is of course a work of far greater psychological subtlety than Yezierska's), she did not appear to take an interest in the craft of fiction itself, and one must read her with expectations appropriate to her intention. The autobiographical energies of a first-person narration (a "confession," a "history," a "defense" of one's present self) need not invariably bring with them a slackening of control, as Bellow's masterpiece *The Adventures of Augie March* makes clear, but Yezierska is so close to her material and to her women protagonists that the ambiguities that disturb and enrich "serious" fiction are largely missing. Yet Yezierska is rarely sentimental about the past, and she certainly does not look back over her shoulder at Europe. The heroine of "The Miracle," an early story, wants *only* to escape her Polish village and come live in America. The heroine of "America and I," exploited by a well-to-do Jewish family for whom she works, goes to work in a sweatshop and reads American history in order to dedicate herself to the mission of building "a bridge of understanding between the American-born and myself."

The City's gift of anonymity, the promise of wages for work—wages agreed upon in advance—make the individual possible for the first time in history: the individual *woman*, one might say.

Mr. Bellow's City, and Others

> *In the end you can't save your soul and life by thought. But if you think, the least of the consolation prizes is the world.*
>
> —Einhorn to Augie in
> *The Adventures of Augie March*

Yet the City does retain its aura of the sacred: it sometimes seems a place of godliness, if no longer a City of God. How else to account for the fascination of the literary mind with the city as a phenomenon— an outrage, a spectacle, an emblem of human ingenuity that seems frankly suprahuman? Quite apart from the somewhat mechanical fatalism of Stephen Crane and the platitudinous pessimism of Dreiser, apart from the deeply moving novels of "social realism" of Anzia Yezierska and her contemporaries and a more recent woman novelist of comparable power, Harriette Arnow[12]—one encounters a celebration of the city as an end in itself: an archetype of amoral dynamism that awakens no emotion more violently than that of simple awe.

William James' extravagant remarks on New York City are as valid for 1980 as for 1907:

The first impression of New York . . . is one of repulsion at the clangor, disorder, and permanent earthquake conditions. But this time, installed . . . in the center of the cyclone, I caught the pulse of the machine, took up the rhythm, and vibrated with, and found it simply magnificent. . . . The courage, the heaven-scaling audacity of it all, and the *lightness* withal, as if there was nothing that was not easy, and the great pulses and bounds of progress, so many in directions all simultaneous that the coordination is indefinitely future, give a kind of *drumming background* of life that I have never felt before. I'm sure that once *in* that movement, and at home, all other places would seem insipid.

Even the Dark Satanic Mills of industrial England are re-imagined in George Orwell's extremely provocative words:

Even in the worst industrial towns one sees a great deal that is not ugly in the narrow aesthetic sense. A belching chimney or a stinking slum is repulsive chiefly because it implies warped lives and ailing children. Look at it from a purely aesthetic standpoint and it may have a certain macabre appeal. I find that anything outrageously strange ends by fascinating me even when I abominate it.

One of the most remarkable achievements of James Joyce's *Ulysses*—more remarkable by far than the dazzling harlequinade of its styles and Homeric structure—is the rendering, in the most supple, sensuous, and precise language possible, of the city of Dublin: that city where "everyone knows everyone else." Joyce's great subject is less his people, memorable as they are, than his setting: that Dublin that is solely and specifically *that* Dublin, on June 16, 1904, with its dissonant harmony of Irish voices. Joyce's mystical nature would have it that God (even the hangman god) is "doubtless all in all in all of us," and that every life, in Stephen Dedalus' words, is "many days, day after day," but the glory of his novel is the city of Dublin itself. Joyce's boldly new art *renders* the city but refuses to *present* it. We experience Dublin in snatches and fragments, catching only glimpses of it, carried along by the momentum of Leopold's or Stephen's subjectivity. We know the city from the inside, though in a sense we "know" it hardly at all. The Dublin of *Ulysses* is subliminally granted. "Everything speaks in its own way," Bloom quietly observes. The City speaks through everyone and everything, in a multitude of voices.

"Moses Herzog" and "Charley Citrine" are Joycean names, if not precisely Joycean people, but we should suspect in any case that Saul Bellow has learned from Joyce (as he has "learned" from any number of writers). For who among twentieth-century American novelists has evoked the City with more passion and more resonance than Bellow? With very little interest in formal experimentation, and no interest at all in following the wild, hilarious Dadaism of certain sections of *Ulysses* ("Nighttown" most famously), Bellow has nevertheless perfected a wonderfully supple and expressive style, a voice uniquely his own. One believes in Bellow immediately, no matter how fanciful the utterances of certain of his male characters. And they speak not simply for themselves but for their epochs, their cities. As the creator of superbly modulated prose and as the observer of character and cityscape, Bellow is Joyce's equal. He has written no novel to rival *Ulysses* (who has?) but the complex riches of his numerous books attest to an imagination as deeply bound up with his subject as Joyce was with his. And if he is less ambitiously experimental than Joyce, it should be noted that he is less self-indulgent as well. Augie March might be speaking for his creator in these arresting opening words of *The Adventures of Augie March*:

I am an American, Chicago born—Chicago, that somber city—and go as I have taught myself, free-style, and will make the record in my own way: first to knock, first admitted; sometimes an innocent knock, sometimes a not so innocent.

Augie March's Chicago—that of the slums and near-slums, of the 1920s and 30s—like Anzia Yezierska's Lower East Side is a place of congestion and drama. European immigrants, blacks, even Mexicans—Jews and Catholics—the Chicago of welfare clinics and ward politics—local millionaires—"bigshots and operators, commissioners, grabbers, heelers, tipsters, hoodlums, wolves, fixers, plaintiffs, flatfeet, men in Western hats and women in lizard shoes and fur coats, hothouse and arctic drafts mixed up, brute things and airs of sex, evidence of heavy feeding and systematic shaving, of calculations, grief, not-caring, and hopes of tremendous millions."[13]—all are eagerly observed by young Augie March, the near-orphan, the innocent who is also a thief, yet still innocent; the boy who senses himself "adoptable" by surrogate parents, yet battens on opposition. Augie is idealistic, but he learns quickly the lessons of the city: to plot, to calculate, to negotiate, to press forward, never to allow himself to be manipulated, never to allow others to define his limits. As a young boy he is taught by his "Grandma" Lausch how to lie convincingly to administrators of a public health clinic. As a teenager he is initiated by his eccentric millionaire employer, William Einhorn, into the pleasure (the paid-for pleasure) of a downtown brothel. Given Augie's frequent romanticism, we are surprised that his first sexual experience should pass by him so quickly, and that in summary: "Yet when the thrill went off, like lightning smashed and dispersed into the ground, I knew it was basically only a transaction." But Augie's judgment is authorative; he knows, being a city boy, that one must pay for everything, and that it doesn't matter. "Nor using what other people used. That's what city life is."[14]

Augie's comic-epic adventures, and his occasional adventures into the near-tragic, school him shrewdly in the strategies of city life. He is acquainted with people who read in German and French, are familiar with Nietzsche and Spengler; in another direction he is acquainted with criminals. "I touched all sides," Augie says, "and nobody knew where I belonged. I had no good idea about that myself." He is there to learn the "lessons and theories of power" in the great city of Chicago, confident (and with justification, as Bellow's career indicates) that these lessons and theories will be generally applicable.

For every Augie March in the near-slums of Chicago there were hundreds of Studs Lonigans, but Augie—of course!—is the survivor, the prince, just as Bellow's unique synthesis of the humanistic and the tragic, his apparently effortless synthesis of the "classic" and the defiantly modern, greatly outdistances the time- and place-locked "naturalism" of James T. Farrell. Like his creator, Augie refuses to be "determined" beforehand. He defines himself; he declares himself a "Columbus of those near-at-hand," a defiantly laughing creature, uncorrupted even by his own diminution of faith. The "universal eligibility to be noble" informs most of his acts and those of his ambitious brother Simon, no matter how frequently these acts cast the brothers down and mock "Grandma" Lausch's inflated hopes for them. Chicago is America writ large, and the American legend is wonderfully seductive: why should one *not* succeed in becoming an American? "What did Danton lose his head for, or why was there a Napoleon," Augie asks passionately, "if it wasn't to make a nobility of us all?"

Darkened by a few degrees, Augie's adventures might well be tragic; his ebullience might swerve into mania or angry despair. (In his youthful idealism he calls to mind the brilliant but doomed Von Humboldt Fleisher of *Humboldt's Gift*—and it has always seemed peculiar, an omission of tact, perhaps, that Augie never declares himself a writer.) After all, Augie's mother is slow-witted, and she has been abandoned by her husband. One of Augie's brothers is an idiot who must be institutionalized, and the March family is always on the brink of actual poverty. Yet Augie's free-wheeling gregariousness manages to absorb (thanks to the elasticity of Bellow's prose) a number of troublesome things: the anti-Semitism of neighborhood Polish Catholics, the disappointments of numerous petty jobs and various sorties into amateur crime, and the gradual disintegration of the March family. For though Augie is very much a loner, *Augie March* is the most generously populated of novels. Chicago emerges as a city of giants who reveal themselves in their speech (eloquent, eccentric, lyric as any in *Ulysses*) and in their possessions (which, like Joyce, Bellow loves to catalog at length). They are reckless, tender, cunning, naive, duplicitous, and loyal by turns. They may be, like the "great" Einhorn, assessed in classical terms, as Augie spiritedly aligns himself with the chroniclers of the great epics of the past: "I have the right," he says, "to praise Einhorn and not care about smiles of derogation from those who think the race no longer has in any important degree the traits we honor in [antiquity]." Or they may be, like Einhorn's son Dingbat, as gigantic in another direction, and as tenderly observed:

> ... without being a hoodlum himself [Dingbat] was taken up with gang events and crime, a kind of amateur of the lore and done up in the gangster taste so that you might take him for somebody tied in with the dangerous Druccis or Big Hayes Hubacek: sharp financial hat, body-clasping suit, the shirt Andalusian style buttoned up to the collar and worn without a necktie, trick shoes, pointed and pimpy, polished like a tango dancer's; he clumped hard on the leather heels. Dingbat's hair was violent, brilliant, black, treated, ripplemarked. Bantam, thin-muscled, swift, almost frail, he had an absolutely unreasonable face. To be distinguished from brutal—it wasn't that, there was all kind of sentiment in it. But wild, down-twisting, squint-eyed, unchangeably firm and wrong in thoughts, with the prickles coming black through his unmethodical after-shave talcum: the puss of an executioner's subject.[15]

Augie understands himself "forced early into deep city aims" in a crowded environment that can, at any moment, turn against him. "You do all you can to humanize and familiarize the world," Augie observes when his fortune declines, "and suddenly it becomes more strange than ever." At the city college he attends for a while, he finds himself one of hundreds, or thousands, the children of immigrants from every part of Chicago, aspiring to be, "the idea was," *American*. Which means to acquire power, by way of wealth, by way of the manipulation of others. Augie resists this Americanization, but he remains a child of Chicago, rather like the playwright Charley Citrine who cannot, for all his cosmopolitan fame, free himself of the nostalgia for Chicago that is also a perverse fascination with and celebration of mortality—death. Whether Bellow composed *Augie March* for the sake of the many ideas it offers, or whether the ideas are mere excuses for his masterful evocations of Chicago, the reader is likely to be most struck by the young author's zestful attention to the details of time and place. Who else would take time to celebrate the "greatness of place" of Gary, Indiana. Though Augie is temporarily wretched, he notes

docks and dumps of sulphur and coal, and flames seen by their heat, not light, in the space of noon air among the black, huge Pasiphaë cows and other columnar animals, headless, rolling a rust of smoke and connected in an enormous statuary of hearths and mills—here and there an old boiler or a hill of cinders in the bulrush spawning-holes of frogs. . . . Thirty crowded miles on oil-spotted road, where the furnace, gas, and machine volcanoes cooked the Empedocles fundamentals into pig iron, girders, and rails.[16]

"If I mentioned a Chicago junkyard as well as Charlemagne's estate," says Augie defensively, "I had my reasons. For should I look into any air, I could recall the bees and gnats of dust in the heavily divided heat of a street of El pillars—such as Lake Street, where the junk and old bottle-yards are—like a terribly conceived church of madmen. . . . And sometimes misery came over me to feel that I myself was the creation of such places."[17]

In the long story, "Looking for Mr. Green," in the volume *Mosby's Memoirs* (1968), the native-born Chicagoan George Grebe is employed by the welfare department to deliver checks in the black district—but he cannot find the crippled black man Green, no matter how courageously or how desperately he tries. The black slums of Chicago will not yield their secrets to him; he *cannot* find the possibly mythical Green. But in his search he learns of a world, and of people, that he had not previously encountered. (He is a university graduate, with a degree in Classics, worthless in the Depression years; his father was a butler in the home of a Lake Shore millionaire.) On the walls of tenement buildings he reads enigmatic scrawls as if they contained a message for him: "So the sealed rooms of pyramids were decorated, and the caves of human dawn." Grebe is one of Bellow's characteristic heroes—ingenuous, eager to be instructed, eager to be of aid. He does not resent his supervisor's amused remarks on the ironies of "superior" education in this "fallen world of appearances": "I'll tell you, as a man of culture," Raynor says pompously, "that though nothing looks to be real, and everything stands for something else, and that thing for a still further thing—there ain't any comparison between $25 and $37 a week, regardless of the last reality." Nor did the Greeks, for all their thoughtfulness, care to part with their slaves.

Herzog (1961) is a richly textured and extremely intense novel about an urban man, Moses Herzog, who shuttles back and forth between Chicago and New York, negotiating the terms of a most unpleasant divorce as he comes closer and closer to a breakdown. Perhaps he is already out of his mind—which is all right with him. At the novel's end, after some feverish activity, Herzog retreats to his mortgaged country home in Ludeyville, Massachusetts, with "no messages for anyone."

Like Augie March, Herzog consciously resists the temptation to be heroic—to be involved in a dramatic (and consequently artificial) sequence of acts. The novel's theme is central to Bellow's mature work, and is stated quite explicitly midway in the narrative: "The real and essential question is one of our employment by other human beings and their employment by us. Without this true employment you never dread death, you cultivate it."[18] In the foreground, however, *Herzog* is near-constant motion. Herzog is always going up or down subway steps, hailing taxis, flying in airplanes, driving (with unfortunate consequences) the Chicago freeway. A highly articulate intellectual (a historian), Herzog manages to get himself arrested by Chicago police for possession of an old revolver. He is very badly treated by his former wife Madeleine and her somewhat comic lover, but he retreats finally to the fairly plausible "idyllic" setting of Ludeyville and, so it would seem, saves himself from collapse. *Herzog* is an unusually self-absorbed novel, far more of an extended monologue than Bellow's other works, and one catches hardly more than glimpses of Herzog's Chicago, though he admits to being deeply involved with it. *His* Chicago, as he says sentimentally, is the Woodlawn Avenue section of Hyde Park:

massive, clumsy, amorphous, smelling of mud and decay, dog turds; sooty façades, slabs of structural *nothing*, senselessly ornamented triple porches with huge cement urns for flowers that contained only rotting cigarette butts and other stained filth; sun parlors under tiled gables, rank areaways, gray backstairs, seamed and ruptured concrete from which sprang grass; ponderous four-by-four fences that sheltered growing weeds. . . . [Here] Herzog did feel at home. He was perhaps as midwestern and unfocussed as these same streets. (Not so much determinism, he thought, as a lack of determining elements—the absence of a formative power.)[19]

Driving to his elderly step-mother's home he broods over "clumsy, stinking, tender Chicago," and notes a species of flower he imagines to be peculiar to Chicago—"crude, waxy things like red and purple crayon bits, in a special class of false-looking natural objects." These foolish plants touch Herzog because they are so "graceless, so corny."

By contrast, there is nothing tender, nothing remotely redemptive, about the City of *Mr. Sammler's Planet*—which is to say, New York City. As one of the "great" cities of the civilized world, it is sharply disappointing: its hold on civilization is extremely tenuous. Not only does society appear to be sinking into madness, but there is, as well, the *excuse* of madness. Sammler passes judgment on a "whole nation, all of civilized society . . . seeking the blameless state of madness. The privileged, almost aristocratic state of madness."[20] As if to mock Bellow's high intentions an opportunistic young man tells Sammler: "You should denounce New York City. You should speak like a prophet, like from another world."

Mr. Sammler's Planet shares with *Humboldt's Gift* and parts of *Herzog* a curious and sometimes uneasy wedding of high, grave, and indeed "prophetic" musings and a plot that is frequently farcical, populated by comic characters. Elderly, half-blind, a distinguished historian and journalist, Artur Sammler looks back upon his friendship with another prophet, H. G. Wells, and his acquaintance with Bloomsbury. He looks back, with distinctly less pleasure, on the madness of nazism, the concentration camps, and a death ditch in Poland in which he almost died. He is a seer, a voice: he exists primarily in his judgments, which are quite savage. Perhaps it is a consequence of his age, as well as the high degree of reflective intelligence he represents, that he is an observer throughout the novel—a protagonist whose passivity and ironic cast of mind alienate him from the City, and forbid him much sympathy with it. The self-absorbed energies of the great city have lost their power to fascinate in the 1960s: too much is happening, very little is comprehended or absorbed, there is a "sexual madness" in the air. In Sammler's words, "You could see the suicidal impulses of civilization pushing strongly." Like anyone who has seen the world collapse once, Sammler entertains the possibility that it might collapse twice.

Though Sammler's reading consists solely of Meister Eckhardt and the Bible (anticipating, perhaps, Charley Citrine's "mystical" leanings), he is very much aware of the chaos around him, and is in fact caught up with it, in the sometimes strained plot Bellow has devised to illuminate one facet of the decade's absurdity. Sammler feels like the time-traveller in Wells' fantasy, *The Time Machine*, and though the curve of the novel brings him to a thematic (and heavily rhetorical) affirmation of this life, this earth—in short, this *planet*—the novel's vitality springs from his general repulsion. This is the symbolic City in which a rat can be mistaken for a dachshund, and sexual experimentation of various kinds is taken up on principle. Simply living in New York makes Sammler think compulsively of Sodom and Gomorrah—a general doom "desired by people who have botched everything." Can the individual transcend this social malaise? Is there a margin of human accountability, quite apart from the lawlessness of civilization's "leaders"? But how, bewitched by the frenzy of the age, is one to "meet the terms of his contract"?

Perhaps because it was written during a particularly tumultuous decade, in which the fairly conservative Saul Bellow was frequently attacked for his political beliefs, *Mr. Sammler's Planet* is the harshest of his novels. It is filled with brooding upon evil and the fascination of evil; the author makes no attempt to link his protagonist with the City, except as an accidental witness; we have come a great distance from the exuberance of young Augie March. Even Sammler's musings upon slum life (as seen from his nephew Elya's Rolls Royce) are oddly devoid of a sense of human kinship with the "underprivileged":

Downtown on Broadway. . . . Tenements, the Puerto Rican squalor. Then the University, squalid in a different way. . . . Except on special occasions . . . Sammler never came this way any more. Walking for exercise, he didn't venture this far uptown. And now . . . he inspected the subculture of the underprivileged (terminology recently acquired in the *New York Times*), its Caribbean fruits, its plucked naked chickens with loose necks and eyelids blue, the wavering fumes of Diesel and hot lard. Then 96th Street, tilted at all four corners, the kiosks and movie houses, the ramparts of wire-fastened newspaper bundles, and the colors of panic waving. . . . Broadway . . . always challenged Sammler. He was never up to it. And why should there be any contest? But there was, every time. For something was stated here. By a convergence of all minds and all movements the conviction transmitted by this crowd seemed to be that reality is a terrible thing, and that the final truth about mankind is overwhelming, and crushing. This vulgar, cowardly conclusion, rejected by Sammler with all his heart, was the implicit local orthodoxy, the populace itself being metaphysical and living out this interpretation of reality and this view of truth. . . . Broadway at 96th Street gave him such a sense of things. Life, when it was like this, all question-and-answer from the top of intellect to the very bottom, was really a state of singular dirty misery. . . . This poverty of soul, its abstract state, you could see in the faces on the street. And he too had a touch of the same disease.[21]

A Schopenhauerian vision. But even here, in this frenzied running-down corner of civilization, one can, by the very act of *thinking*, detach himself from the fury of the world's blind Will: by way of the Idea which is not overpowered by *maya* in any of its forms. The irony of Sammler's (and Bellow's) position, freely acknowledged in the looser, wilder *Humboldt's Gift*, is that the novel's energies depend entirely upon the repulsiveness of what is being denounced. Nor is the "fallen" world dramatized: it is *only* denounced.

(By contrast, Hubert Selby, Jr.'s extraordinary collection of stories, *Last Exit to Brooklyn*, and John Rechy's rather more reticent, but still deeply disturbing *City of Night* attempt to illuminate from the inside the nightmare qualities of the City in more or less the stage of deterioration that so upsets Sammler. The near-primitive nature of Selby's characters and the almost consistently uninflected rhythm of his prose should not obscure the fact that *Last Exit to Brooklyn* is, in its way, a formal experiment: an attempt to force the reader to *feel* the repulsiveness of its subject. One does not tour Brooklyn in a Rolls Royce or its moral equivalent in *Last Exit*, nor is one allowed an aesthetic distance from the cities of night [New York at Times Square, Los Angeles at Pershing Square, New Orleans during Mardi Gras] in Rechy's deeply moving and surprisingly lyric novel of the homosexual sub-culture. To use Schopenhauer's terminology, these naturalistic works give verbal life to the Will—and if the Idea is present, it must be inferred by the reader, who should not, on that account, imagine himself superior to the "singular dirty mystery" of these fictions.)

Humboldt's Gift, Bellow's most recent novel—it was published in 1975 and brought Bellow, after a distinguished career, both the long-withheld Pulitzer Prize and the Nobel Prize—resolves in comedy of a frequently outsized, loony nature many of the tragic paradoxes of Sammler's world. In *Humboldt's Gift*, discursive and moralizing passages seem, at times, set down almost at random in the text, and the novel's protagonist Charley Citrine, a "famous" and commercially successful playwright, often earns the impatience his ex-wives and other critics ("Reality Instructors") feel for him. Yet beneath the carnival-like plot there is the constant brooding upon death—mortality and love and fame and death in America—that Bellow has elsewhere explored. As Augie said long ago, "There is a darkness. It is for everyone."

Humboldt is, of course, Von Humboldt Fleischer, the beautiful brilliant boy-genius of a poet who becomes—all too quickly, and too plausibly—a dishevelled ruin of an alcoholic whose fate is a lonely death in a hotel off Times Square. Charley Citrine, his old friend, is obsessed with Humboldt, not simply because he feels that, in complex ways, both he and Humboldt betrayed each other (and loved each other, like brothers), but because Humboldt's fate is illustrative of the fate of the poet in America at the present time:

The country is proud of its dead poets [Citrine thinks]. It takes terrific satisfaction in the poet's testimony that the USA is too tough, too big, too much, too rugged, that American reality is overpowering. And to be a poet is a school thing, a skirt thing, a church thing. The weakness of the spiritual powers is proved in the childishness, madness, drunkenness, and despair of these martyrs. . . . Poets are loved, but loved because they just can't make it here. They exist to light up the enormity of the awful tangle and justify the cynicism of those who say, "If *I* were not such a corrupt, unfeeling bastard, creep, thief, and vulture, I couldn't get through this either. . . ." So this . . . is how successful bitter hard-faced and cannibalistic people exult.[22]

And Citrine is convinced that Chicago with its "gigantesque outer life" contains the problem of poetry and the inner life in America. For if power, fame, and money—but particularly power—are all that matter, how is the poet to compete as a man among men? (For Bellow's point has very much to do with competition.) Where once the poet was considered to have divine powers, now his relative impotence is shown for what it is: "Having no machines, no transforming knowledge comparable to the knowledge of Boeing or Sperry Rand or IBM or RCA. . . . For could a poem pick you up in Chicago and land you in New York two hours later? Or could it compute a space shot? It had no such powers. And interest was where power was. . . . It was not Humboldt, it was the USA that was making its point: 'Fellow Americans, listen. If you abandon materialism and the normal pursuits of life you wind up at Bellevue like this poor kook.' "[23]

Beneath Citrine's comic despair is the heartcry of Bellow himself, who has written, elsewhere, frankly and thoughtfully of the failure (that is, the refusal) of the nation's "leaders" to pay the most minimal attention to novelists and humanists like himself. One hardly wants the State to show an interest in literature like that of Stalin's—yet the situation is rather discouraging for a writer with Bellow's justifiable claims of "leadership" in his own field. In a self-interview published in 1975 shortly after the appearance of *Humboldt's Gift*, Bellow attacks the "formulae, the jargon, the exciting fictions, the heightened and dramatized shadow events" selected by the media and accepted by the public, and "believed by almost everyone to be real." Is the reading of serious literature at all possible for such people? In the universities, where one might expect something very different, "the teaching of literature has been a disaster." Interpretation, critical methodology, and "learned" analyses are substituted for the actual experience of the work of art itself. And the cultural-intelligentsia (professors, commentators, editors) have become politicized and analytical in temper, and hostile to literature. The members of this élite, Bellow says, *had* literature in their student days and are now well beyond it.[24]

The City of *Humboldt's Gift* is background primarily, experienced in snatched moments, though greatly bound up with Citrine's meditation upon death. (Indeed, *Humboldt's Gift* is a novel whose very spirit feeds upon a sustained communion with the dead.) Citrine is not so obsessed with his guilt over Humboldt and his love for Renata, however, that he fails to pause for characteristically Bellovian moments of sharply observed commentary. New York City, for instance, seen from a high window of the Plaza Hotel, reveals itself in its myriad dazzling lights as similar to "cells in a capillary observed through a microscope, elastically changing shape, bumping and pulsatory." And, in one of the book's strongest passages, Citrine broods:

On hot nights Chicagoans feel the city body and soul. The stockyards are gone, Chicago is no longer slaughter-city, but the old smells revive in the night heat. Miles of railroad siding along the streets once were filled with red cattle cars, the animals waiting to enter the yards lowing and reeking. The old stink still haunts the place. It returns at times, suspiring from the vacated soil, to remind us all that Chicago had once led the world in butcher-technology and that billions of animals had died here. And that night the windows were open wide and the familiar depressing multilayered stink of meat, tallow, blood-meal, pulverized bones, hides, soap, smoked slabs, and burnt hair came back. Old Chicago breathed again. . . . I heard fire trucks and . . . ambulances, bowel-deep and hysterical. In the surrounding black slums incendiarism shoots up in summer. . . . Chicago, this night, was panting, the big urban engines going, tenements blazing in Oakwood with great shawls of flame, the sirens weirdly yelping, the fire engines, ambulances, and police cars—mad-dog, gashing-knife weather, a rape and murder night. . . . Bands of kids prowled with handguns and knives.[25]

Have we come full circle, to the demonic sub-human city of Stephen Crane's *Maggie?*

Yet Citrine, and presumably Bellow, would leave us with the conviction that the individual is, indeed, capable of transcending the physical limits set for him by the City. Citrine appears convinced—as a consequence of his reading in the mystic Rudolf Steiner, and his involvement with people out of his and Humboldt's shared past—that one's existence is "merely the present existence, one in a series," and that there is more to any experience, connection, or relationship than ordinary consciousness, the daily life of the ego, can grasp. "The soul belongs," Citrine says, "to a greater, an all-emb̶ ̶cing life outside."

The City has so fascinated contemporary writers of prose and poetry alike that no paper can do justice to the variety of "images" that has been explored. Some are deservedly famous, like Bellow's, and that of Ralph Ellison (whose *Invisible Man* of 1952 is still very much a contemporary work). Others, for instance Anne Tyler's Baltimore, deserve closer attention. Philip Levine has written less of Detroit than of lives passed in the haze of Detroit's industrial slums and near-slums; his most powerful poems fairly pulse with the beat of that infinitely sprawling city, and take their life from a perverse nostalgia which is all the more disturbing for its authenticity:

Coming Home, Detroit, 1968

A winter Tuesday, the city pouring fire,
Ford Rouge sulfurs the sun, Cadillac, Lincoln,
Chevy gray. The fat stacks
of breweries hold their tongues. Rags,
papers, hands, the stems of birches
dirtied with words.

                   Near the freeway
you stop and wonder what came off,
recall the snowstorm where you lost it all,
the wolverine, the northern bear, the wolf
caught out, ice and steel raining
from the foundries in a shower
of human breath. On sleds in the false sun
the new material rests. One brown child
stares and stares into your frozen eyes
until the lights change and you go
forward to work. The charred faces, the eyes
boarded up, the rubble of innards, the cry
of wet smoke hanging in your throat,
the twisted river stopped at the color of iron.
We burn this city every day.[26]

New York City—that most mythical of cities—tends to emerge in recent literature as hellish, or at any rate murderous; yet its presence is the occasion for some of the most subtle and intelligently graceful prose of our time. Consider Hortense Calisher's classic "The Scream on 57th Street" in which a lonely woman hears, or believes she hears, a scream of terror five flights below her bedroom window: *Some of us,* Mrs. Hazlitt thinks with desperate pride, *are still responsible.*[27] Consider the New York observed in Renata Adler's novel of anecdote and collage, *Speedboat* (in which an unsolved murder is noted, but is not dwelt upon); and the New York of Elizabeth Hardwick's *Sleepless Nights* (in which another murder—among numerous disturbing events—is noted in passing). The City cannot be comprehended, but the vertiginous nature of its threat can be translated into language—a language necessarily oblique and circumspect. In Donald Barthelme's prose poems the City is re-imagined from every possible angle: its suprahuman dynamism is a *given,* like the Milky Way, like the passage of time. A typically anonymous Barthelme hero sets out upon a "legendary" quest one day, hoping to climb the glass mountain (which might be confused with a high-rise office building) on the corner of Thirteenth Street and Eighth Avenue. At the base of the mountain are the corpses of innumerable knights who have died attempting this climb, but the hero perseveres, and at the top—after ninety-odd numbered sentences—he encounters the "beautiful enchanted symbol" in its golden castle. He approaches the symbol with its "layers of meaning" but, unfortunately, when he touches it, "it turned into only a beautiful princess" whom he then throws headfirst down the mountain and into the street.[28]

In another Barthelme fantasy, "The Balloon," a gigantic balloon appears in Manhattan, covering forty-five blocks north-south and an irregular area east-west, about six crosstown blocks on either side of Fifth Avenue. The balloon is an anti-city, an artifice of the imagination, hence disturbingly controversial. Everyone contemplates it; everyone has a theory. But it is reasonable to assume that the balloon's fascination lies partly in the fact that it is not limited or defined. It changes constantly. "This ability of the balloon to shift its shape, to change, was very pleasing, especially to people whose lives were rather rigidly patterned, persons to whom change, although desired, was not available. The balloon, for the twenty-two days of its existence, offered the possibility, in its randomness, of mislocation of the self, in contradistinction to the grid of precise, rectangular pathways under our feet."[29]

In "City Life" the anonymous narrator expresses a view of the City not dissimilar to Artur Sammler's: it is muck, but a multi-directional muck with its own mayor. It is a creation of the muckish nation-state, in itself the creation of that muck of mucks, human consciousness. And in one of Barthelme's most elaborately pessimistic stories, "Brain Damage," a finale of despair takes on the rhythms of a litany: "There's brain damage on the horizon, a great big blubbery cloud of it coming this way—This is the country of brain damage . . . these are the rivers of brain damage . . . where the damaged pilots land the big, damaged ships. . . . Skiing along on the soft surface of brain damage, never to sink, because we don't understand the danger—"[30]

In one of the penultimate stories of the elegiac *Too Far to Go*, John Updike positions his soon-to-be-divorced protagonist Richard Maple in a Boston apartment with a view of a locally famous skyscraper. This skyscraper is a beautiful disaster, never completed, and Richard, in his solitude, finds much to contemplate in it. The skyscraper is disastrous—glass keeps falling from it—precisely because it is beautiful. "The architect had had a vision. He had dreamed of an invisible building, though immense; the glass was meant to reflect the sky and the old low brick skyline of Boston, and to melt into the city. Instead, the windows of mirroring glass kept falling to the street, and were replaced by ugly opacities of black plywood." Richard comes to equate the skyscraper with his own soul: even unseen, it is always present.

One day, however, Richard takes a walk, and finds himself at the base of the skyscraper. A mistake: the skyscraper close-up is hideous.

Heavily planked and chicken-wired tunnels, guarded by barking policemen, protected pedestrians from falling glass. . . . Trestles and trucks jammed the cacophonous area. The lower floors were solid plywood, of a Stygian black; the building, so lovely in air, had tangled mucky roots.[31]

The building, so lovely in air, had tangled mucky roots.

Notes

1. Saul Bellow, *Humboldt's Gift* (New York: Viking Press, 1975), p. 10.

2. Anzia Yezierska, "My Last Hollywood Script," in *The Open Cage: An Anzia Yezierska Collection* (New York: Persea Books, 1979), p. 187.

3. Saul Bellow, *Mr. Sammler's Planet* (New York: Viking Press, 1970), p. 26. Bellow's Sammler broods: "The many impressions and experiences of life seemed no longer to occur each in its own proper space, in sequence, each with its recognizable religious or aesthetic importance, but human beings suffered the humiliations of inconsequence, of confused styles, of a long life containing several lives. In fact the whole experience of mankind was now covering each separate life in its flood. . . . Compelling the frail person to receive, to register, depriving him because of volume, of mass, of the power to impart design."

4. Donald Barthelme, "City Life," in *City Life* (New York: Farrar, Straus & Giroux, 1970), p. 172.

5. Stephen Crane, *Maggie: A Girl of the Streets* (New York: Fawcett Paperback, 1978), pp. 26–28.

6. Theodore Dreiser, *Sister Carrie* (New York: Boni and Liveright, 1917), p. 2.

7. Ibid., p. 83.

8. Anzia Yezierska, *Bread Givers* (New York: Persea Books, 1979), p. 9.

9. Ibid., p. 138.

10. Ibid., p. 155.

11. Ibid., p. 231.

12. Harriette Arnow is the author of a number of novels, but her masterpiece is *The Dollmaker*, first published in 1954 and reprinted by Avon Books in 1972. Since I wrote the Afterword for this edition I hesitate to repeat myself, except to emphasize the fact that *The Dollmaker*, set in Kentucky and Detroit during the closing months of World War II, is as significant a work as any by

John Steinbeck and may bear comparison, in some respects at least, with the novels of William Faulkner.

13. Saul Bellow, *The Adventures of Augie March* (New York: Modern Library Edition, 1965), p. 39.

14. Ibid., p. 124.

15. Ibid., p. 62.

16. Ibid., p. 90.

17. Ibid., p. 330.

18. Saul Bellow, *Herzog* (New York: Fawcett, 1964), p. 333.

19. Ibid., p. 317.

20. Bellow, *Mr. Sammler's Planet*, p. 89.

21. Ibid., p. 280.

22. Bellow, *Humboldt's Gift*, p. 128.

23. Ibid., p. 169.

24. See "Self-Interview" by Saul Bellow in *The Ontario Review* (Fall–Winter 1975–76): 51–60.

25. *Humboldt's Gift*, p. 124.

26. Philip Levine, *They Feed They Lion: Poems* (New York: Atheneum, 1972), p. 22.

27. *The Collected Stories of Hortense Calisher* (New York: Arbor House, 1975), p. 502.

28. Donald Barthelme, "The Glass Mountain," in *City Life*, pp. 59–65.

29. Donald Barthelme, "The Balloon," in *Unspeakable Practices, Unnatural Acts* (New York: Farrar, Straus & Giroux, 1968), p. 28.

30. Donald Barthelme, "Brain Damage," in *City Life*, p. 146.

31. John Updike, "Gesturing," in *Too Far to Go* (New York: Fawcett, 1979). pp. 222–223.

FERNALD LIBRARY
COLBY-SAWYER COLLEG
NEW LONDON, N.H. 032

85517

City Limits, Village Values: Concepts of the Neighborhood in Black Fiction

Toni Morrison

> We come to Chartres . . . for the cathedral that
> fills our ideal.
> > —Henry Adams,
> > Mont-Saint-Michel and Chartres

> I am terrified by the slippery bottomless well to
> be found in the crypt down which heretics were
> hurled to death, and by the obscene,
> inescapable gargoyles strutting out of the stone.
> > —James Baldwin,
> > "Stranger in the Village," Notes of a Native Son

When James Baldwin looked at Chartres, he was doing more than reflecting on the schizophrenia of Western civilization. He was responding to what are universally believed to be the best and the most magnificent features of pre-industrial life from the singular position of a Black writer. His is an extraordinary observation for many reasons, one of which is that it brings up the question of how a dispossessed people, a disenfranchised people, a people without orthodox power, views the cities that it inhabits but does not have a claim to. Like Black American writers before and after him, Baldwin could not ruminate elegantly and with subjective pride in the achievement of Chartres as Henry Adams could—not because of any want of intellect or skill, but because the intimacy between the writer and the historical artifact that Adams felt did not exist in the same way for Baldwin, and neither did the impetus to relish whatever was fine in those achievements. If Baldwin could respond in that manner to Chartres, how much more despairing we would expect him to be in his view of twentieth-century post-industrial urban America. In fact

© 1981 by Toni Morrison.

he is, but not for the same reasons his white colleagues appear to have been.

It is true, of course, that by and large, the national literature of this country has always deplored the city. Mainstream writers are appalled by the urban. "Viewing 'progress' with alarm" has the frequency of a cliché. And there is a similar hostility among Black writers as well. Yet the assumptions of white writers are markedly different from those of Black ones. Although the anti-urbanism of white writers from Melville to Dos Passos and Hemingway to Cheever is couched in terms of blight, automation, and Babbittry, it nevertheless seems to originate not from any intrinsic hatred of the idea of a city over life in and with nature, but from a wholehearted acceptance of the mandates of individualism, which, presumably, cities curtail. From Huck Finn to the disengaged intellectual, from Paul Bunyan to Jay Gatsby, "society" is seen as a diminishing of freedom—corrupting. In their writings, a commitment to a social cause is doomed to failure (inevitably and rightly doomed in their point of view) because such commitments curtail individual freedom and dehumanize issues and people.[1] We live, after all, in a country where three Italian immigrants were jailed in the same decade: one, Al Capone, a greedy pursuer of individual freedom, was a folk hero; two others, Sacco and Venzetti, who put society above personal comfort, deserved execution according to the wisdom of the time.

The country, on the other hand, represents to these mainstream writers the possibility of personal freedom, nobility, privacy, and purity. Just as their anti-urbanism does not seem to be directed toward the idea of cities per se, so their professed love of nature is questionable. Hemingway's "earth that abideth forever" is a holiday excursion—not a way of life where the character actually lives. It is an opportunity to be heroically alone, to transcend society and define one's single, private self. Although Gatsby's dream is, according to Carraway, "unadaptable to Eastern [urban] life," and although Hemingway's people are busy excluding society and living by private codes of self-discipline, endurance, and stubborn individualism, none is seen as having fulfilled lives in the natural environment. Not only is this fulfillment unavailable in the city, it isn't even available in a rural town. The delicious, regenerative qualities of nature are outside even Gopher Prairie, which is described as being as lethal in its own way as New York City. Perhaps the anti-urbanism is not anti-urban at all, but anti-social.

In *The Enormous Room*, E.E. Cummings lauds the anarchic, the illiterate, the primitive, precisely because he sees those characteristics as being against the social order and therefore rife with individualism. Nothing could be further from the truth. Dos Passos's deserter wallows in the sun and air and water, but his communion with them is escape from commitment and orders, not toward the inexorable rules that a genuine communion with nature would demand. Even when we see an attraction toward the village, it is not reverence for nature. The village—unlike the city—of white writers seems to have no moral life or manners. For Cheever or Updike, the village is merely suburbia, where privacy is a real value; where society is washed and comes in smaller numbers; where, in fact, society as masses does not intervene or require any limitations on personal freedom or the constant effort to avoid unmanageable minglings with the lower classes. The urbanism, pro or con, of Black American writers, however, is mixed in a different cauldron.

When Black artists write, whether they profess love of urban life as Langston Hughes did, or despise it as Baldwin does, whether they are awed by the city or terrified of it, the emotion cannot be compared to Sandburg's or Fitzgerald's or Henry James's, simply because its sources are not the same. Collectively they have not contributed to the major decisions in founding or shaping the city. Minor decisions, yes. The specious power of numbers, yes. The fraudulent repulsive power of the "patient," yes. For Black people are generally viewed as patients, victims, wards, and pathologies in urban settings, not as participants. And they could not share what even the poorest white factory worker or white welfare recipient could feel: that in some way the city belonged to him. Consequently, the Black artist's literary view of the city and his concept of its opposite, the village or country, is more telling than the predictable and rather obvious responses of mainstream American writers to post-industrial decay, dehumanization and the curtailing of individualism which they imagined existed in the city but not in the country. It may be that the positive and negative aspects of urbanism can best be articulated by those who know it, but who have no vested political, cultural, or philosophical interests in supporting or rejecting it as it presently exists, and who seldom see themselves as disengaged from society.

In spite of their labor and enterprise—the Black-owned oyster houses of Wall Street, the Black stone masons of Manhattan, the iron workers of New Orleans—the affection of Black writers (whenever displayed) for the city seems to be for the village within it: the neighborhoods and the population of those neighborhoods. The city itself was "a crypt down which heretics were hurled." It was Ellison's underground hideout, Wright's nightmare violence. But what repelled them was not Eliot's Wasteland nor was it the mechanization of life. (The horror of industrialization seems to me mostly an elite preoccupation. Laborers seemed to have an affinity for machines when allowed dominion over them rather than a hostility toward them, perhaps because they are the ones who work with them.) The anti-urbanism among Black writers is not an attitudinal response to that which they perceive as ugly or newly decayed, or nostalgia for something once grand. Nor is it the suffocation of Paul Bunyan robotized by the city. Similarly, pro-urban views of city life among these writers are not the result of the pride and excitement of having created something with one's own hands, or solved some problem of social order. The Black writer's pro-urbanism, his eagerness for acceptance in the city, his anxiety to be individually free there, seeking entrance in and associations with the very institutions his white brethren deride, is clearly a statement against segregation rather than a respect for the intrinsic value of the institution itself. The rewards the city can bestow on him are rewards for proving the stereotype to be wrong. This makes for some ambivalence and contradiction. Langston Hughes professed to love Harlem and the glittering skyscrapers downtown. The "I" in "I, too, am America" is obviously "we" and the thrust is integrationist. But unlike Eliot's river, Hughes's river is an urgent connection with and celebration of racial past—not the scene of modern man's futility.

While individualism and escape from the community was frequently a major theme in Black writing, it should be regarded for what it was: "A devotion to self-assertion can be a devotion to discovering distinctive ways of expressing community values, social purpose, mutual regard or . . . affirming a collective experience."[2] These community values (I call them village values) are uppermost in the minds of Black writers, and it may be this feeling for village values as opposed to Gopher Prairie despair that causes so much misadventure in white criticism of Black writers: such critics tend not to trust or respect a hero who prefers the village and its tribal values to heroic loneliness and alienation. When a character defies a village law or shows contempt for its values, it may be seen as a triumph to white readers, while Blacks may see it as an outrage.

Harlem, the closest thing in American life as well as literature to a Black city, and a mecca for generations of Blacks, held this village quality for Black people—although on a grand scale and necessarily parochial. The hospitals, schools, and buildings they lived in were not founded nor constructed by their own people, but the relationships were clannish because there was joy and protection in the clan.

We can generalize easily about those writers who are familiar to us, but something rather fascinating seems to be showing up in the writing of more recent Black authors. Black music—jazz—may have misled us into thinking of Black people as essentially urban types, relishing or at least preferring to deal with city life rather than small towns. Automatically the effort to view country life through Black eyes produced visions of lynchings, share croppers, slavery, and all the fear and facts of Black life in America. An effort to view the city through those same eyes dredges up Blacks who may roam, but never walk—the violence of the powerless coupled with a kind of stylized adroitness, cunning, and subterranean rip-off tactics. But in fact, almost all of the fiction of recent Black writers, even when its theme is unequivocally pro-city, even when its mode and style is urbane, hip, consistently reveals characters disappointed by a marked and poignant absence of some vital element of city life that is all the more startling because of the presence of this same element or quality in their descriptions of rural or village settings.

This missing quality in city fiction is not privacy or diminished individual freedom, not even the absence of beauty. Nor is the quality present in stories about the country, nature, serenity, or peace, for the country holds as many terrors for the Black American writer as the city does. What is missing in city fiction and present in village fiction is the ancestor. The advising, benevolent, protective, wise Black ancestor is imagined as surviving in the village but not in the city. The general hostility to the city is not the result of the disappearance of grandeur or the absence of freedom. And the idealization of the country is not a pastoral delight in things being right with God. Writer after writer after writer concedes explicitly or implicitly that the ancestor is the matrix of his yearning. The city is wholesome, loved when such an ancestor is on the scene, when neighborhood links are secure. The country is beautiful—healing because more often than not, such an ancestor is there.

When the Black American writer experiences the country or the village, he does so not to experience nature as a balm for his separate self, but to touch the ancestor. When he cannot (because the ancestor is not there, or because he cannot communicate with him), then and only then is he frustrated, defeated, devastated, and unregenerated. When he is able to, he is regenerated, balanced, and capable of operating on a purely moral axis. It is obvious what role the missing or misunderstood ancestor plays in Baldwin's writings. It should be equally obvious what Invisible Man's difficulties are, having left the ancestor, having misunderstood him and felt guilty because of this misunderstanding. The wantonness described in much urban Black literature is really the wantonness of a character out of touch with the ancestor. But lest this appear too happy a generalization, I would like to look at some contemporary writers, male and female, city-bred and country-bred who are prolific enough and whose talent is dazzling enough to bear fruit in this investigation.

Contemporary Black writers seem to view urban life as lovable only when the ancestor is there. The worst thing that can happen in a city is that the ancestor becomes merely a parent or an adult and is thereby seen as a betrayer—one who has abandoned his traditional role of advisor with a strong connection to the past.

Toni Cade Bambara has written two collections of short stories and one novel. She is a New Yorker, born and educated in that city with an intimate and fearless knowledge of it, and although the tone of most of her stories is celebratory, full of bravura, joyfully survivalist, the principal fear and grief of her characters is the betrayal of an adult who has abandoned not the role of providing for, but the role of advisor, competent protector. Of the sixteen stories in *Gorilla, My Love*, only two stories cannot fit that description. And one of the two, "The Survivor," describes a girl going to the country for help, succor, and regeneration at the hands of an elderly aunt who lives up to the demands of an ancestor exactly. In the title story, Hazel, the young protagonist, is at odds with the world because her favorite uncle who promised to marry her is not only engaged to somebody else, but has changed his name. When she confronts him with his promise, he

look[s] at [her] real strange like he never saw me before in life. Like he lost in some weird town in the middle of night and lookin for directions and there's no one to ask. Like it was me that messed up the maps and turned the posts round.

The uncle says to her that he was simply teasing her; she says she was not teasing and replies to him in a voice

just how he said it so he can hear what a terrible thing it is. . . . "You a lyin dawg," I say, when I meant to say treacherous dog, but just couldn't get hold of the word. It slipped away from me. And I'm crying and crumplin down in the seat and just don't care. And Grandaddy say to hush and steps on the gas. And I'm losin my bearins and don't even know where to look on the map cause I can't see for cryin. And Baby Jason cryin too. Cause he is my blood brother and understands that we must stick together or be forever lost, what with grownups playin change-up and turnin you round every which way so bad. And don't even say they sorry."[3]

In "The Survivor," a rural story, Jewel, pregnant and reeling from an unfortunate marriage, has traveled from New York to her grandmother in a small town. When they first meet they stand in a field: "Miss Candy dainty but sinewy and solid, never hid from weather of any kind." And when she stoops to touch some roots, remarking on the need for rain, she "traced the travels of the tree roots barely bulging beneath the bristly grass. 'A good woman does not rot,' she said on her haunches like some ancient sage.'" Jewel has gone there because

family ties [are] no longer knitted close and there was no one to say let's get our wagons in a circle when someone was in crisis. So she'd come to M'Dear, Miss Candy, the last of that generation who believed in sustaining.

In her novel, *The Salt Eaters*, the theme is totally explicated.[4] A would-be suicide is literally and metaphorically healed by the ancestor: the witch woman, the spiritual sage, the one who asks of this oh so contemporary and oh so urban daughter of the sixties, "Are you sure you want to be well?" Here is the village, its values, its resources, its determination not to live, as Stevie Wonder has put it, "just enough for the city," and its requisities for survival only. The village is determined to flourish as well, and it is that factor that makes it possible for Velma to rise from the ancestor's shawl and drop it to the floor "like a cocoon."

Another writer of this high caliber, Henry Dumas, is a special case in point. Born in Sweet Home, Arkansas, he wrote brilliantly of both the village and the city. In the former, there are innumerable examples of the connection (not conflict) between the ancestor and personal fulfillment. In his collected stories, *Ark of Bones*, the title story concerns two young boys who have an encounter with a mysterious ship that appears at night on the Mississippi.[5] When they board, they find an old man and a crew whose job it is to retrieve the bones of Black people murdered and thrown into the river. Their job is to reflesh them and await restitution. The ceremony is religious in its ritual, and Dumas speaks of the old man as a priest. Oaths are taken, the responsiblity for collecting the bones and living in the "house of generations" is passed on, with the narrator as witness. In "Echo Tree," the characters are involved in calling spirits from a sacred tree. One of them was taught how to do this by Leo who had gone to New York where he got "messed up" and is now dead. The consequence of laughing, of not taking the spirits seriously, is being turned into an albino. The instruction from the dead brother was to "get that hard city water out of your gut, you liable to taint yourself," which is the sign of being on one's way to becoming an albino. Obviously in the cursing of the ancestor, the spirit is to become white, which equals evil or dead—a state of existence available inevitably in the city, away from the spirits that guide and protect.

In his novel, *Jonoah and the Green Stone*,[6] the central character is returning from a sojourn in the city, and unlike most in mainstream fiction, he is regenerated by his return to the village, is met there, tested there, and judged and received by those whose values he once betrayed. Sweet Home is not Gopher Prairie. In "A Harlem Game," the "game" is not just the cards being played by the adults, or even the trick the boy's father plays on him. The game that is typically Harlem is the betrayal of the ancestral functions. What is there is the treachery of one parent and the indifference of another. For Dumas the country, the village, is always a place of magic testing under the watchful eye of a benevolent ancestor. The city is always devoid of this presence. In "Strike and Fade" the men go to seek counsel of an elder who has that position simply because he is a Vietnam veteran. He advises them on guerrilla warfare. Jonoah's "green stone" is the watermelon turned into a saving ark, an ark of deliverance manned by the ancestors.

It is not just recent Black fiction that reveals this predilection. In Jean Toomer's "Cane," the longest piece in *Cane*,[7] the protagonist returns to the South (an ancestral South). And the story pivots on the presence of Father John, the sage, the one who speaks one sentence, the one who is cared for and revered as though he were a living saint. Elsewhere in the book, Washington, D.C., is a "bastard of Prohibition and the War . . . crude-boned, soft-skinned wedge of nigger life breathing its loafer air, jazz songs and love, thrusting unconscious rhythms, black reddish blood into the white . . . washed wood of Washington. Stale soggy wood of Washington." In "Avey," the heroine is a city girl described as an "orphan-woman" who cannot find a wholesome life or home in the city. Rhobert, in the story of that name, wears his house on his head like a "monstrous diving helmet," and succumbs to its pressure—alone.

The fiction of James Alan McPherson, Leon Forrest, Albert Murray, Paule Marshal, and R. Fischer—of so many Black writers—becomes doubly fascinating when examined from this point of view; and since the attitudes expressed toward the city and the village do not stem from reactions to post-industrialism, horror of mechanization, the comfort of an urban intellectual society, the fulfillment or even the promise (these days) of a better economic life, I think it is possible to get a deeper, more profound perception of what cities have to offer writers and what villages do from their work rather than from the work of mainstream writers.

This love of ancestor should not be confused with some simple-minded cant about Black families, broken families, or historylessness. Dumas does not seek a history; he describes it. Wright does not miss a past; he hates it. And what beguiles me is the way in which the absence or presence of an ancestor determines the success of the protagonists. For the ancestor is not only wise; he or she values racial connection, racial memory over individual fulfillment. Fighting the ancestor frequently occurs, but the devastation of the protagonist never takes place unless he succeeds in ignoring or annihilating the ancestor.

Like Baldwin, these writers have seen the "slippery bottomless well to be found in the crypt" in the city at its best, its most beautiful and ideal. But that is not what impales them, what gashes life. It is the absence of the ancestor, who cannot thrive in the dungeon of the city. For the true ancestor is frequently a social or secret outlaw like Ellison's Grandfather on his death bed saying, "I never told you but our life is a war and I have been a traitor all my born days, a spy in the enemy's country." The ancestor must defy the system, be cautious of Chartres, provide alternate wisdom, and establish and maintain and sustain generations in a land. Huck Finn lights out for the territory as escape. Nigger Jim is hiding there, but his wish is to go home—to the village. Without that presence and recognition there is no life. And it is for this reason, I believe, that among Black writers, the city has huge limits and the village profound values.

Notes

1. Society here means "masses" and dehumanize is meant to suggest taking away a character's singularity.

2. Robert Elias, *Entangling Alliances with None* (New York: Norton, 1973), p. 190.

3. Toni Cade Bambara, *Gorilla, My Love* (New York: Random House, 1972), pp. 19–20.

4. Toni Cade Bambara, *The Salt Eaters* (New York: Random House, 1980).

5. Henry Dumas, *Ark of Bones and Other Stories* (Carbondale: Southern Illinois University Press, 1971).

6. Henry Dumas, *Jonoah and the Green Stone* (New York: Random House, 1976).

7. Jean Toomer, *Cane* (New York: Boni and Liveright, 1923).

Poetry and the Modern City

Stephen Spender

Athens, Alexandria, Rome, Paris, Vienna—all echo through the work of poets. But ever since the industrial revolution, the poets, instead of regarding the cities as centers of civilization, have regarded them as destructive of the conditions out of which the supreme achievements of poetry in the past were created. The modern urban environment is ugly, overwhelming, materialistic. Its power is expressed in a scientific, sociological vocabulary which is alien to the image-making vocabulary of past poetry.

In the view of Romantic poets such as Wordsworth or Blake, the city with its smoke and slums, its factories—Blake's "dark satanic mills"—its businessmen, and its false religion empties men, women, and children—city-dwellers—of their individual lives and fills them with its annihilating smoke and ugliness (far from the countryside) and the obligation to perform the mechanical tasks which enslave its inhabitants.

The consequences of seeing the post-industrialized urban environment as essentially anti-poetic and destructive of all the arts differ with different poets. Blake viewed the world of his time as the battlefield of an apocalyptic struggle between the forces of materialism (hypocritically supported by official religion) and the spiritual and sexual energies of individual men and women. Wordsworth saw it as necessitating a separation by the poets of the countryside—nature—where people still lived lives unaffected by industrialism, from the towns where people were corrupted by it. The poets driven from the towns must withdraw into the surroundings of nature. They must go and live in the country and write poetry in the language of the simple but uncorrupted people there, describing the joys and sorrows of their lives, entering into their natural and traditional religion, and relating their experiences and feelings to the awesomeness and beauty of nature in plain, straightforward language which is comprehensible to people who live in the country.

© 1981 by Stephen Spender.

The Romantic poets wrote great poetry in their total rejection of the modern city. Looking back on them now, we can see their work as the result of their withdrawal from the urban environment into the English countryside (Wordsworth and Coleridge); into mysticism (Blake); into the greatest and purest moments of the world of the Shakespearean imagination (Keats); into the Mediterranean landscape and culture (Byron and Shelley); or into their own inner lives and autobiography (again, Byron and Shelley). The Romantic movement from this point of view—seen as a reaction to industrialism—was an immense rearguard action. It had its splendid achievements, but it left poetry with a vocabulary capable of dealing only with the poet in some Romantic situation. The inheritance which it left to the Victorian poets was a highly inflated poetic vocabulary and a vision of the poet as completely isolated within, or alienated from, the powerful forces of the industrial society: not only from the cities but also from science. Moreover, the original impetus of Romanticism had passed. The poet was driven back on the resources of the countryside, the past, escape from the city. Yet although, as poets, men like Tennyson and Browning felt isolated, as citizens, living in Victorian society and accepting many of its views and standards, they lacked the hysterical inner passion of Byron, Keats, and Shelley. And Wordsworth's countryside had become a shrine visited by lovers of Wordsworth.

In these circumstances, Tennyson, Browning, and Matthew Arnold did what they are scarcely given credit for: they attempted to come to terms with modern life—with the industrial environment of their time, with Darwin's theories of evolution, modern science, and the crisis of religion. But the ideas of poetry which they inherited from the Romantics left them without a vocabulary which was responsive to their environment. They tried to write about the urban environment, but they did so in the vocabulary and with ideas about form which were entirely derived from the Romantics who had rejected the world of industrialism. Browning was the most successful of the Victorians in inventing a modern idiom—a lot of his poetry reads like that of a nineteenth-century Ezra Pound. Moreover, like Pound he chose to live in and write from Italy. He even wrote about Italian politics of his time, though fortunately for him, there was in his day no Italian leader corresponding to Mussolini. His most successful works were dramatic monologues in which he discussed some of the problems, such as marital relations, which stirred Victorian readers, but he was as remote as Shelley from the industrial environment.

The slums, all the sordid conditions of Victorian London, were resistant to treatment by poetry in the Romantic tradition. What was required was not a poetry which discussed in an outworn idiom of escape from the realities of the age of progress, the ugliness, the squalor, the materialism, the science, and the loss of faith characteristic of the age, but a modern idiom which was strengthened by absorbing some of the brutal strength of the period, speaking its own language of industrial imagery and abstract thinking, and yet able to make poetry out of this unpromising material. Towards the end of the century, this aim was partly realized in the work of one poet—who went unpublished, almost, in his lifetime—the Jesuit priest Gerard Manley Hopkins, who for some years worked in the Liverpool slums. Hopkins realized that to express in poetry his religious faith, the poetry had to employ imagery borrowed from the industrial scene and must meet the world of machinery on its own terms:

> The world is charged with the grandeur of God,
> It will flame out like shining from shook foil;
> It gathers to a greatness, like the ooze of oil
> Crushed. Why do men now not reck his rod?

"Charged" as an electric battery is charged; "shook foil" like the light reflected from a sheet of metal foil shaken; "ooze of oil" like the industrial oil on a wharf into which someone has trod.

But the *Poems* of Hopkins were not published till 1917 because their editor, the friend of Hopkins, Robert Bridges, did not think there was a British public prepared to receive them until that date. And apart from Hopkins, with the possible exception of Thomas Hardy, the Victorian poets had not invented a modern idiom for poetry. When they tried to write poetry about science, politics, and the urban environment, the results were slightly embarrassing, like the remarks of some Anglican bishop of the time about Darwinism. They were happiest writing poetry that invoked the world of medieval legend.

The failure of the poets to write about the century they lived in had one important result for literature, the consequences of which are still with us. This was the novel which in some respects has the characteristics of a poem. Dickens in *Bleak House* takes the London fog as a metaphor for the suffocating entanglements of the law in which the main characters of his novel get caught up. And the law itself—or, rather, the law firm of Jarndyce and Jarndyce—becomes a metaphor for the British constitution, the Houses of Parliament, and the whole British governmental system. *Bleak House*, through the force of the imagination drawing into its plot a cast of characters which seems at times as vast as the population of London itself, approaches being a prose epic poem: and we have had examples of this, of course, in the twentieth century with Joyce's *Ulysses* and *Finnegans Wake*, the great novel of Proust, and novels by D. H. Lawrence and Virginia Woolf. Poets of the present century have gone to these novelists as to batteries, in order to charge up their poetry with Joycean, Proustian, or Laurentian electricity.

There was also, late in the nineteenth century, another development within poetry itself. This movement, which began in France, proudly called itself the Decadence. It was associated with the mood appropriate to the end of the century—the *fin de siècle*—and it embraced the city, not on account of its material achievements (which the Decadents disliked as much as did the Romantics), but on account of the corrupting effects it had on its inhabitants. Poetry was found in the vices, the prostitution, the absinthe drinking, the sexual and drug addictions of the low life of the cafés and bars, as well as in the misery and sickness of people living in the city. Here Romanticism, which had fled from the urban environment, met the decadence which embraced it. For the Romantics, in their extreme individualism and their alienation from the world they lived in, were halfway to decadence.

Translating the physiological decadence of people in the city into spiritual terms, Decadence showed preference for the spiritual life of the damned to institutionalized religious life: the priests having, in the opinion of a poet like Baudelaire, sold their religion to the values of an industrialized urban environment. In the city, conditions made it impossible to be really good. Therefore it was better to be consciously wicked than to be spiritually dead, in the manner of the successful bourgeois inhabitant of the urban environment. Baudelaire called his great collection of poems—for which he was prosecuted—*Les Fleurs du Mal*—the Flowers of Evil.

Regarding the city as wicked, the poet could write, in the Decadent manner, about its shadowy back streets, its dens of vice, and their depraved inhabitants. This new urbanism was the opposite of the Wordsworthian pastoral.

The achievement of the Decadents was to break completely with the Romantic convention that poetry must be about the beautiful. Or to put it differently, but more exactly, they sought to prove that the ugly was beautiful. But in doing so they discovered features of Romanticism which already suggested this, for example the attraction of the Romantics to incest, and the deliberate diabolism of Lord Byron.

At the beginning of the present century, the association of artists—themselves rejected—with the rejected members of society in great cities and the equating of what had been thought to be ugly with the beautiful led to the association of revolutionary artists with revolutionary politics, based on the self-identification of many poets and painters with the poor.

In the course of time, this meant that the poet and artist, associating with the politics of the proletariat, began to see himself as redeeming the city, making it anew. The German Expressionists and the Italian Futurists—to take two examples—accepted the urban environment, preferred it to the countryside. They came to feel that through their art, allied with powerful forces in the society, they could transform the city, making it—according to their own aesthetic standards—beautiful, and creating an urban environment which would transform the lives and attitudes of the inhabitants. This point of view is expressed energetically by Wyndham Lewis, in the early twenties, when he was very much in sympathy with the Futurists:

Art, however, the greatest art, even, has it in its power to influence everybody. Actually the shapes of the objects (houses, cars, dresses and so forth) by which they are surrounded have a very profound subconscious effect on people. A man might be unacquainted with the very existence of a certain movement in art, and yet his life would be modified directly if the street he walked down took a certain shape, at the dictates of an architect under the spell of that movement, whatever it were. Its forms and colours would have a tonic or a debilitating effect on him, an emotional value. Just as he is affected by the changes of the atmosphere, without taking the least interest in the cyclonic machinery that controls it, so he would be directly affected by any change in his physical milieu.

A man goes to choose a house. He is attracted by it or not, often, not for sentimental or practical reasons, but for some reason that he does not seek to explain, and that yet is of sufficient force to prevent him from, or decide him on, taking it. This is usually an example of the functioning of the aesthetic sense (however undeveloped it may be in him) of which we are talking.[1]

This reads to us today as absurdly optimistic. Looking at our cities with their architecture of glass boxes of almost uniform design, we cannot feel that modern art has influenced more than a very few architects, far less, through the media of architecture and design, transformed cities and the lives of men and women in them. All we can say is that through the diverse energies of modern movements in art, the poets of the early twentieth century did evolve a poetic idiom in which it was possible to carry on a dialogue with those conditioned in their consciousness by the urban environment.

Note

1. Wyndham Lewis, "A Preamble for the usual public," *The Tyro, a Review of the Arts of Painting, Sculpture and Design* 2 (1922): 5.

The Poet and the City:
Robert Lowell

Helen Vendler

Late in his volume *History*, Robert Lowell looked back on "Red and Black Brick Boston," as he called it: it is Boston seen in the brilliant winter sunshine of a life's latter days. The city is in part the red of life's blood, in part the black of death, and yet the bricks are identical in size and shape, different only in color. Under the dazzling clarity the red itself turns black, but the poet knows it to be still alive: in Shakespearean terms, he is seeing "the glowing of such fire / That on the ashes of his youth doth lie." Yet Boston, soiled, chequered with heat and cold, is still "worthy," still, says Lowell, offers difference in homogeneity, still abounds in those facts—of architecture, history, population, event—that awaken his imagination. Not all the past, however, could draw Lowell like the present, and no city subsequently known ever became as dear to him as Boston. I quote the lines I have been paraphrasing:

> The arctic brightness bakes the red bricks black,
> a color too chequered to splash its happiness—
> the winter sun in shining on something worthy,
> begging the visible be eternal.
>
>   *   *   *
>
> I glow with the warmth of these soiled red bricks,
> their unalikeness in similarity,
> a senseless originality for fact,
> "Rome was," we told the Irish, "Boston is."[1]

Lowell spent his life begging the visible to be eternal through his poetry; one of the visible things commanding his sensibility was the modern city, with all its original facts. He not only told the Irish, he told himself, that the invisible city was not to be preferred to the

© 1981 by Helen Vendler.

51

visible one: "Much against my will," he announced in "Beyond the Alps," "I left the City of God where it belongs."

The Boston he writes about in *History* is not only his place of imaginative origin, but his place of eventual imaginative departure: even in leaving life he will leave, Lowell says, from Boston:

> We will follow our skeletons on the girder,
> Out of life and Boston, singing with Freud:
> "God's ways are dark and very seldom pleasant."[2]

Lowell's reference is to a painting by Frank Parker, showing Death galloping on a bridge of red rail ties and girders against a background of archaic Boston—"this the eternal, provincial / city Dante saw as Florence and hell."[3] This, not the City of God, is Lowell's eternal city; he lived in Boston from the time he was seven till he went to Kenyon. After living in New York he returned to Boston; still later, after his years in New York and London, he returned to live in Cambridge, and was dividing his time between New York and Cambridge when he died. He wrote about many cities—Paris, Belfast, Florence, ancient and modern Rome, Buenos Aires, Caracas, Cuernavaca, Washington, and Dublin; but it was to Boston and Cambridge, on the one hand, and to New York, on the other, that he returned as to inexhaustible subjects. For inhabitants of both cities, he made the visible eternal. And it would be sufficient to praise him for doing only that, for rendering "fast and fallen New York"[4] and "dour, luxurious Boston."[5]

I will be dwelling in part on the visible qualities in cities which Lowell wished to make eternal, but I would like to reflect, too, on the difficulties that the city poses as a subject for the lyric poet, and on the changes in Lowell's use of the city over time.

The first difficulty for the lyric poet is the actual constitution of the city—large, heterogeneous, full of unknown people, political, land-scaped, historical. Its largeness must be reduced to fit the brief scope of lyric; its heterogeneity must be preserved, at least symbolically; its inhabitants must be sorted out into populations (with risks of stereotyping); its politics must be made intelligible; its landscape given a shape and perspective; its history seen in its visible and invisible traces. The scale of lyric has made it the form taken up chiefly for domestic and private concerns. Like other poets attempting to reclaim terrain conventionally reserved to fiction, Lowell looks outward from his houses—on Marlborough Street, on West Sixty-seventh Street, on Redcliffe Square—to the cities in which they stand, not without dangers to his art.

Lowell's first impulse in recording cities was to symbolize them in architecture, streets, and monuments. The first poem in *Lord Weary's Castle* situates its exile in the midst of the Hôtel de Ville, the Holstenwall, an ancestral house, the Market Square, the Rathaus, and a cathedral. The first Boston poem, "Christmas Eve under Hooker's Statue," places us in wartime outside the State House (opposite the St. Gaudens memorial), and lets the statue of Hooker, enshrined above cannon and cannonballs, stand for all the anti-pacifist evil in patriarchal Boston:

> Hooker's heels
> Kicking at nothing in the shifting snow,
> A cannon and a cairn of cannon balls
> Rusting before the blackened Statehouse, know
> How the long horn of plenty broke like glass
> In Hooker's gauntlets.[6]

In just the way that Hooker's statue dominates its poem, the King's Chapel Burying Ground dominates "At the Indian Killer's Grave": rich, emblematic, isolated enough to be a single pregnant image, the cemetery drew out Lowell's best writing in his first book—writing at once prophetic in moral wrath, elegant in precise visualization, biblical in language, and yet compelled out of its historical fascination with gravestones by the demotic pull of subway and city laborer:

> Blacker than these black stones the subway bends
> About the dirty elm roots and the well
> For the unchristened infants in the waste
> Of the great garden rotten to its root;
> Death, the engraver, puts forward his bone foot.[7]
>
> *   *   *
>
> A public servant putters with a knife
> And paints the railing red
> Forever, as a mouse
> Cracks walnuts by the headstones of the dead
> Whose chiselled angels peer
> At you, as if their art were long as life.[8]

Lowell's economic reduction and selection makes the city landscape gleam with the clarity of a Dürer: every detail is locked into place—the engraved skulls, the grisly well, the indolent workman, the indifferent mouse, the silent headstones, the lurking angels, and under it all the black subway.

The single most famous picture of Boston in *Lord Weary's Castle* is drawn by the same rule: choose a single impressive piece of the city and etch it in moral acid:

> The wild ingrafted olive and the root
>
> Are withered, and a winter drifts to where
> The Pepperpot, ironic rainbow, spans
> Charles River and its scales of scorched-earth miles.
> I saw my city in the Scales, the pans
> Of judgment rising and descending.[9]

We know the argument against such writing about the city: it forces the city to be gripped in the poet's moral vise, leaves the city no independent heterogeneous existence as a natural fact. It was a long time before Lowell could resist his powerful intellectualizing enough to let the city be wholly itself, but his "senseless originality for fact" pressed against his emblematic tendency even in the first book. Boston strives rebelliously to remain itself, and details not entirely governed by emblematic plot, but rather by the genius of memory, sift almost effortlessly into certain poems. Boats, for instance, the shells on Boston Basin, and the swanboats in the Public Garden, appear emblematically present in Lowell's elegy for his grandfather in order to foreshadow Charon's bark. But the Public Garden, Lowell's childhood playground, eludes the iron grasp of the poem, and is simply itself:

> Grandfather Winslow, look, the swanboats coast
> That island in the Public Garden, where
> The bread-stuffed ducks are brooding, where with tub
> And strainer the mid-Sunday Irish scare
> The sun-struck shallows for the dusky chub.[10]

We can perhaps find reasons for the ducks, the chub, and the sun-struck shallows, but they are not emblematic as Hooker and the Pepperpot and King's Chapel Burial Ground are. They are essentially ahistoric, and represent the counterpoise, in Lowell, to the weight of the historic. He sees his city in the Scales, we may say, but in one pan is the historic Boston, in the other the contemporary city; is he to be archivist or journalist?

This question is present as a dilemma, I believe, for Lowell, as it is not for Pound. Pound saw the contemporary *as* historical; from his perspective, all history is simultaneously present, and the present is no more immediate to him than the Homeric. Lowell's historical

vision was fundamental to his art, so much so that the phantasma-
goria of history served him as his chief adolescent fantasy-life. The
bedrock of Lowell's imagination, when excavated, yields the fossils of
Rome, Napoleon, Lincoln, Verdun. But the embedded past, of unequivocal moral fixity, appears to have been important to Lowell
chiefly in his adolescence and young manhood. Later, the ahistoric
present began to seem for him a truer resting-place.

The historic and the unhistoric debate in Lowell's soul. The origin
of the debate may be glimpsed in his elegy for his mother, "Sailing
Home from Rapallo." When he thinks of the family cemetery in
Dunbarton, he divides it into historic Winslows and the hopelessly
unhistorical single Lowell buried there, his father:

> A fence of iron spear-hafts
> black-bordered its mostly Colonial grave-slates.
>
> The only "unhistoric" soul to come here
> was Father, now buried beneath his recent
> unweathered pink-veined slice of marble.
> Even the Latin of his Lowell motto:
> *Occasionem cognosce,*
> seemed too businesslike and pushing here,
> where the burning cold illuminated
> the hewn inscriptions of Mother's relatives:
> twenty or thirty Winslows and Starks.
> Frost had given their names a diamond edge.[11]

The compulsion to be a Winslow and see the present as only the
newest inscription on the palimpsest of history was very strong in
Lowell, and remained strongest in his treatment of Boston. But it was
to struggle permanently, even in his writing on Boston, with the
unhistoric, the businesslike, and the pushing—with unlovely pink-
veined marble, so less pleasing to the eye than the rigid grave-slates of
the maternal past, but so much more indubitably quarried in the
present.

The textbook illustration of the city in the Scales, where the historic
is balanced against the contemporary, is the famous elegy, "For
the Union Dead," where the two forces have come to a shuddering
standoff: the State House shakes over the excavation of the Common
Garage; St. Gaudens' Civil War relief shakes too. The one is braced by
girders, the other propped by a plank splint. Old statues and old
churches still stand, but against them rise the malignancies of
Hiroshima and segregation. Colonel Shaw still rides; around him "a
savage servility / slides by on grease." The struggle is melodramatic,

and the poet's sympathies are still with the historic (though, interestingly enough, Robert Gould Shaw was related by marriage to
Lowell through the Lowell, not the Winslow, side). For all the poem's
moral indignation, it is nevertheless visually entranced by the unhistoric:

> Behind their cage,
> yellow dinosaur steamshovels were grunting
> as they cropped up tons of mush and grass
> to gouge their underworld garage.
>
> Parking spaces luxuriate like civic
> sandpiles in the heart of Boston.
> A girdle of orange, Puritan-pumpkin colored girders
> braces the tingling Statehouse.[12]

But "For the Union Dead," like so many other Lowell poems,
declares by its choosing of the palimpsest as its form that the present
must not be left unsupported by a historical underpinning; it is in fact
to that underpinning that we must turn, the poem warns, in order to
find a moral standard by which to judge the present. Having left the
City of God where it belongs, the poet looks to the secular city, but in
its historical aspect, to provide an ethical referent. But historic Boston
is not, as we know from its history of killing Indians and denying
Christian burial to unbaptized infants, an entirely reliable moral
guide. It was Lowell's ambivalence toward the maternal Puritan ethos
that first drove him towards Catholicism, and the backward look in
"For the Union Dead," not toward Puritanism but toward Civil War
heroism as a moral rule-of-thumb, is in fact an unsatisfactory and only
temporary solution for Lowell.

The interest in the contemporary city exhibited in *Life Studies* and
For the Union Dead brings with it an interest in contemporary language, far from the high rhetoric of the early poetry. Increasingly,
Lowell's language mirrors the struggle evident in his images between
the historic and the contemporary. Slang enters the poems—we meet
"hopped up," "hits the streets," "cruise" (in the sexual sense), "free-
lancing," "screwball," and "What makes him tick?" in the space of
nine lines. In another poem, two "Hollywood pimps" are said to
"blow their tops" and beat someone named Abramowitz "black and
blue." The Public Garden is full of "sailors and their pickups," as
mallards dive toward "muck." The poem which, together with "For
the Union Dead," most bluntly forces at this epoch in Lowell's writing
the confrontation of historic city and contemporary city, and does so

as much by language as by imagery, is "July in Washington." In July, the month of Washington, Adams, Jefferson, and National Independence, the radiating avenues of L'Enfant's city seem to touch only corruption. The pun on the Puritan elect and the contemporary elected is the fulcrum on which the poem turns:

> The stiff spokes of this wheel
> touch the sore spots of the earth.
>
> On the Potomac, swan-white
> power launches keep breasting the sulphurous wave.
>
>   *   *   *
>
> On the circles, green statues ride like South American
> liberators above the breeding vegetation—
>
> The elect, the elected . . . they come here bright as dimes,
> and die dishevelled and soft.[13]

We might expect, were it not for the disheartened reference to the vestigial and the nameless statues, some reference to an earlier standard of civic virtue. And it does come, but without the rebuking uprightness of Colonel Shaw: the poet's wish for civic virtue is now seen as his own nostalgic invention of a Golden Age that never was, and which, because of its romance and false ideality, repels us, as do all Paradises:

> . . . We wish the river had another shore,
> some further range of delectable mountains,
>
> distant hills powdered blue as a girl's eyelid.
> It seems the least little shove would land us there,
>
> that only the slightest repugnance of our bodies
> we no longer control could drag us back.[14]

Dragged back to the real by the body's repugnance from ideality, Lowell nonetheless still resists any approval of the real. The sulphurous wave of the Potomac echoes the "sulphur-yellow sun / of the unforgivable landscape" of New York and New Jersey in "The Mouth of the Hudson."[15] How is Lowell to discover America if he cannot look for guidance to its past? The landscape seems full of meaningless and random objects, as unmanageable as the "wild ice / ticking seaward down the Hudson, / like the blank sides of a jig-saw puzzle." There is, without history, no figure in the carpet; the eyes alone cannot see; the puzzle-pieces are reversed, and elusive.

New York always presented a blank face to Lowell. Because the family had no history there, for him the city is a priori ahistorical. Every landscape in New York is blankly itself and nothing else. On the other hand, Manhattan has form, unlike those "cities without a center, as hideous / as Los Angeles,"[16] but the penalty it pays for its compactness is its crime and its unholy density ("It's not the crowds, but crowding kills the soul").[17] Even in the midst of disgust, however, Lowell admires the civilization of the city:

> Man is the root of everything he builds;
> no nature, except the human, loves New York.[18]

In a deliberate reference to Wordsworth's attempt to find the sleeping London beautiful, Lowell writes,

> Nothing more established, pure and lonely,
> than the early Sunday morning in New York—
> the sun on high burning, and most cars dead.[19]

Finally, for the American artist, it seems that no city but New York, for all its ugliness, will suffice:

> Yet people live here . . . Paris, Wien, Milano,
> which had more genius, grace, preoccupations?
> We pass up grace, our entrance fee and tithe
> for dwelling in the heavenly Jerusalem—
> small price for salience, and the world is here.[20]

To pass up the heavenly Jerusalem for New York to give up grace in exchange for salience—these are aesthetic choices as well as religious ones.

"Salience"—a word we hear frequently in Lowell's contemporary Archie Ammons—is a word of moral, but not perceptual, neutrality. It directs its gaze to what is, not to what ought to be or to what might be implied. If the ice on the Hudson no longer needs to be thought of as an emblem, but unreadable because reversed and therefore irritating to the emblematic mind, it can be seen simply as one of the saliences, present, ungraced by import, but nevertheless beautiful:

> The slush-ice on the east water of the Hudson
> is rose-heather this New Year sunset; the open channel,
> bright sky, bright sky, carbon scarred with ciphers.[21]

Once "salience" provides a more reposeful aesthetic, the ahistorical city becomes, if not more comforting than before, at least material for art (as, when it stimulated only puzzled disgust, it could scarcely be). The severe geometry of the Manhattan skyscrapers becomes, in "Castine 1860," the grid of elemental design, comparable to Aquinas' strict geometry of the Trinity. Once again the ice of the Hudson reappears, this time neither a wild blank puzzle nor a purely aesthetic rose-glow, but an element undergoing metamorphosis, as the visible becomes eternal, as ice turns to water, as life melts into death and art.

The patron saint of "salience" in this poem becomes Emerson, the archetypal moment of "salience" the absolute clarity of the American paintings of the Luminist School, and the aesthetic predecessor becomes Fitz Hugh Lane, the painter of hard-edged brilliance. In Lane's 1860 painting of Castine Harbor we see a ship,

> its bright flywings fixed in the topographical
> severity of a world reworked as glass.[22]

Emerson was "drowned in luminism, the vast serenity of emptiness." "Skyscraper villages" are "elemental material, line to line to line, / the skeletal Trinity of Thomas Aquinas." The aesthetic of salience takes everything as material, and sets it in high or low relief; it is the aesthetic of the man carrying a notebook through his trapped life, taking notes on everything as his life melts away:

> One should take a notebook into jail,
> nothing is real until set down in words—
> we are ice returning to water.[23]

I do not wish to minimize the aesthetic problems set by the modern city, even in *Notebook*, but Lowell's relaxing of those defenses against its multiplicity which forced it to be emblem or palimpsest, defenses stemming, as I see it, from unexamined loyalty to a rigid civic ethic and a family past, enabled him to see more widely and more truly. The wonderful photographic eye that roams over many cities in *Notebook* is an eye liberated to notice whatever is most salient, from the "hideous concrete dome of MIT" to "the Charles itself, half ink, half liquid coaldust," to the brilliant Cambridge blizzard, where Lowell finds himself "Risen from the blindness of teaching to bright snow,"

> to snow-trekking the mile from subway end to airport,
> to all-flights-canceled, to the queues congealed
> to telephones out of order, to the groping buses,
> to rich, stranded New Yorkers staring with the wild, mild
>   eyes
> of steers at the foreign subway.[24]

Wrapped up in his teaching, the poet has not noticed the snow; but what an original eye for noticing he displays, once he lets it loose. There is a pure unbodied joy in such seeing, which frees a vein of tender humor in Lowell, and lets him relish, for instance, in an overdone Chicago apartment, "the little girl's bedroom, perfect with posters: / 'Do not enter,' and 'Sock it to me, Baby.' "[25]

It is not that Lowell entirely trusts the generous aesthetic of salience. The difficulty of judging just what is salient seems to him the peril of modernism. Modernist invention is

> . . . dangerously distracted by commonplace,
> [its] literal insistence on the letter,
> [making] trivia indistinguishable from tragedy.[26]

Nonetheless, the commonplace variety of the city kept an appeal to Lowell to the end: "Why should a landscape painter ever leave Central Park?" he asks in *Day by Day*; "His subject lies under his nose . . . / his prison?"[27] Prisoner of variety (there are many Central Park poems), the poet sometimes seems, through *Notebook* and its derivatives, to be helpless in his sea of data. When he abandons the aesthetic of the journalist with his notebook for the aesthetic of the diarist with his journal inscribed each day, day by day, the hectic pace—so reflective of New York—slows in the landscapes of England and Ireland.

Day by Day is not an urban book, though there are occasional glimpses of Boston, London, and New York. The city no longer presents itself with the urgency of an aesthetic problem to be solved. The emblematic vision, with its stereotypes ("the Irish," "the Yankee") has been rejected as coercive and false. The historical palimpsest calling on Jonathan Edwards or Robert Gould Shaw appears largely irrelevant to the irremediably personal terms on which, with private pain and joy, life must be lived. Lowell has replaced the Puritan prophetic view and the long historical view with the successive imperatives of the painter doing life studies, the journalist keeping a notebook, the diarist keeping a journal, and, finally, the photographer writing with light, like Vermeer.

The city was judged emblematically by the Puritan prophet, "placed" against other historical times by the historian, recorded in all its variety by the journalist, and then faded into the background. The painter of life studies, the diarist of the everyday, and the amateur photographer take an essentially domestic view of life, and contract the focus of lyric, in "the photographer's sacramental instant," to a single domestic relation or incident. In *Day by Day*, the public life of the urban anthill recedes in favor of romance:

> Ants are amazing but not exemplary;
> their beehive hurry excludes romance.[28]

Urban surroundings in *Day by Day*—Harvard sidewalks, a New York playground, a municipal court, a billboard, a Boston brick house, a hospital—are only a minor part of that "universal consolatory / description without significance"[29] which solaces Lowell's last worn nobility, in which he wished to dwell again, not on the crowded vitality of cities, but on single beloved figures, to "give / each figure in the photograph / his living name."[30]

Notes

1. "Death and the Bridge," in *History* (New York: Farrar, Straus & Giroux, 1973), p. 205.
2. Ibid.
3. Ibid.
4. "Off Central Park," in *Day by Day* (New York: Farrar, Straus & Giroux, 1977), p. 45.
5. "To Mother," in ibid., p. 78.
6. "Christmas Eve under Hooker's Statue," in *Lord Weary's Castle* (New York: Harcourt Brace and Co., 1946), p. 17.
7. "At the Indian Killer's Grave," in ibid., p. 54.
8. Ibid., p. 57.
9. "Where the Rainbow Ends," in ibid., p. 69.
10. "In Memory of Arthur Winslow," in ibid., p. 19.
11. "Sailing Home from Rapallo," in *Life Studies* (New York: Farrar, Straus & Cudahy, 1959), pp. 77–78.
12. "For the Union Dead," in *For the Union Dead* (New York: Farrar, Straus & Giroux, 1964), p. 70.
13. "July in Washington," in ibid., p. 58.
14. Ibid., p. 59.
15. "The Mouth of the Hudson," in ibid., p. 10.
16. "Caracas I," in *Notebook*, 3rd ed., rev. and enl. (New York: Farrar, Straus & Giroux, 1970), p. 53.
17. "The Well," in ibid., p. 60.
18. "The Heavenly Rain," in ibid., p. 65.
19. "Alba," in ibid., p. 57.
20. "Elizabeth Schwartzkopf in New York," in ibid., p. 113.
21. "New Year's Eve 1968," in ibid., p. 173.
22. "Castine 1860," in ibid., pp. 245–246.
23. Ibid., p. 246.
24. "Blizzard in Cambridge," in ibid., p. 93.
25. "Fear in Chicago," in ibid., p. 229.

26. "Square of Black," in *Day by Day*, p. 32.
27. "Off Central Park," in ibid., p. 45.
28. "Ants," in ibid., p. 66.
29. "Shifting Colors," in ibid., p. 120.
30. "Epilogue," in ibid., p. 127.

The Puzzle of Anti-Urbanism in Classic American Literature

Leo Marx

Whenever American attitudes toward the city are under discussion, we are likely to hear a familiar note of puzzlement. We hear it, for instance, near the end of the influential study by Morton and Lucia White, *The Intellectual Versus the City: From Thomas Jefferson to Frank Lloyd Wright* (1962). After making their case for the centrality of anti-urban motives in American thought and expression, the Whites invite us to share their perplexity. "How shall we explain this persistent distrust of the American city?" they ask. "Surely it is puzzling, or should be."[1]

But should it be? My aim here is to reconsider the bias against the city that allegedly makes itself felt in our classic American literature. At the outset it must be admitted that many of our greatest writers have not displayed anything like a fondness for or even, for that matter, much interest in the actualities of urban experience in America—far from it. To recognize just how far, we need only try to recall the way city life is depicted in the work of the poets in the main line that leads from Emerson to Whitman, Frost, and Stevens, or in the central tradition in prose that includes Cooper, Emerson, Thoreau, Hawthorne, Melville, James, Mark Twain, Fitzgerald, Hemingway, and Faulkner. Which of these writers may be said to have given us an adequate specification of city life in this country? Which is not vulnerable to the charge of neglect, whether benign or malign, of urban reality? The two who on first thought may seem most deserving of exemption from that charge are Whitman and James. But only at first. For though it is true that New York is the setting for much of Whitman's poetry, his New York is less like a city anyone ever inhabited than it is, in Richard Chase's apt words, "a paradoxically urban-pastoral world of primeval novelty."[2]

© 1981 by Leo Marx.

63

As for James, it is true that he also set his most important work in cities, but he made a sharp point of the fact that they were *not* American cities. His explanation hardly could be more pertinent to my argument. Invoking a musical analogy, James observed that the major key of urban life in the United States is, "absolutely, exclusively," the key of "down-town." Only by writing in that key, he admitted, could a novelist hope to attune himself to what really mattered in the American city, but to the key of "down-town" he nonetheless confessed to being incurably deaf.[3] A further inference of James's remark is that in London, Paris, and Rome—the sites he chose for his most ambitious novels—the key of "up-town" still had resonance enough to yield novelistic significance. On second thought, then, neither James nor Whitman is an exception. Their work manifests no more concern than that of the other writers mentioned for the exact rendering of urban reality in America.

Should we be puzzled by this fact? I think not, but even if I am correct in suggesting that much of the puzzle can be dispelled by ridding ourselves of the false assumptions which underlie it, the puzzle's very existence is an interesting, perhaps even significant datum of our cultural history, and it calls for some explanation. Why is it that our writers, artists, and intellectuals are *expected* to convey a fond approval of the modern city? If we can account for this largely misguided expectation, we will be in a better position, I think, to address the more important issue: how to understand the implicit attitude to the city in the work of so many of our most gifted writers. Let me say at once that I do not think it makes sense to interpret their neglect of urban reality as evidence of a deep bias against "the city" as such. In imaginative literature, indeed, the concept of "the city" must be understood as in large measure an abstract receptacle for displaced feelings about other things. I shall be arguing that the attitude the Whites and others have mistaken for anti-urbanism is better understood as an expression of something else: a far more inclusive, if indirect and often equivocal, attitude toward the transformation of society and of culture of which the emerging industrial city is but one manifestation.

First, however, let us consider a few of the more compelling reasons for expecting American writers to convey an affirmative attitude toward city life. Behind this expectation there is a view of history, and its starting point is the ineluctable fact that we have been a city-building people. From the very beginning, indeed, the European occupation of North America has been a process of relentless urbanization. During the Atlantic crossing in 1630, John Winthrop envisaged the colony the Puritans were about to establish as "a city upon a hill." The trope was conventional, to be sure, but it nonetheless expressed an important attribute of the Calvinist mentality. Though many of these migrating Englishmen were of rural origin, they were carriers of an essentially bourgeois culture, or what Max Weber was to call "the Protestant ethic." They were burghers in spirit, and like most other European settlers, they conceived of the colonizing enterprise as an affair of organized communities. Their aim was to set up villages, towns, and potential cities in the wilderness. During the colonial period, settlement by the unaffiliated was discouraged, and historians long since have discarded the beguiling notion of a westward-moving frontier comprised of individual "pioneers" like Daniel Boone or Natty Bumppo. The effective cutting edge of population until the end of the nineteenth century was a chain of small communities which often, as in the dramatic instance of Chicago, became cities overnight. Demographers have shown us that for many people the movement of population from east to west was a movement from one city to another, and it was accompanied by a simultaneous movement throughout the nation from country to city. When the Republic was founded, roughly nine out of ten Americans lived in a rural environment; by now that fraction is less than three out of ten. On this view of the past we are a city-building, city-dwelling people, and so it would seem reasonable to expect our high culture to "reflect" that ostensible preference for an urban way of life.

To this conception of the American past it is necessary to add the received wisdom concerning the ancient and virtually timeless affinity between city life and the life of the mind. Cities, after all, are the places where scholars, artists, and writers naturally congregate. They do so because, for one thing, most of the vital institutions of mental production—universities, libraries, theaters, museums, galleries, publishers, printers—almost invariably have been located in cities. (Monasteries perhaps are the outstanding exception.) Cities are the places where ideas travel most quickly, where one can most readily become knowing or, so to say, urbane. The origins of civilization itself are thought to have been closely bound up with the invention of settled agriculture and cities, and historians of early man often cite the relative size and prosperity of a people's cities as a more or less reliable index of the level of culture to which it has attained.

The long history of cities as the environment most conducive to thought lends credence to the claim that city life has been held in special favor by most intellectuals in the West. More often than not, they have chosen urban settings for their literary accounts of utopia, and by the same token many influential thinkers from Socrates to Karl Marx have looked upon the countryside as a region of mindlessness, not to say idiocy. All of which would seem to justify the notion that the anti-urban motives that make themselves felt in American literature, if that indeed is what they are, constitute a puzzle in need of explanation.

Now the first thing to be said about this argument is that it posits a banal and finally misleading conception of the relations between that urbanizing America out there in reality and the imagined world we encounter in literature. It assumes that a national literature invariably should "lend expression to" or "reflect" (as in a sort of copy image) the dominant features of national experience. But that is to universalize the specific aesthetic program of certain writers, especially the modern realistic novelists, whose chief aim indeed has been to create a fictive illusion of social actuality.

Think of all those important American writers, not yet mentioned, who in fact did make an effort to render the concrete particulars of urban experience in the United States. I have in mind, for example, Howells, Wharton, Norris, Crane, Dreiser, Dos Passos, Wright, Farrell, Baldwin, Ellison, and Bellow. It is significant that these names, often assigned to the categories of "realism" or "naturalism," seldom appear in the roster of "classic" American writers. When we stop to think about the tacit criteria for membership in that amorphous literary society,* as roughly defined in the work of several modern critics and scholars, notably D. H. Lawrence, Van Wyck Brooks, F. O. Matthiessen, and Charles Feidelson, Jr., we soon realize that a chief criterion has been a commitment to an essentially nonrepresentational and often expressly *anti*-realistic method of composition.[4] Nathaniel Hawthorne might have been speaking for most of the other classic American writers when he explicitly repudiated realism or, as he described it, that "form of composition . . .

---

*The privileged status accorded to the "classic" writers by this honorific label is of course open to question. That the label carries with it a burden of class, ethnic, regional, and other unacknowledged assumptions seems obvious enough. For present purposes, however, the existence of this subcategory within the prevailing conception of American literature may be taken for granted. A certain academic legitimacy has been conferred upon it by the standard anthologies and course syllabi of our schools and universities, and by the mutually supporting judgments of writers, critics, teachers, and audiences which created the entire canon. However skewed, in other words, it is in a sense an authentic product of the dominant culture.

presumed to aim at a very minute fidelity, not merely to the possible, but to the probable and ordinary course of man's experience." Instead, he claimed for himself the artist's privilege of rearranging everyday experience and presenting it, as he put it, "under circumstances, to a great extent, of the writer's own choosing or creation."[5]

This is an absolutely vital distinction for anyone concerned to discriminate among the various literary treatments of urban life. Granted that no verbal composition actually can provide a mirror image of anything, much less a whole city, there still is an immense difference between a realistic novel aimed at creating some such illusion and an avowed "romance" of the sort Hawthorne defines. As he surely realized, the line between those two compositional types can become terribly fuzzy or disappear entirely, and yet the usefulness of the distinction, where it is discernible, cannot be exaggerated.

In *Sister Carrie*, for example, Dreiser immediately reveals his documentary purpose. It is apparent in the opening pages that he wants his readers to respond by saying, in effect, "Yes, of course, this is a perfect picture of Chicago, just the way it must have been when Carrie Meeber got off the train on that day in August, 1889." When a writer manifestly sets out to present us with an exact, detailed, seemingly comprehensive imitation of urban reality, then it certainly makes sense to ask whether he has selected truly significant details and has got them right. But such a test is beside the point in reading the work of a writer like Hawthorne, who immediately signals his unconcern with any such accurate, solidly specified rendering of the environment.

Hawthorne's practice in *The Scarlet Letter* exemplifies the way a writer's concept of form—in this case an explicitly non-representational form—governs his treatment of the city. Since this romance is set in seventeenth-century New England, moreover, we can assume that it will not provide us with any *direct* evidence (the sort we might expect to derive, for instance, from descriptive imagery) of Hawthorne's attitude to American cities of his own time. The nearest thing to a city here is Boston, and though it is only a small outpost of civilization on the edge of a vast continental wilderness, we may think of it as a city because we know it is going to become one, and also because it already is the Puritan capital, the center of power and authority as well as the most densely populated place in Massachusetts Bay.

At the outset, Hawthorne exercises his romancer's privilege by singling out three visible features of the town—the prison, the cemetery, the scaffold—and by casting a high light upon them. He is not in the least interested in conveying a literal image of the way Boston looked at the time, a fact whose significance was lost, unfortunately, upon the makers of the recent television production who went to such disconcertingly great lengths to create an historically accurate and detailed naturalistic set. On the contrary, Hawthorne deliberately focuses all of our attention upon three tangible manifestations of the hard, reality-oriented, authoritarian spirit of the Calvinists whose power is concentrated there.

As decreed by the characteristically American moral geography, the original source of that iron-hearted spirit lies to the east, in Europe, and it is only natural that the deepest yearnings of someone like Hester Prynne, a victim of Puritan repression, are identified with the untrammeled forest that stretches out to the west. On the quotidian plane of the action, of course, the forest is the only place where she and Dimmesdale can risk any gestures of intimacy. Nature, the wild territory beyond the confines of Boston, is Hester's true orbit, the locus of the freedom and self-fulfillment of which she dreams. The moment she is released from prison, accordingly, she moves out of Boston to a comparatively remote cottage facing the forest towards the west.

On the outskirts of the town, within the verge of the peninsula, but not in close vicinity to any other habitation, there was a small thatched cottage. It had been built by an earlier settler, and abandoned because the soil about it was too sterile for cultivation, while its comparative remoteness put it out of the sphere of that social activity which already marked the habits of the emigrants. It stood on the shore, looking across a basin of the sea at the forest covered hills towards the west. . . . In this little, lonesome dwelling, . . . Hester established herself, with her infant child.[6]

To live on the outskirts of Boston proper is important to Hester. Her choice of this half-in-half-out relation to the town is one of the first signs we get of her concealed but obdurate resistance to the dominant culture. As it turns out, of course, she is anything but your typical have-it-both-ways suburbanite, and her peninsula home proves to be only a way station on the spiritual route to the great climactic forest episode. There in the moral wilderness, she finally discloses to Dimmesdale the heretical extremism of her ruminations, and her bold plan to gain freedom for them both. It entails nothing less than his willingness to join with her in a public repudiation of everything for which Boston stands. " 'Doth the universe lie within the compass of yonder town?' " she asks him. " 'And what hast thou to do with all these iron men, and their opinions? They have kept thy better part in bondage too long already.' "[7]

On its face, admittedly, this is an unlikely choice of a text to exemplify the way the city is represented in our classic American literature. The animus Hester directs against the Puritan town obviously is not evoked by its comparatively urban character. Boston is made to seem grim and repressive, it is true, but we are given no reason to suspect that Hawthorne (or Hester) considers those qualities intrinsic to urban life. It is not Boston's cityness, realized or potential, that she would repudiate; it is the kind of society whose power is concentrated there. Express attitudes toward the city qua city, in short, have little or nothing to do with the matter, and that is just the point I am trying to make. To Hawthorne the significant attributes of this place—its essential qualities as a human habitat—are part of something else: the Puritan way of life. His judgment of that culture, not his personal feelings about cities as places to live, is what governs the way he writes about Boston in *The Scarlet Letter*.

The point would be too obvious to mention if it were not so often ignored. It is chiefly ignored by academicians who regard the literary treatment of cities as a question, at bottom, of representational accuracy. I have in mind the kind of investigation of "the image of the city" in art or literature which is conducted in American studies these days. The investigator proceeds on the assumption that literature "reflects" reality. In spite of frequent denunciations by critics, incidentally, the metaphor of "reflection" still seems to be the most popular figure available for conveying a sense of the relationship between art and life. In any case, a corollary of the representational theory of literature is the assumption that passages dealing with a particular subject, such as the city, have inherent significance when detached, more or less arbitrarily, from their immediate literary context and compared with each other and with what we know about those real cities out there in the writer's society.

But of course no work of art, including the work of the most literal-minded, programmatic, realistic novelist, bears any such direct, unmediated relation with raw experience. There are significant differences, however, between the planes of abstraction on which the relationship—that mediation of form—may be established. Hence the first problem for a critic is to identify that plane or, to put it differently, to grasp the principles, explicit or implied, governing the way literary form mediates the transmutation of experience in a particular piece of writing. It makes no sense to approach the work of the classic American writers in search of "responses" to the city on the plane of direct sensory experience, as if the writers were attempting to convey exact images of the real thing.

Hawthorne's conception of Boston is formed on that relatively high plane of abstraction where his most general ideas about art converge with his most general understanding of society and its history. That conjunction is apparent, for example, in his choice of the scaffold as a focal point of Boston life in The Scarlet Letter. It is at once an expression of his theory of fiction, or romance, as a symbolic reconstruction of reality, and of his recognition of the centrality, in our collective experience, of those large organizing symbol systems we now refer to, in the anthropological sense, as "cultures." His ambivalent attitude toward Puritan culture, rather than an effort to imitate the character of daily life in seventeenth-century Boston, is what governs his treatment of that town in The Scarlet Letter.

In opting for a non-representational method, Hawthorne had no intention of cutting all ties between his kind of fiction and social reality. He did not want to create a free-floating world of pure imagination, but rather a "neutral territory," as he put it, "somewhere between the real world and fairyland, where the Actual and the Imaginary may meet, and each imbue itself with the nature of the other."[8] Hawthorne believed that in fiction, to cite Melville's cogent formulation of their shared understanding, we should look for "even more reality" than in "real life." Like religion, Melville said, fiction "should present another world, and yet one to which we feel the tie."[9] As Melville understood, I believe, Hawthorne had dismissed the too literal program of the realistic novel in the service of what Dostoyevski would call a higher realism. That is the meaning of Hawthorne's famous stricture to the effect that a "romance" must "rigidly subject itself to laws, and . . . sins unpardonably so far as it may swerve from the truth of the human heart."[10] This statement usually has been taken as a brief for "psychological realism," but its implications reach far beyond the sphere of individual motives. Judging by his best work, the "laws" of mental life to which he refers apply to collective as well as individual, public as well as private, experience. Indeed, Hawthorne is propounding a more ample method of literary representation, designed with a view to the particularly complex conception of reality it aims to convey. Because this reality includes the mental set of those who experience and, in a measure, create it, it cannot be apprehended by any merely pictorial "reflection" of the external world, or by any rendering, however detailed, of individual sense experience. To represent the shared mentalities through which the experience of Hawthorne's characters have been screened, only a symbolic rearrangement of "real life" will suffice.

All of this enables us to account for the seeming anti-urbanism in Hawthorne's work. The tacit key to any one of his characters' attitudes to the city is the degree of that person's identification with the dominant culture. The Puritans in *The Scarlet Letter* presided over the building of Boston. It is their town; hence the ruling elect and those who most nearly identify with them understandably exhibit the most affirmative attitude toward the place. At the other extreme, comporting with her embrace of a radical antinomian, or separatist, viewpoint, is Hester's alienation and her scheme for getting away. Between these polar viewpoints, presumably, a hypothetical spectrum of attitudes may be imagined, and a vital aspect of this dialectical concept of culture—dialectical in the sense that Hawthorne posits a conflict of value as its essence—is continuity over time. Thus each of the opposed attitudes toward Puritan life (including the Puritan city) has its nineteenth-century equivalent, and much of the power of *The Scarlet Letter* derives from Hawthorne's skill in suggesting how the conflict it dramatizes is being replayed in his own day.

T.S. Eliot once observed that Hawthorne had "a very acute historical sense,"[11] and in truth he had recognized, long before Max Weber or Perry Miller, that the first settlers had brought with them, embedded in their theology, the seeds of the narrowly utilitarian, acquisitive ethos which had burst into full secular bloom two centuries later. In the self-righteous saints who had persecuted Hester Prynne, Hawthorne would have us recognize the ideological forebears of Judge Pyncheon of *The House of the Seven Gables*. He is the kind of successful man of affairs who dominates the nineteenth-century New England city, and who is described at one point as "subtle, worldly, selfish, iron-hearted, and hypocritical."[12]

The epithet "iron-hearted" here helps to convey Hawthorne's sense of the historical continuity of culture. Indeed, the image of iron is the nucleus of a recurrent cluster of images in his work which includes rust, fire, smoke, and blackness, and it serves to make graphic the connection between the hell-fired mentality of the first generation and the prevailing belief system in that society in the era of emerging industrial capitalism. Iron connotes the practical and specifically technological bent that was to become a distinguishing feature of the new industrial order, and it accords with the Puritan view of nature and the natural as the sphere of the satanic: a fallen world redeemable only by the elect. In a deft satirical sketch, "The Celestial Railroad," Hawthorne depicts Calvinism as the incubator of that belief in material and technological progress which had replaced Christianity as the dominant American faith; it was an ideological transformation closely bound up with the metamorphosis of the Puritan town into the modern Vanity Fair or capitalist city.

But it would be wrong to imply that the critical attitude to the American city implicit in Hawthorne's work derives only—or even chiefly—from a negative view of the dominant culture. In the forest, when Hester disdainfully refers to "yonder town" as a place she and her lover ought to leave forever, she is not merely impelled by her contempt for its iron-hearted ruling class. As important in hardening her will is her impassioned belief in the attainability of an alternative way of life. In imploring Dimmesdale to forget the past and begin a new life elsewhere, she repeatedly refers to the presence of nature— represented, initially and most tangibly at least, by the forest that surrounds them—as evidence that the necessary conditions for a new beginning are accessible to them. She perceives untrammeled nature as the embodiment of a moral and metaphysical as well as a literal (physical) sanction for her extravagant conception of the freedom and happiness she and Dimmesdale might gain by leaving Boston. " 'Doth the universe lie within the compass of yonder town,' " she asks,

which only a little time ago was but a leaf-strewn desert, as lonely as this around us? Whither leads yon forest track? Backwards to the settlement, thou sayest! Yes; but onward, too! Deeper it goes, and deeper into the wilderness, less plainly to be seen at every step! until, some few miles hence, the yellow leaves will show no vestige of the white man's tread. There thou art free! So brief a journey would bring thee from a world where thou hast been most wretched, to one where thou mayest still be happy!

Hester's language, like the natural setting, conveys the continuing ideological force of her visionary individualism two centuries later— in Hawthorne's own time. At the outset, to be sure, he had taken pains to associate her with "the sainted Ann Hutchinson," the antinomian heretic banned by the Puritan orthodoxy. The honorific epithet indicates that Hawthorne's narrator is sympathetic with this native strain of radical non-conformism, and the doctrine Hester espouses in her effort to strengthen Dimmesdale's will (" 'What we did had a consecration of its own. We felt it so!' "), closely approximates the root theological assumptions of antinomianism. But Hawthorne also describes Hester's secret reflections in a way calculated to evoke the largely secularized radicalism of his dissenting contemporaries, the transcendentalists. When he says, in chapter XIII, that Hester's repudiation of authority had reached the extremity at which "the world's law was no law for her mind," he manifestly is echoing Emerson (in "Self-Reliance"): "No law can be sacred to me but that of my nature." A constant feature of this Protestant viewpoint is that degree of assurance, or self-trust, consonant with a non-deferential attitude to received modes of thought and behavior. But whereas Ann Hutchinson would have attributed a "consecration" like that claimed by Hester to the intervention of a transcendent deity, Hester's language places her closer to Emerson and his belief in nature as "the present expositor of the divine mind."[13]

Hester's susceptibility to an Emersonian feeling for Nature is what lends her views a seeming anti-urban bias. In pleading with Dimmesdale to leave Boston she does sound, it must be admitted, as if she were asking him to reject all forms of social habitation—whether village, town, or city—in favor of some other sort of life "closer to nature." She urges him to contemplate the happiness that awaits them in the trackless forest (" 'There thou art free' "), as if she took literally the metaphor of a journey into the deep heart of Nature. Given the tone of the duplicitous narrator, moreover, a careless or gullible reader might be led to suppose that Hawthorne was ratifying Hester's belief. But as the subsequent action reveals, she had been carried away by the rapture of the moment, and it seems evident that the entire forest episode is meant to expose what Hawthorne regards as the large element of projection, or wish-fulfillment fantasy, in transcendental pastoralism.

Much of this becomes clear in the chapter of virtual parody in which Hawthorne "so manages his atmospherical medium" as to have the clouds reciprocate the lovers' mood.[14] When they are completely intoxicated by the prospect of their imminent liberation, the gloomy forest ("Such was the sympathy of Nature . . . with the bliss of these two spirits!") suddenly is lit by a burst of sunshine. But of course this is not much more ridiculous than Hester's notion that she and Dimmesdale have only to plunge off into the forest to be free and happy. That idea is of a piece with the rest of Hester's extravagantly utopian expectations. It has nothing whatever to do with a bias against "the city" as such, a fact which becomes evident when we learn that the lovers actually had decided not to escape into nature after all. "It had been determined," Hawthorne casually reveals in chapter XX, after the aura of the forest idyll has been dispelled, "that the Old World, with its crowds and cities, offered them a more eligible shelter and concealment than the wilds of New England, or all America."

I want to suggest that Hawthorne's theory and practice will serve as an almost paradigmatic example of the way the classic American writers treat the environment. Their work is non-realistic in the sense that they represent place not chiefly for what it is, but for what it means. The meanings they attach to forests, oceans, mountains, prairies, villages, towns, cities, and so forth, are dialectical, not univocal: they derive from a play of conflicting ideas and feelings represented in the narrative. (The town and the forest in *The Scarlet Letter* have diametrically opposed significance for the orthodox and for Hester.) This enacted conflict of values and meaning within the text usually can be aligned with a similar conflict in that extra-literary realm we call, for shorthand purposes, American society or culture.

A distinguishing feature of this body of writing is its domination by protagonists, like Hester, whose deepest yearnings are expressed in numinous visions of the natural landscape. She might be speaking for any one of them when she urges Dimmesdale, in the forest, to " 'Begin all anew! Hast thou exhausted possibility in the failure of this one trial?' " I am thinking of that familiar roster of pastoral figures: Natty Bumppo, the "I" of Emerson's *Nature* and Thoreau's *Walden*, Ishmael, Christopher Newman,* Huckleberry Finn, Jay Gatsby, Nick Adams, and Ike McCaslin. All of these characters enact the ideal life of the American self journeying away from the established order of things into an unexplored territory we tend to think of as Nature. The object of the journey, implied or avowed, is the nearest possible approximation to the situation of the autonomous unencumbered self.

The entire canon might be described, in other words, as a continuous replaying or testing of the Emersonian doctrine of self-reliance as the epitome of "the natural." (It is interesting that Lawrence, who evidently was fascinated by Emerson but for some reason ended up not writing about him, initially had called his *Studies in Classic American Literature*, "The Transcendental Element in American Literature."[15]) To realize that ideal condition of the self is to disengage from ordinary social reality, but to describe this omnipresent pastoral motive as an expression of a bias against cities is grossly reductive and misleading. The topography here—place in a literal sense—is a vitally important but nonetheless secondary subject, or vehicle, of the great central figurative conception whose primary subject, or tenor, is the search for inner freedom and fulfillment.

*Although Newman, like the protagonists of James's later international theme novels, finally goes to Europe, his idea of disengagement from his business vocation initially comes to him when he impulsively leaves Wall Street and drives out to Long Island to contemplate the rustic landscape.

As Thoreau said about his ardent cultivation of the bean-field, these repeated moves away from society—or the city—are undertaken chiefly for the sake of tropes and expression. To call *Walden* "a bible of anti-urbanism," as the Whites do, is a grand impertinence.[16]

That anti-urbanism is largely beside the point is further indicated by the fact that the pastoral impulse enacted in these typical American fictions seldom is rewarded with success. The outcome of the action in *The Scarlet Letter* reinforces Hawthorne's judgment of Hester's vision, implicit in the ironic rigging of the forest episode, as magnificently extravagant and infeasible. The truth is that not one of the works in question finally can be described as an unqualified "pastoral of success."[17] *Walden* comes as close as any to being that, but the more carefully one reads the book, the more narrowly personal and limited Thoreau's triumph seems. Since Thoreau's time, in any event, our best writers working in this mode increasingly have tended to compose pastoral romances of manifest failure. They continue to enact the retreat/quest, but it would seem that they do so chiefly in order to deny it, and the resulting state of mind is one of structured ambivalence.

Perhaps the most revealing twentieth-century instance of this mode of rendering the modern industrial city by an American writer is *The Great Gatsby*. Fitzgerald's fable is particularly useful for our purposes because he has Gatsby (and, to a lesser extent, Nick Carraway) assimilate their conceptions of New York to an illusionary pastoral viewpoint. That that is Gatsby's mode of perception becomes evident to Nick, in his role as narrator, in the famous ending when he finally discovers the clue to Gatsby's character. Lying on the beach, looking across the Sound at dusk, Nick suddenly recognizes that all of the incongruities of Gatsby's behavior can be explained by his characteristically American propensity to credit the pastoral hope. It is a view of life which initially had been fostered in Europeans by the image of the beautiful, rich, vast, seemingly unclaimed continent. The physical reality of the place, all that it promised in the way of material satisfaction, also was assumed to have made available an inner freedom and fulfillment such as Gatsby seeks. In the beginning of the European settlement of America, at least, there had been reason to believe that the actualizing of the ancient pastoral dream really might be feasible in such a "new" world. A palpable sense of that possibility is another distinctive quality of American pastoralism. As Nick puts it, Gatsby's dream of Daisy, represented by the green light, "must have seemed so close that he could hardly fail to grasp it"—another way of saying what Hester had tried to convey to her self-hating lover by pointing to the unbounded forest: " 'There thou art free! So brief a journey would bring thee from a world where thou hast been most wretched, to one where thou mayest still be happy!' " But that possibility had existed a long while ago, Nick realizes, and what Gatsby did not know is that it "was already behind him, somewhere back in that vast obscurity beyond the city [before America had become an urban industrial society], where the dark fields of the republic rolled on under the night."

Gatsby's failure to grasp this historical truth is of a piece with his distorted view of certain realities before his eyes, and Nick's view of the world is only somewhat less skewed by a similar susceptibility to illusion. Nowhere is this more obvious than in Nick's account of New York itself. He sees the city from the vantage of an ambitious young man, like Gatsby, just in from the western provinces. To him it is a ceaselessly beckoning fairyland.

Over the great bridge, with the sunlight through the girders making a constant flicker upon the moving cars, with the city rising up across the river in white heaps and sugar lumps all built with a wish out of non-olfactory money. The city seen from the Queensboro Bridge is always the city seen for the first time, in its first wild promise of all the mystery and the beauty of the world.[18]

Nick pastoralizes the streets of Manhattan as naturally as Thoreau does the landscape at Walden Pond. "We drove over to Fifth Avenue," he says, "so warm and soft, almost pastoral, on the summer Sunday afternoon that I wouldn't have been surprised to see a great flock of white sheep turn the corner." This image occurs to Nick shortly after he has described an appalling urban wasteland—a passage which in fact gives us our first sight of the city proper in The Great Gatsby. It is the opening paragraph of chapter II. Before that Nick has described the white palaces and spectacular green lawns of Long Island suburbia where his main characters live. But this is quite another New York.

About half way between West Egg and New York the motor road hastily joins the railroad and runs beside it for a quarter of a mile, so as to shrink away from a certain desolate area of land. This is a valley of ashes—a fantastic farm where ashes grow like wheat into ridges and hills and grotesque gardens; where ashes take the forms of houses and chimneys and rising smoke and, finally, with a transcendent effort, of men who move dimly and already crumbling through the powdery air. Occasionally a long line of gray cars crawls along an invisible track, gives out a ghastly creak, and comes to rest, and immediately the ash-gray men swarm up with leaden spades and stir up an impenetrable cloud, which screens their operations from your sight.

This is a modern city at its worst, and it has no place in a green vision of America like Gatsby's. His inability to recognize the discrepancy between the underside of urban industrial society, as embodied in the valley of ashes, and the idealized world of his aspirations is the direct cause of his death and his failure. Every significant element of the tale, indeed—the characters and landscape and action—has discrepant meanings in accord with this duality. As Nick describes it, this other city is utterly remote and unreal. Its ashen inhabitants, who dimly go about their obscure operations, already are crumbling in that polluted air. These are people, like the auto mechanic, Wilson, whose lives are largely circumscribed by material conditions, and who share none of Gatsby's gratifying sense of a dream about to be consummated. Glimpses of this other New York, composed of the material and human detritus of industrial society, are fleeting but crucial in *The Great Gatsby*. They provide the measure by which we know that the main characters inhabit a realm shaped by myth as well as wealth. Near the end, when Nick tries to imagine how the world might have looked to Gatsby when divested of its mythic veil, he describes it hauntingly as "A new world, material without being real, where poor ghosts, breathing dreams like air, drifted fortuitously about . . . like that ashen, fantastic figure gliding toward him through the amorphous trees." The ashen figure is Wilson on his way to kill Gatsby. He kills him because of Gatsby's unwillingness—or inability—to let go of his patently false conception of Daisy and, by extension, of the world.

In *The Great Gatsby* and *The Scarlet Letter*, human habitations derive their meanings from essentially the same conflict of views. At one extreme we are shown a town or city as it exemplifies the writer's highly critical conception of the dominant culture. This is a real place represented at its worst by emblems of oppression and suffering like the valley of ashes or the scaffold. At the other ideological extreme, we are given the perception of that place by a pastoral figure like Hester or Gatsby. It is true, of course, that Hester is alienated from Puritan Boston—is eager to get away—whereas Gatsby and Nick are more or less enthralled by the glamour and excitement of New York. But this difference is not as significant, finally, as the similarity in their viewpoints and its ultimate implications. Gatsby and Nick (until the very end) see New York from an idealized perspective very much like the one to which Hester lends expression in the forest. (" 'I'm going to fix everything just the way it was before,' " Gatsby says of his relations with Daisy.) But Fitzgerald points to Europe as the truly significant place from which the symbolic disengagement has been made, and for Gatsby all America—urban, rural, wild—retains the attributes of that fresh green breast of the New World envisaged by arriving Europeans. This is the illusion that ashen-faced Wilson finally destroys. Thus the outcome of the action in both works may be understood as exposing the glorious impracticality of the alternative each has posed to urban reality.

What we have then, in our classic American literature, is not a single, fixed attitude to the city, but rather a kind of semantic, or ideological, field in which a range of attitudes, some of them diametrically opposed, is generated. The field is bounded on one side by representations of the status quo, which is to say, by various embodiments of the dominant culture of industrial capitalism. (These are likely to be negative images like the scaffold or the valley of ashes.) On the other side, however, the field is bounded by the distinctively intense demands and expectations of a restless, journeying American self impelled by pastoral visions of possibility. Pastoralism seems to be the alternative program to the established order most attractive to Americans. It proposes not to change or resist the system as it is, but simply to withdraw in the direction of Nature in search of alternatives. (Nature, as we have seen, refers to the presocialized resources of the self, as well as to relatively undeveloped social and political areas of the environment.) Although the illusory character of the alternative is insisted upon, and often made to have tragic consequences, it retains a remarkably powerful hold on the imagination. As the closing sentences of The Great Gatsby imply, we are prisoners of this dead dream: "So we beat on, boats against the current." And in their continuing fascination with it, our greatest writers attest to its vitality even as they expose its falsity.

This fictional charting of American attitudes is far more persuasive, I submit—it captures more of historical actuality—than the notion that Americans harbor some special bias against cities as such. Indeed, it casts a reasonable doubt upon the validity of the abstract conception, the city, for it stresses the difference, rather than the similarity, between American cities and the classic preindustrial cities of Europe. Most American cities, after all, have been built since the onset of industrialization, and unlike London, Paris, or Rome, they embody relatively few features of any social order other than that of industrial capitalism. If the American city is perceived chiefly as the locus of a particular socio-economic order, that view accords with the historical fact that millions of Americans have moved to cities, not because they preferred urban to rural life, but rather because of the inescapable coercion of a market economy.

The idea that the distinguishing features of the American city do not reside in its cityness becomes more evident when we consider, for example, the mass exodus of the white middle class from our cities in the recent past. Why did they leave? The usual explanation has to do with poverty and race and violence and the decline of services. Our cities are close to bankruptcy because, for one thing, the social resources of the nation have had to be deflected from the satisfaction of immediate human needs to meet the ostensible imperatives of "national defense" and the overall "health" of the economy. In other words, the reason for the exodus from the city, like the reason for the influx of rural white and black southerners after World War II, has little or nothing to do with the intrinsic character of cities. Nor does it have much to do with the personal preferences of the people involved for the inherent attributes of rural or suburban as against urban life. It is a consequence, like so many of our "urban problems," of the larger socio-economic system and its accompanying culture. All of which suggests that the bias of American intellectuals against "the city" is more apparent than real, and not a cause for puzzlement so much as a misconception.

Notes

1. *The Intellectual Versus the City: From Thomas Jefferson to Frank Lloyd Wright* (Cambridge: Harvard University Press, 1962), p. 221.

2. Richard Chase, *Walt Whitman Reconsidered* (London: Victor Gollancz Ltd., 1955), p. 95.

3. Henry James, "Preface" to *Daisy Miller*, in *The Art of the Novel: Critical Prefaces*, ed. Richard P. Blackmur (New York: Charles Scribner's Sons, 1955), pp. 272–274.

4. Consider, especially, Lawrence's *Studies in Classic American Literature* (1923), Brooks's *Emerson and Others* (1927) and *The Flowering of New England* (1936), Matthiessen's *American Renaissance* (1941), and Feidelson's *Symbolism and American Literature* (1953).

5. Nathaniel Hawthorne, "Preface," *The House of the Seven Gables* (1851).

6. Hawthorne, chapter V, "Hester at Her Needle," *The Scarlet Letter*.

7. Hawthorne, chapter XVII, "The Pastor and His Parishioner," *The Scarlet Letter*.

8. Hawthorne, "The Custom House," Introductory to *The Scarlet Letter*.

9. Herman Melville, chapter XXXIII, *The Confidence Man* (1857).

10. Hawthorne, "Preface," *The House of the Seven Gables*.

11. T.S. Eliot, "Henry James," in *The Shock of Recognition*, ed. Edmund Wilson (New York: The Modern Library, 1955), p. 861.

12. Hawthorne, chapter XVIII, "Governor Pyncheon," *The House of the Seven Gables*.

13. Ralph Waldo Emerson, chapter VII, "Spirit," *Nature* (1836).

14. Hawthorne, chapter XVIII, "A Flood of Sunshine," *The Scarlet Letter*.

15. D.H. Lawrence, *The Symbolic Meaning, The Uncollected Versions of "Studies in Classic American Literature,"* ed. Armin Arnold (New York: Centaur Press, 1962).

16. *The Intellectual Versus the City*, p. 30.

17. For the concept of pastorals of "success" and "failure," see Harold E. Toliver, *Marvell's Pastoral Vision* (New Haven: Yale University Press, 1960), pp. 88-89.

18. F. Scott Fitzgerald, chapter IV, *The Great Gatsby* (New York: Charles Scribner's Sons, 1925).

New York from Melville to Mailer

Alfred Kazin

> My impression is that in New York anything
> might happen at any moment. In England
> nothing could happen, ever.
>
> —John Sparrow,
> Warden of All Souls, Oxford,
> The New Yorker, February 26, 1972

> Have you ever seen an inch worm crawl up a
> leaf or twig, and there clinging to the very end,
> revolve in the air, feeling for something to reach
> something? That's like me. I am trying to find
> something out there beyond the place on which
> I have a footing.
>
> —Albert Pinkham Ryder
> (visionary painter, 1847–1917),
> quoted in Lewis Mumford, The Brown Decades

> It is because so much happens. Too much
> happens.
>
> —Mrs. Hines, in William Faulkner,
> Light In August

> In New York who needs an atom bomb? If you
> walked away from a place they tore it down.
>
> —Bernard Malamud,
> The Tenants

No New York streets are named after Herman Melville, Henry James, Walt Whitman, or Edith Wharton. New York does not remember its own: it barely remembers Poe in Fordham, Mark Twain on lower Fifth Avenue, William Dean Howells on West Fifty-seventh Street, Stephen Crane in Chelsea, Dreiser and O'Neill in Washington Square, Willa Cather on Bank Street, Thomas Wolfe and Marianne

© 1981 by Alfred Kazin.

Moore in far-off Brooklyn, Hart Crane on Columbia Heights, Allen
Tate in the Village, Cummings in Patchin Place, Auden in St. Mark's
Place, Lorca at Columbia. It will not remember Ellison and Bellow on
Riverside Drive, Mailer in Columbia Heights, Capote in the U. N.
Plaza, Singer on West Eighty-sixth Street any more than it remembers
having given shelter to European exiles from Tom Paine to John
Butler Yeats, Gorky to Nabokov. It, and you, will be astonished to hear
that the following effusion was written by Ezra Pound:

> My City, my beloved, my white! Ah, slender,
> Listen! Listen to me, and I will breathe into thee a soul.
> Delicately upon the reed, attend me.[1]

New York the city has been one of the great subjects of American
writing. More than New England, the South, the West, it has been a
great home to American writers as well as the chief marketplace. But
New York is so intent on whatever it is that is more important than
writing that its writers usually feel as ignorable, evanescent, and
despisable as those poor storekeepers on newly smart, renovated
Columbus Avenue now being removed because they cannot pay
$4,000 a month for a grocery that last month rented for $900. "In New
York who needs an atom bomb?" someone says in Bernard Malamud's *The Tenants*. "If you walked away from a place they tore it
down."

The ever accelerating pace of New York, its historic fury, its ex-
tremes of culture and deprivation, ostentation and misery, leave
whole segments of the population historically mute, not even aware
of a greater life that goes on far away from them at the Manhattan
center of the storm. Anonymous particles of dust trudging invisibly
within places that could be Yazoo City for all their connection with
New York. My parents lived out their lives in total insignificance, not
even knowing that a child of theirs might some day speak for them.

But a writer can himself be the wound that remembers. Herman
Melville, born to what Edith Wharton called those "qualified by birth
to figure in the best society," was always to feel that New York was his
nemesis, and that living in it again the last twenty-five years of his life,
he had to be as indifferent as it was to him. New York uprooted him as
a little boy after his father's sudden bankruptcy and death. New York
(or the savage ups and downs of economic life that seem New York
incarnate) broke up his family, forced him to become a sailor, deserter, adventurer—and thus an author howling against this most hazard-
ous of trades. When he finally confessed his wordly failure as an

author and returned to New York in 1866 to eke out a living as a customs inspector, the New York in which he was totally forgotten as an author was somehow bearable *because* it ignored him. He now confined himself to poetry, privately published and paid for by relatives, though his anxious wife was afraid to have the family know that he was writing poetry at all, because his reputation for instability was already so dark. At the very end, conserving in retirement the energy left him, he wrote the now famous short novel *Billy Budd* that he may not have intended to have published at all. Long after his death the entangled and barely legible drafts were recovered from a tin box by a graduate student, Raymond Weaver, the first to resurrect obliterated Herman Melville.

Yet without all this disorder and early sorrow, without New York, "the terrible town" as Henry James called it, Melville might very well have lived the sterile upper-class life that Edith Wharton fled to live in Europe. The protagonist of James's marvellous story, "The Jolly Corner," returns to New York from many years abroad to seek what *he* would have been if he had lived the life of his class. He finds it in the ghost of himself, in the old house off Fifth Avenue he grew up in—a figure beautifully elegant in appearance but brutalized and frightening.

Melville was swept out of this life into an oceanic space that for sheer extent and metaphysical terror resembles the outer space into which our astronauts go—those heavenly spaces into which, as Melville well knew, man carries forever the image of himself and tries to transcend it—"The immense concentration of self in the midst of such a heartless immensity, my God! who can tell it!"[2] Melville confronted his self not as Narcissus but as Ahab: strike through the mask! New York was the threshold, the jumping-off place. *Moby-Dick* opens at the Battery on "a dreamy Sabbath afternoon, . . . thousands of mortal men fixed right here in ocean reveries. . . . Nothing will content them but the extremest limit of the land; loitering under the shady lee of yonder warehouses will not suffice. No. They must get just as nigh the water as they possibly can without falling in."[3]

This longing for the sailor's life, pointedly compared to Cato throwing himself upon his sword, was all too soon to be crushingly realized by the young boy bound for Liverpool, the sailor on the whaler *Acushnet*. The sea turned out to be the open universe. Beyond the happy valley of the Typees, the Galápagos where he had a premonition of what Darwin was to publish in *The Origin Of Species*, and all that mystery buried in "my dear Pacific" lay the enigma of man's relationship to what is forever unchangeable by man. This presses hardest on Americans, the people who thought they could change anything. . . . By contrast New York was the closed world: fashionable Grace Church on lower Broadway from which Melville describes himself in "The Two Temples" being ejected by the sexton; Wall Street in "Bartleby the Scrivener," where a man had to starve himself to death to demonstrate his freedom; *Pierre*, where in Chapter 22 Melville describes the throes of finishing *Moby-Dick*; and finally "The House-Top," the extraordinary Coriolanus poem in Melville's *Battle-Pieces* that describes Melville on the rooftop of his house in East Twenty-sixth Street scorning the immigrant mob that in the heat of August, 1863, violently attacked the city in its protest against the draft.

The life of an author in the New York summer! To Hawthorne he wrote in 1851: "In a week or so, I go to New York, to bury myself in a third-story room, and work & slave on my 'Whale' while it is driving thro' the press. That is the only way I can work now—I am so pulled hither and thither by circumstances." Later in the same month: "The Whale is only half through the press; for, wearied with the long delays of the printers, and disgusted with the heat & dust of the Babylonish brick-kiln of New York, I came back to the country to feel the grass, and end the book by reclining on it, if I may."[4]

In Chapter 22 of *Pierre* we read:

The chamber was meager even to meanness. No carpet on the floor, no picture on the wall; nothing but a low, long, and very curious-looking singled bedstead, that might possibly serve for an indigent bachelor's pallet . . . a wide board of the toughest live-oak, about six feet long, laid upon two upright empty flour-barrels, and loaded with a large bottle of ink, an unfastened bundle of quills, a pen-knife, a folder, and a still unbound ream of foolscap paper, significantly stamped, "Ruled, Blue."

Now look around at that most miserable room, and at that most miserable of all the pursuits of a man, and say if here be the place, and this be the trade, that God intended him for. A rickety chair, two hollow barrels, a plank, paper, pens, and infernally black ink, four leprously dingy white walls, no carpet, a cup of water, and a dry biscuit or two. . . . Civilization, Philosophy, Ideal Virtue! behold your victim![5]

Melville's distrust of authorship extended to his distrust of literature as a vehicle for his agonized search for a constant in the duplicitous universe. Failure on failure: *Moby-Dick*, 1851; *Pierre Or The Ambiguities*, 1852; the intended hack novel *Israel Potter*, 1855; *The Piazza Tales*,1856, first sold to New York magazines like *Putnam's* for less than $20 a story; and *The Confidence Man*, 1857, the last work of prose fiction he was to publish in his lifetime—the veritable end to Melville's career as a professional author as well as the most tangled secret assault on shallow American Christianity as the support of an American optimism that lasts only so long as the money holds out.

From 1866 to his death in 1891 Melville is captive in the city he associates with failure, indigence, and anonymity. In the aftermath of the Civil War, when so many were seeking a new start, Melville becomes an out-of-door inspector of customs at a salary of $4 a day (it was later reduced to $3.60 a day). At a time when bright prophetic Britishers, like Robert Buchanan, for whom the author of *Moby-Dick* was "a Titan," came looking for him, astonishingly important literary mediocrities of the day like E. C. Stedman, who could only report that Melville was "dwelling somewhere in New York," Melville did not even have assurance of tenure in his job. His brother-in-law John Hoadley wrote to the secretary of the treasury,

to ask you, if you can, to do or say something in the proper quarter to secure him permanently, or at present, the undisturbed enjoyment of his modest, hard-earned salary, as deputy inspector of the Customs in the City of New York—Herman Melville. Proud, shy, sensitively honorable—he had much to overcome, and has much to endure; but he strives earnestly so as to perform his duties as to make the slightest censure, reprimand, or even reminder,—impossible from any superior. Surrounded by low venality, he puts it all quietly aside, quietly declining offers of money for special services—quietly returning money which has been thrust into his pockets behind his back, avoiding offence alike to the corrupting merchants and their clerks and runners, who think that all men can be bought, and to the corrupt swarms who shamelessly seek their price; quietly steadfastly doing his duty, and happy in retaining his own self-respect.[6]

During the Gilded Age, the Brownstone Decades, the Iron Age that made New York (until our day) the supreme capital, of money, money-making, of the power panorama in architecture, art, publishing, the cosmopolitan intellectualism fused by mass immigration, Melville in his evenings, "nerve-shredded with fatigue," as his wife said, worked at poetry that she was afraid to tell the family he was writing—"you know how such news gets around"—but which a relative paid to have published. *Battle-Pieces*, his poems on the Civil War impelled, he said, by the fall of Richmond, had already been above the battle, just as in "The House-Top," the most personal poem in the collection, he was on his rooftop scorning the New York mob whose insurrection against the Draft Act he heard as

> a mixed surf
> Of muffled sound, the Atheist roar of riot.
> Yonder, where parching Sirius set in drought,
> Balefully glares red Arson—there—and there.
> The Town is taken by its rats—ship-rats
> And rats of the wharves. All civil charms
> And priestly spells which late held hearts in awe—
> Fear-bound, subjected to a better sway
> Than sway of self; these like a dream dissolve,
> And man rebounds whole aeons back in nature.[7]

Now, in *Clarel*, he was in the Holy Land; in *Timoleon*, in the Villa Albani—removed from the city just a century ago that Edith Wharton remembered with a shudder as row on row of brownstones put up by venal landlords in the 1860s. "Out of doors, in the mean, monotonous streets, without architecture, without great churches or palaces, or any visible memorials of an historic past ... cursed with its universal chocolate-covered coating of the most hideous stone ever quarried, this cramped horizontal gridiron of a town without towers, porticoes, fountains or perspectives, hide-bound in its deadly uniformity of mean ugliness."[8]

Melville, who was to spend many Sundays with his granddaughter Eleanor in the newly opened Central Park, had nothing to say about the urban scene in this first great public park in the New World, nothing about the thousands pouring every year into New York harbor. Henry Adams, in his *Education*, at least did the huddled masses seeking to breathe free the courtesy of attacking them. Melville, writing in his poetry of the Pyramids, of tormented Confederate veterans in Jerusalem, of the Age of Antonines, of conflict with his own androgyny, had nothing to say of the rapacity of finance capitalism in the age of Jay Gould and Jim Fiske; nothing of the crime and squalor of the lower New York streets so conveniently adjacent to police headquarters. Jacob Riis, taking his extraordinary photographs of destitution for *How The Other Half Lives*, used to obtain his flash in the dark rooms by firing a pistol; this often set off a fire, but a cop laughed that dust was so thick on the walls that it smothered the fire.

If there is nothing in Melville "dwelling somewhere in New York" of the world that Stephen Crane was soon to describe in *Maggie* and in his sketches of the Bowery and the Tenderloin district—material that enraged the police forever shaking down prostitutes and that practically excluded Crane from New York—neither is there anything of Whitman's feeling for the people, the streets, the sheer life-giving vitality that made Whitman describe *Leaves Of Grass* and his city as counterparts. "I can hardly tell why, but feel very positively that if anything can justify my revolutionary attempts & utterances, it is such *ensemble*—like a great city to modern civilization & a whole combined clustering paradoxical unity, a man, a woman."[9]

The port, the greatest harbor as it used to be thought of, was to stupefy and alarm Henry Adams at the end of the old century and Henry James at the beginning of the next. But Melville the "isolato" (his word) reminds us in his New York secretiveness of so many poets, artists, and visionaries who in New York found perfect solitude even if they were afraid of dying in it—a creative race that tolerated New York, even loved it from the distance of Washington Heights, Brooklyn, and Queens. Like Ishmael clinging for life to the coffin that Queequeg had lovingly cut into designs showing the gods and the whole cycle of life, they had more freedom than they ever could in a small town. Freedom to write, to love as you please, freedom to write of your own Spoon River, Winesburg, Asheville, without your neighbors looking into your pots.

But is Melville the last of these New York hermits—after Albert Pinkham Ryder, Edward Arlington Robinson, O. Henry, Louise Bogan, Joseph Cornell? Can a writer or painter now get away from the radio and television next door, the tenants' association, the investigator, the drug pushers, the muggers? Immigrant New York, ethnic New York—making a living from the streets, living in the streets, making it, living the dream of making it, faster, faster!—forced its children out into the open, made them seek every public arena in the city, and turned the city itself into their chief image of love and frustration, the city as the great preoccupation of American thought. From the same period of Melville's retreat into New York, the late 1860s, we get the conjunction of New York with creativity *about* the future: as in the Roeblings' Brooklyn Bridge, the incomparable center promenade overlooking New York harbor (the last of its kind), as well as the curveship that Hart Crane from Ohio described as lending a myth to God:

> O harp and altar, of the fury fused
> (How could mere toil align thy choiring strings!)
> Terrific threshold of the prophet's pledge,
> Prayer of pariah, and the lover's cry.[10]

The best things written about the American city as a stupendous new fact were written usually by midwesterners who caught the new sense of scale involved just in moving to a city—Dreiser, Anderson,

Cather, Lindsay, Sandburg, Fitzgerald, Lewis, Dos Passos, Hemingway, Bellow. Much of modern American writing was conceived in the outsider's dream of the big city, by those relatively new to it—and much of America was still new to it up to 1945. Only those amazed by the commonplace, like Dreiser, could uncover the clash of interests, the vital struggles below the surface, the shock and clamor of the unexpected, the savagery that is so rooted in temptation and so precious to temptation.

This is where American writing came of age, if you like; or ceased to find the New World new. What vanished openly, with New York as the theater and great arena of modern corporate life and mass life, had subtly vanished long before—the totally independent sense of divinity that Emerson, Thoreau, and Whitman knew as essential to their own modern quest for personality; that bitter Melville never ceased to look for; that Dickinson in far-off Amherst handled as traditional allegory rather than as an article of belief. The problem of the nineteenth century *was* the death of God, precisely because, as Marx said, man cannot confront his pressing conviction of immortality so long as he is brutalized by the struggle for existence. The modern world is not so much political as ideological; the new wars of religion, left wing and right wing, reveal their character by proving interminable.

But this is getting ahead of our story; the onset was physical in every sense, starting with the freedom of the body. Eros, as Auden wrote in New York, is the builder of cities. Dreiser's Carrie, Crane's Maggie, even James's New York heroine Milly Theale in *The Wings Of The Dove*, along with his other two spacious and astonishing novels from London in the earliest 1900s, *The Ambassadors* and *The Golden Bowl*, turn on a long-buried sexuality that only Whitman the commoner had had the wit to celebrate in himself because it was so wickedly and beautifully alive in New York. The connection between sex and the physicality of New York was equally clear to Gertrude Stein after her first affair with a woman—the very look of New York conveyed to her a message about purity; it corresponded to her new, cleansed state of mind. "I simply rejoiced in the New York streets, in the long spindling legs of the elevated, in the straight high undecorated houses, in the empty upper air and in the white surface of the snow. It was such a joy to realize that the whole thing was without mystery and without complexity, that it was clean and straight and meagre and hard and white and high."[11]

Yehudi Menuhin said in 1943 that one of the great war aims was to get to New York. This became a great rush just before and after what

Dos Passos called "Mr. Wilson's War," when many native sons stopping in New York on their way to Paris came to love New York. To this day Francis Scott Key Fitzgerald of St. Paul remains the dramatic poet of New York's luxurious upper-class landmarks, like the Plaza Hotel. New York was a dreamland to Fitzgerald, as it was to his acolyte, John O'Hara from Pottsville, Pennsylvania. But O'Hara's mind was too ordinary, a mirror of his own brutal characters, to duplicate Fitzgerald's delicate and tragic triumph. O'Hara loved and aped the privilege that lies in large amounts of cash, the chance to sit with the racing set and to name their horses. To Fitzgerald upper-class New York represented the imagination of whatever is charming, touched by the glamour of money, romantically tender and gay.

No writer born to New York's constant pressure can ever associate so much beauty with it—can ever think of New York as the Plaza Hotel. Fitzgerald felt about New York that it was a woman too exciting to be trusted. New York was the pleasure capital, and thus, to the active American conscience, unreal, a mirage, surely treacherous. At the end of *The Great Gatsby*, when the tale of Gatsby's foolish hopes has all been told, Fitzgerald suddenly, piercingly, begins a great litany over the Middle West as the source of American innocence and hope. Nick Carraway the narrator is gripped by the realization that New York—the East incarnate—has spoiled and ruined all his midwestern friends. "That's my Middle West—not the wheat or the prairies or the lost Swede towns, but the thrilling returning trains of my youth, and the street lamps and sleigh bells in the frosty dark and the shadows of holly wreaths thrown by lighted windows on the snow."[12]

Of course Fitzgerald never wrote about St. Paul as much, or as brilliantly, as he did about New York. He had the feeling for the textures and lights of the great metropolitan glitter that the enraptured guest gets—or used to get?—at the great New York feast. He wrote of "the enchanted metropolitan twilight," of "forms leaning together in taxis," of New York on summer afternoons as "overripe, as if all sorts of funny fruits were going to fall into your hands," of "Negroes in cream-colored limousines being driven by white chauffeurs across Queensboro Bridge."[13] For Fitzgerald, all paradoxes then were spectacles. The name of the American dream was still New York.

Fitzgerald's dream was not shared by the writer who admired him so much that he was killed at thirty-seven rushing to Fitzgerald's funeral—Nathan Wallenstein Weinstein—who became Nathanael West. Those immigrants of a century or so ago might see America as promises, but certainly not as beauty. When their descendants became the authors of *Miss Lonelyhearts, Jews Without Money, Call It*

Sleep, Awake And Sing, Franny and Zooey, Barbary Shore, An American Dream, The Victim, Seize The Day, The Assistant, and *The Little Disturbances of Man,* books with which one must associate such testaments of hard American experience by the descendants of slaves as *Native Son, Notes Of A Native Son, Invisible Man,* no one could miss a grimness behind certain lives projected on the imperial city. This gave release to a few, all too few, new imaginations. Despite the masses of Jews, Italians, Blacks, and Hispanics who have found opportunity in the big cities if nothing else—and often not even that—it is chilling to remember how few *lasting* works have come out of their lives, have done justice to the mass experience in the big city.

Fitzgerald wrote proudly of "the stamp that goes into my books so that people can read it blind, like braille."[14] It is possible, in the current reign of conceptualism and ideological rage, that literature itself is out of date. In the best universities, criticism has been replaced by literary theory, which is convenient when you consider how little students read for pleasure. In lesser places, it has been replaced by sawdust for the intellect like Black studies, women's studies, and that chain of fraudulent liberations that clanks its way through every convention of the Modern Language Association—the novel of androgyny in New South Wales. It is hard for the children of oppression to think of art as engaging faculties subtler than anger. Black writing often seems drowned in the urgency of struggle, and since there is little interest outside the once liberal community, which now seems to be evaporating, it is not surprising that most Black authors have never published a second book.

It is hard to be a Jew, said Sholem Aleichem; it is peculiarly hard to be a Jewish writer. The enemies of the Jewish writer predominate in his own household, demanding to know why Isaac Bashevis Singer writes about sex, Norman Mailer about violence, Saul Bellow about himself. It was not until the end of the nineteenth century that Jews from eastern Europe, which used to mean orthodoxy, felt free to flout the commandment against engraving images. Though there seem to be legions of Jewish novelists today, the so-called Jewish novel, the novel of emancipation from the commandments, the bourgeoisification of the immigrants' children, is visibly over. The real subject that haunts the Jew cannot be treated in literature, for a civilization capable of accepting the murder of a million Jewish children is still the only civilization we know.

The creative element ungraspable by criticism, the element that makes for independent beauty, for the touch of life in itself, the psychic moment, the particular scene that brings the wonder of our existence home to us—that is not easy to find in the literature of an always beleaguered people, precarious, isolated, and unloved. What the Israeli novelist Amos Oz complains of is true for more than Jews—"I'm not terribly happy with the Jewish-American novelists. . . . too wise, their characters always exchange punchlines instead of talking to each other, their books are just clever sociology. They don't have the echo of the universe, you don't see the stars in their writing."[15]

One reason for this weakness among Black writers is the exaggeration of powerlessness, the discursiveness that as in the case of so talented but floundering a writer as James Baldwin shows itself in the projection of sexual tangles onto a political cause—the latest cause year after year. Baldwin doesn't seem to have recovered from the onslaught against him by Black nationalists. Political anger is hardly his natural turf, and of course he has never had an audience in the Black community anyway. But novel by novel Baldwin, who is actually an expatriate and a very elegant writer, writes books out of an unforgettable family situation that afford him no catharsis, that seem to get bigger and windier with each reiteration of the fraternal tangle.

His old sidekick and rival, Norman Mailer, *is* a political imagination. Whatever may be said of Mailer's career as a whole—I admire him because he really gives and destroys himself with each hallucinating subject—it is a fact that while fascinated with outlaws, murderers, criminals, people broken on the wheel of American disorder, he knows that his characters are *not* powerless and spiritually indigent. They are alive and fighting. It revolts me to sit in a New York subway car mucked up from floor through seats to ceiling with graffiti so thick on the windows already crusted with dirt that you cannot see where to get out. But only Mailer had the solidarity with the unknown vandals working through the night in the subway barns to imagine what they felt, what they wanted, what in their secret writing *they* are dreaming.

What Mailer recognizes, especially in the context of destructive and ferocious New York, is that Americans are drunk on a sense of power, induced by good money and the wars that bring in the good money and the cars they drive without listening to the drivel on the radio. The good life is their idea of freedom. Mailer, secretly obsessed with the ancestral idea of God as the only lasting power, has made this duplicitous American freedom the obsessive theme of his work. It is the labyrinth of his own guilt as a moralist in this profane world. Pent-up maddened New York is the symbol. He has not been afraid to look ridiculous, reeling like a possessed man from one dispossession to another, from subject to subject, book to book. The excessiveness, the unreality, the violence, and the *dreck* that weigh on my battered sensibility in the big city—Mailer has made these his preoccupation, has turned himself into an urban laboratory. I admire and envy his recklessness. These days it may indeed be necessary to plunge into a book as into a jungle, not knowing what you will meet—or whether you will come out at all.

Notes

1. "N.Y." (*Riposte*, 1912), *Collected Early Poems of Ezra Pound*, ed. Michael John King (New York: New Directions, 1946), p. 185.

2. Herman Melville, *Moby-Dick*, ed. Alfred Kazin (Boston: Houghton Mifflin, 1951), p. 321.

3. Ibid., p. 23.

4. *Herman Melville: Representative Selections*, ed. Willard Thorp (New York: American Book Company, 1938), p. 390.

5. Herman Melville, *Pierre, or The Ambiguities*, ed. Henry A. Murray (New York: Farrar & Strauss, 1949), p. 355.

6. *A Melville Log*, ed. Jay Leyda (New York: Harcourt Brace & Co., 1951), vol. II, p. 731.

7. Herman Melville, *Battle-Pieces and Aspects of the War*, ed. Sidney Kaplan (Amherst: University of Massachusetts Press, 1972), p. 86.

8. Edith Wharton, *A Backward Glance* (New York: D. Appleton Century Co., 1934), pp. 54–55.

9. *The Correspondence of Walt Whitman*, ed. Edwin Haviland Miller (New York: New York University Press, 1961), vol. IV, p. 299.

10. *The Collected Poems of Hart Crane* (New York: Liveright, 1933), p. 4.

11. Gertrude Stein, quoted in *Literary New York: A History and Guide*, eds. Susan Edmiston and Linda D. Cirino (Boston: Houghton Mifflin Co., 1976), pp. 251–252.

12. F. Scott Fitzgerald, *The Great Gatsby* (New York: Charles Scribner's Sons, 1925), p. 218.

13. Ibid., pp. 69, 70, 50.

14. F. Scott Fitzgerald, *The Crack-Up* (New York: New Directions, 1945), p. 180.

15. Amos Oz, quoted in "A Talk with Amos Oz," Herbert Mitgang, *New York Times Book Review*, Oct. 26, 1975, p. 22.

Cities of Mind, Urban Words:
The Dematerialization of Metropolis
in Contemporary American Fiction

Ihab Hassan

*The city is a fact in nature, like a cave, a run of
mackerel or an ant-heap. But it is also a
conscious work of art, and it holds within its
communal framework many simpler and more
personal forms of art. Mind takes form in the
city; and in turn, urban forms condition mind.
. . . With language itself, it [the city] remains
man's greatest work of art.*

—Lewis Mumford,
The Culture of Cities

*With cities, it is as with dreams: everything
imaginable can be dreamed, but even the most
unexpected dream is a rebus that conceals a
desire or, its reverse, a fear. Cities, like dreams,
are made of desire and fears, even if the thread
of their discourse is secret, their rules are
absurd, their perspectives deceitful, and
everything conceals something else.*

—Italo Calvino,
Invisible Cities

*Our language can be seen as an ancient city: a
maze of little streets and squares, of old and
new houses, and of houses with additions from
various periods; and this surrounded by a
multitude of new boroughs with straight regular
streets and uniform houses.*

—Ludwig Wittgenstein,
Philosophical Investigations

© 1981 by Ihab Hassan.

I

The city: grime, glamour, geometries of glass, steel, and concrete. Intractable, it rises from nature, like proud Babel, only to lie athwart our will, astride our being. Or so it often seems. Yet immanent in that gritty structure is another: invisible, imaginary, made of dream and desire, agent of all our transformations. It is that other city I want here to invoke, less city perhaps than inscape of mind, rendered in that supreme fiction we call language. Immaterial, that city in-formed history from the start, molding human space and time ever since time and space molded themselves to the wagging tongue.

And so to commence, I shall tersely review the founding of that ideal city, which even the naturalist tradition in American fiction—from Frank Norris, Upton Sinclair, Theodore Dreiser, through James Farrell, Henry Roth, Nelson Algren, to Willard Motley, Hubert Selby, and John Rechy—failed to make into mortar and stone. I shall regard it as concept, project, field, a magic lantern through which the human condition may be viewed. Next, I shall consider some examples of fiction, largely postwar, uniquely American, omitting, alas, both international trends and historical antecedents. Last, from this special perspective, I shall assay some in-conclusion, which my brief scope must make even briefer.

II

In its earliest representations, the city—Ur, Nineveh, Thebes, or that heaven-defying heap turned into verbal rubble, which we call Babel—symbolized the place where divine powers entered human space. The sky gods came, and where they touched the earth, kings and heroes rose to overwhelm old village superstitions, and build a city. As Lewis Mumford says: "All eyes now turned skywards. . . . Those who made the most of the city were not chagrined by the animal limitations of human existence: they sought deliberately, by a concentrated act of will, to transcend them."[1] And so they did, with language: "with glyphs, ideograms, and script, with the first abstractions of number and verbal signs."[2] All cities, it seems, are sacred, symbolic, heavenly at their origin, made of unconscious promptings as they grow into mind, made of mind that grows into purer mind through the power of language.

Thus the dematerializing metropolis coincides with the first temple or palace stone, and dimly evokes, farther back, the burial mound, around which village life fearfully gathered. The "twin cities," biopolis and necropolis, stand for the visible and invisible demesnes that all human endeavor, however profane, assumes. Arnold Toynbee, we recall, thought that cities helped to "etherialize" history. But etherialization, as Mumford knows, carries also its counterpoint—"The rhythm of life in cities seems to be an alternation between materialization and etherialization: the concrete structure, detaching itself through a human response, takes on a symbolic meaning, uniting the knower and the known; while subjective images, ideas, intuitions . . . likewise take on material attributes. . . . City design is thus the culminating point of a socially adequate process of materialization."[3]

Yet as the universe became conscious of itself in *homo sapiens*, so do we now reflect upon the city through abstractions the city itself generates. To "see" a city whole is also to apprehend its theoretical nature, its hidden functions, and ideal forms. For the city acts as mediator between the human and natural orders, as a changing network of social relations, as a flux of production and consumption, as a shadowy financial empire, as an arena of violence, play, desire, as a labyrinth of solitudes, as a system of covert controls, semiotic exchanges, perpetual barter, and, withal, as an incipient force of planetization. In short, at once fluid and formal, the city apprehends us in its vital grid.[4]

Modern theoreticians of the city variously recognize this aspect of its character. Max Weber, for instance, conceives the city not as a large aggregate of dwellings, but as a complex "autocephalic" system of self-maintaining forces; while Robert E. Park, founder of urban "ecological" sociology in America, describes it as "a state of mind, a body of customs and traditions, and of organized attitudes and sentiments." Practical and street-wise, Jane Jacobs still insists that the "ubiquitous principle" of cities is their need "for a most intricate and close-grained diversity of uses that give each other a constant mutual support," a need that dishonest city planning invariably conceals. Raymond Williams, though historically alert to the forces of production and consumption in the city, also perceives it as a "form of shared consciousness rather than merely a set of techniques," about which everything "from the magnificent to the apocalyptic—can be believed at once."

As for McLuhan, we know his theme: the old metropolitan space must eventually dissolve into electric information, a "total field of inclusive awareness." Similarly, Charles Jencks considers the urban environment as a communicating system, a cybernetic or semiotic mesh; hence the efforts of such architects as Nicholas Negroponte to use computers (URBAN 5) in designing cities. Finally, stretching the cybernetic metaphor to its limit, Paolo Soleri speculates that in "the urban organism, the mind remains in independent but correlated parcels divided spatially and coincidental with the parceled brains, the whole forming the mental or thinking skin of the city." His "arcology" presages no less than the passage from matter to spirit.[5]

Such visions may seem intolerably angelic to citizens inured to the diabolic occlusions and exigencies of the modern metropolis. Yet the city remains an alembic of human time, perhaps of human nature—an alembic, to be sure, employed less often by master alchemists than sorcerer's apprentices. Still, as a frame of choices and possibilities, the city enacts our sense of the future; not merely abstract, not mutable only, it fulfills time in utopic or dystopic images. This expectation strikes some thinkers as peculiarly American. Nearly half a century ago, Sartre remarked: "For us [Europeans], a city is, above all, a past; for them [Americans], it is mainly a future; what they like in the city is everything it has not yet become and everything it can be."[6] But Sartre was never the most reliable observer of America; and what he perceives as an American impatience merely avows the city's own high-handedness with history.

Utopia, dystopia, futuropolis: these cities of mind have occupied a space in the western imagination since Plato's Republic. In Christian times, the City of God, the Heavenly City, even the medieval Church Triumphant, became structures of a pervasive spiritual energy whose absence in nether regions suffered the Infernal City to rise. (Pieter Brueghel's paintings of Babel attest to this doubleness in their equivocation between heaven and hell.) But the great architects of the Italian Renaissance—Brunelleschi, Alberti, Bramante, Leonardo—its painters—notably Lorenzetti, Piero della Francesca, Francesco di Giorgio—and its authors—especially Tommaso Campanella in *City of the Sun*—turned to the dream of reason; circular or square, radial or polygonal, their urban visions revealed logic, will, clarity, purest tyranny of the eye.[7]

English utopian writers, like More and Bacon, also implicated their utopic concepts into urban space. So did, later, the pictorial architects of the eighteenth century, Etienne-Louis Boullée and Claude Nicholas Ledoux, the nineteenth-century planners of Garden City, inspired by Ebenezer Howard, and those eccentric designers of the early twentieth century, Tony Garnier and Sant' Elia, who ushered in the austere shapes of Futurism and Constructivism, of the Bauhaus and Le Corbusier. Closer to our time still, "plug-in cities" of Archigram illustrate the immanent structuralist principle; Buckminster Fuller's geodesic forms enclose us all in nearly invisible technology; and Doxiadis' "entopias" offer blueprints of "the city of dreams that can come true." Abstract urbs all, bright geometries of desire, they share with Disneyland and Disney World—indubitably our two most solvent cities—a commitment to effective fantasy.

Yet as Jane Jacobs warns: "Designing a dream city is easy; rebuilding a living one takes imagination."[8] Since our cities seem still to beggar the imagination of planners, our urban afflictions persistently defy our sense of a feasible future. Thus dystopia becomes a synonym of megalopolis. Disneyland will not rescind Harlem; and against the visions of Soleri, Doxiadis, or Fuller, those of Fritz Lang in "Metropolis" or of Godard in "Alphaville" may yet prevail. Writers and illustrators of speculative fiction certainly continue to envisage island cities in space, mobile, radiant, noetic, all Ariel and no Caliban, communicating with each other and the universe by means of unique mental powers. Yet these mind-cities yield, in darker speculations, to vast conurbations of discorporate brains, floating in innumerable cubicles, ruled all by a sublime computer or despot brain.[9] Here time and space, transcended by mind, betray the ultimate terror of dematerialization—complete control.

III

I have not erred altogether from my subject, "the city in fiction"; I have tried rather to perceive it from a certain angle, which reveals the city as a fiction composing many fictions. Baudelaire, perhaps first among moderns, knew this well enough, though some might claim for Restif de la Bretonne or Eugène Sue earlier knowledge of nocturnal streets. Baudelaire, at any rate, allegorized Paris in various poems; one in particular, "Les Sept Vieillards," found an echo in Eliot's poem about another "unreal city":

> Fourmillante cité, cité pleine de rêves,
> Où le spectre en plein jour raccroche le passant!
> Les mystères partout coulent comme des sèves. . . . [10]

This spectral note pervades, in diverse timbres, all modern as well as postmodern literature—fiction, poetry, or drama, naturalist, symbolist, or absurd. Certainly, the city as a formal dream or internal shape of consciousness emerges in fiction before the postwar period. Proust's Paris, Joyce's Dublin, Döblin's Berlin, Musil's Vienna, the

London of Virginia Woolf, the Manhattan of Dos Passos, Henry Miller's Brooklyn, Nathanael West's L.A., all attest to a longer historical view. Perhaps I can make the point by adverting to the last two.

In *Black Spring* (1936), Miller declares himself a patriot of the "Fourteenth Ward," where he was raised, to which he continually returns "as a paranoiac returns to his obsessions":

We live in the mind, in ideas, in fragments. We no longer drink in the wild outer music of the streets—*we remember* only. . . . Here there is buried legend after legend of youth and melancholy, of savage nights and mysterious bosoms dancing on the wet mirror of the pavement, of women chuckling softly as they scratch themselves, of wild sailors' shouts, of long queues standing in the lobby, of boats brushing each other in the fog and tugs snorting furiously against the rush of tide. . . .

The plasm of the dream is the pain of separation. The dream lives on after the body is buried.[11]

One might add: after the city vanishes too. For Miller really dissolves the city into his emotions, into remembrances more vivid than the city ever was, splashing his words on the page as Pollock threw colors on a canvas, exorcising his death in images drenched in nostalgia. Sensations, perceptions, observances of the city thus obey, in "The Fourteenth Ward," the imperative of his soft need.

This absorption or ingestion of the object—a whole borough here—typifies the romantic sensibility. But Miller could suddenly exchange the romantic egoist for—perhaps no less romantic—the selfless cosmologist.[12] Thus, in the surrealist section of *Black Spring* entitled "Megalopolitan Maniac," he collapses the city not into the self but into the universe:

The city is loveliest when the sweet death racket begins. Her own life lived in defiance of nature, her electricity, her frigidaires, her soundproof walls. Box within box she rears her dry walls, the glint of lacquered nails, the plumes that wave across the corrugated sky. Here in the coffin depths grow the everlasting flowers sent by telegraph. . . . This is the city, and this the music. Out of the little black boxes an unending river of romance in which the crocodiles weep. All walking toward the mountain top. All in step. From the power house above God floods the street with music. It is God who turns the music on every evening just as we quit work.[13]

The city as self, the city as cosmos: thus Henry Miller draws the far limits of urban conceptualization. Nathanael West, however, conceptualizes the city with cooler art: in *The Day of the Locusts* (1939), Los Angeles finds its consummation in a painting that Tod Andrews wants to create. West—employing throughout various devices of style

and impersonal narration to distance himself from the lunatic scene—
ends his novel with a vision of chaos, within another vision of chaos,
rendered in the very act of experiencing that chaos amid the crowds
assaulting Kahn's Persian Palace Theatre. Here is the passage depict-
ing Tod's apocalypse within apocalypse:

> Despite the agony in his leg, he was able to think clearly about his picture,
> "The Burning of Los Angeles." After his quarrel with Faye, he had worked on
> it continually to escape tormenting himself, and the way to it in his mind had
> become almost automatic.
>
> As he stood on his good leg, clinging desperately to the iron rail, he could
> see all the rough charcoal strokes with which he had blocked it out on the big
> canvas.[14]

A description of the fiery and fantasmic picture ensues, as Tod imagines himself at work on his painting. Thus, Nathanael West gives us
in his novel the work of art that Tod Andrews fails to complete. Can
this mean that Hollywood, city of dreams, lends itself to our
apprehension only as another kind of dream (Tod's painting) within
still another form of art or dream (West's fiction)? The question
offends our sense of the real. Yet how different, finally, does Hollywood seem from all those modern cities which drive us to fictions of
survival amidst their desperate confusions?

IV

The modern city compels us into certain idealizations of its orders or
disorders. Moreover, all art selects, abstracts, and so must further
conceptualize its objects, dense or ethereal. The great Naturalists, I
suspect, knew this subliminally, as did Symbolists and Modernists to
a fuller degree. In the postwar period, however, Fabulism, Irrealism,
Absurdism abet the conceptual tendency further. I have no leisure
here to survey the entire fictional landscape. Nor perhaps should I
endeavor to do so, since the urban element in many novels seems
often extraneous.[15] In certain works, though, urban setting and fictive
form are inseverable. I cite—all too cursorily, I fear—two early examples: Ralph Ellison's *Invisible Man* (1952) and Saul Bellow's *The
Adventures of Augie March* (1953).

Ellison's novel transmutes Harlem into a dance of characters, a
music of ideas and illusions; realism and surrealism here are seam-
less. Thus the protagonist always moves between an act and its
shadow: "I leaped aside, into the street, and there was a sudden and
brilliant suspension of time, like the last ax stroke and the felling of a

tall tree."[16] All New York becomes the image, the sound, the very texture of a dramatic theme; and the coal cellar, in which Invisible Man at last confronts his invisibility, burns with an ironic intelligence more luminous than the 1369 light bulbs improbably affixed to its ceiling. Similarly, Bellow's Chicago shapes Augie's high call to freedom, his quest for the fabled "axial lines."[17] Deadly, fluent like money, omnific like love, the city becomes the very form of American experience in mid-century. And when Augie wonders in a dejected moment if cities, cradles once of civilization, can ever become wholly barren of it, he thus refutes himself: "An inhuman thing, if possible, to have so many people together who beget nothing on one another. No, but it is not possible, and the dreary begets its own fire, and so this never happens."[18]

To the classic fictions of Ellison and Bellow, one may add others that variously render or vivify the American city. But I should turn now to another kind of novel, more shadowy in its urban inscapes, more cunning. I allude to William Burroughs' *Naked Lunch* (1959), Thomas Pynchon's *The Crying of Lot 49* (1966), and Donald Barthelme's *City Life* (1970).

In Burroughs' entropic world, whether earthly or galactic, the city becomes a machine for dying. Fueled on sex, junk, and money, this infernal machine invariably regulates, violates, exterminates; in short, it both controls and negates, relying on the calculus of absolute human need. "Junk is the mold of monopoly and possession," Burroughs grimly notes; it is the "ultimate merchandise," no "sales talk necessary."[19] The need, beyond eroticism, is for forgetfulness. Artaud understood this: "I believe the opium we now have, the black juice of what we call the poppy, is the expulsion of an ancient eradicating power, which man no longer wanted, and those who were weary of the seminal fluid and of the erotic twistings of the self in the fluid of the first offense recoiled toward opium as toward a different lubricity."[20] This lubricity, in the metabolism of the addict, aspires to "Absolute ZERO."[21]

But if Burroughs' spectral city finds its center in the human body, locus of desire and decay, it meets its circumference in language. Death first enters the erotic body, and spreads through the body politic, carried by the virus Word. Hence Burroughs' injunction against the Logos: "RUB OUT THE WORD FOREVER."[22] Or if this prove impractical, then let the word, testifying against the world, testify also against itself. Cut-up, desiccated, phantasmagoric, Burroughs' language reaches heights of savage poetry, grisly humor, metaphysical outrage, grotesque conceit, yet must finally expend itself, as the city must, in prophetic waste:

The Word is divided into units which be all in one piece and should be so taken, but the pieces can be had in any order being tied up back and forth, in and out fore and aft like an innaresting sex arrangement. This book spill off the page in all directions, kaleidoscope of vistas, medley of tunes and street noises, farts and riot yipes and the slamming steel shutters of commerce, screams of pain and pathos and screams plain pathic, copulating cats and outraged squawk of the displaced bull head, prophetic mutterings of brujo in nutmeg trances, snapping necks and screaming mandrakes, sign of orgasm, heroin silent as dawn in the thirsty cells, Radio Cairo screaming like a berserk tobacco auction, and flutes of Ramadan fanning the sick junky like a gentle lush worker in the grey subway dawn feeling with delicate fingers for the green folding crackle.[23]

Naked Lunch, then, attempts to become itself the feculent city, an expanse of shameful words, deeds, deaths, dreams. The shame of cities? It is of existence itself.[24]

Pynchon, another wizard of words and waste, in *The Crying of Lot 49*, offers a city ruled (perhaps) by the expectation of WASTE ("We Await Silent Tristero's Empire") and DEATH ("Don't Ever Antagonize The Horn"). His Los Angeles, indeed the whole of urban California if not of the United States, seems a lunatic semiotic system, both immanent and indeterminate, the breath of some universal paranoia. The mystery that Oedipa Maas pursues through the labyrinths of signs remains a mystery; for self and society in America have dissolved into these same esoteric signs—hieroglyphs of concealed meaning or meaninglessness (we never know which).

Still, though entropy affects the physical, the social, the linguistic universes—*pace* Maxwell's demon—the mind insists on weaving and unweaving patterns, creating and decreating fictions, including Pynchon's own. Consider these communicative devices the author devises to guide or misguide his heroine through the book; a cryptic will; stamp collections; the mails; telephone; television; radio; graffiti and drawings; plays; movies; lapel buttons; wrecked cars; hallucinogens; maps; transistor circuits; motel signs; rock music; inaudible voice frequencies; striptease shows; impressions on a dirty mattress; footnotes; forged editions; doodles; puns; typographic errors; sign languages; children's games; tapes; arm bands; bullet shots; epileptic fits; sex; silence, and so forth. Semiosis unending: can we wonder that the city, that all existence, turns for Oedipa into a cryptogram? Here she muses the nature of language:

Behind the initials was a metaphor, a delirium tremens, a trembling unfurrowing of the mind's plowshare. The saint whose water can light lamps, the clairvoyant whose lapse in recall is the breath of God, the true paranoid for whom all is organized in spheres joyful or threatening about the central pulse of himself, the dreamer whose puns probe ancient fetid shafts and tunnels or truth all act in the same special relevance to the word, or whatever it is the word is there, buffering, to protect us from. The act of metaphor then was a thrust at truth and a lie, depending where you were: inside, safe, or outside, lost. Oedipa did not know where she was.[25]

The world, the city, the book: all promise some hierophany, always deferred. But is a malignant Logos or the encapsulated human Self here at fault? Locked in an imaginary tower, Oedipa once dreams of letting her hair down to serve as ladder for another, only to discover that her hair is a wig. Narcissism, then, defines our city's limit, as in San Narciso. And the opposite of narcissism, which we call love, breaks through these limits, and in so doing releases "the unnamable act, the recognition, the Word."[26] In short, Pynchon's city of treacherous signs may stand in the void or hold some occult meaning that only love can yield. Or perhaps only the "unimaginable Pacific," the "hole left by the moon's tearing-free and monument to her exile," can redeem it.[27] But which?

Burroughs' and Pynchon's are cities of entropy and mystery; Barthelme's, no less entropic or mysterious, is one of parody. *City Life*, of course, tells us nothing overtly about New York City. A collage of stories, a catena of fragments, it provides rather an experience of *urban being*, under the aspects of parody, pastiche, parataxis, under the aspect of the most delicate irony. The experience resists interpretation, battens on absurdity and irrelevance; and so we fasten on such words as "dreck," "detritus," "trash," "waste," and "sludge," which Barthelme slyly supplies. "It's that we want to be on the leading edge of this trash phenomenon," he writes, "the everted sphere of the future, and that's why we pay particular attention, too, to those aspects of language that may be seen as a model of the trash phenomenon." And again: "We like books that have a lot of *dreck* in them, matter which presents itself as not wholly relevant (or indeed, at all relevant) but which, carefully attended to, can supply a kind of 'sense' of what is going on. This 'sense' is not be to obtained by reading between the lines (for there is nothing there, in those white spaces) but by reading the lines themselves."[28] The dreck, sludge, or trash, may strike us as the unassimilable detritus of an urban mass civilization; yet they become available to us as epistemic units of city life, parodies of parodies—and parodies of parodies of parodies, etc.—which finally inhabit the mind as a unique mode of urban consciousness.

The transformation of dreck into mind is style in action. Barthelme's consummately ironic style employs catalogues, drawings, photographs, puns, vignettes, aphorisms, clichés, neologisms, jokes, innuendos, stutters, fragments, metafictions, non sequiturs, recondite allusions, odd juxtapositions, asides, absurd humor, and typographic horseplay, not only to "defamiliarize" his art but also to "dematerialize" his city. (Defamiliarization and dematerialization have been for nearly a century concomitants in various arts—cubist, surrealist, and abstract.) Above all, Barthelme's rhetoric of irony deconstructs, displaces, defers urban reality—to use three voguish terms—precisely because it declines to make it whole.[29] The city, radically discontinuous, becomes a mental construct, reconstructed from verbal shards, sad, zany, or wise. As Barthelme remarks in an interview:

New York City is or can be regarded as a collage, as opposed to, say, a tribal village in which all the huts (or yurts, or whatever) are the same hut, duplicated. The point of collage is that unlike things are stuck together to make, in the best case, a new reality.[30]

This is more urbane than Ramona's urban statement, near the end of *City Life*:

Ramona thought about the city. —I have to admit we are locked in the most exquisite mysterious muck. This muck heaves and palpitates. It is multidirectional and has a mayor. To describe it takes many hundreds of thousands of words. Our muck is only a part of a much greater muck—the nation-state— which is itself the creation of that muck of mucks, human consciousness. Of course all these things also have a touch of sublimity.[31]

And so the city, "dreck," "collage," or "palpitating muck," leads us directly to the problem of the "nation-state" in the twentieth century, and to "that muck of mucks, human consciousness"—touched with "sublimity," of course.

V

The city conceived as a machine for dying (Burroughs), as a paranoiac semiotic system (Pynchon), and as mental dreck or palpitating muck (Barthelme), presumes on the novelist's freedom from verisimilitude. Such freedom becomes constitutive in a number of works that we may unabashedly call fantasy or science fiction.

Marge Piercy's *Woman on the Edge of Time* (1976) stands at the
edge of this genre. Poised between three worlds—the desolate present, a utopic future, a dystopic alternative—the book refracts reality in
the lens of several mental institutions; the madhouse becomes both
metaphor and microcosm of the modern city, which ruthlessly ex-
ploits the poor, the powerless, and the deviant. At its core, Piercy's
book seethes with poetic outrage, in the honored naturalist mode,
threatening to explode its fantastic frame. Yet the frame holds because
the present does contain all versions of its future; the modern city
does enact the convulsions of its fate. Thus the incarceration of
Connie Ramos in Rockover Mental Hospital not only betrays the
violence of our civilization; it further tests its potential for survival.

Connie communes mentally with two futures. One seems ideal,
arcadian, impeccable in its advanced views of sex, race, ecology,
technology, education, political life, yet earthy withal. The other
looms like an urban nightmare of windowless skyscrapers, gray suns,
fetid air, cyborg police, and unspeakable vulgarity. But the crucial
insight of the novel identifies the war between these two possible
futures with the actual war between Connie and her captors—that is,
the struggle between two cities, one of human fulfillment, the other of
inhuman deprivation. Here is Connie's cry of pain:

Whoever owned this place, these cities, whoever owned those glittering
glass office buildings in midtown filled with the purr of money turning over,
those refineries over the river in Jersey with their flames licking the air, they
gave nothing back. They took and took and left their garbage choking the air,
the river, the sea itself. Choking her. A life of garbage. Human garbage.[32]

Garbage (or dreck) this city really is not, but rather something more
sinister; electroencephalic control through brain implants. Thus the
good doctor explains:

You see, we can electrically trigger almost every mood and emotion—the
fight-or-flight reaction, euphoria, calm, pleasure, pain, terror! We can monitor
and induce reactions through the microminiaturized radio under the skull.[33]

The novel, as I have said, tells a tale of two cities. To their struggle—
a struggle also between unborn futures, virtual worlds clashing in a
crux of time—the novel can offer no denouement, except the rage of
Connie, her poisoned will to survive. Relentlessly ideological in
parts—all the men, for instance, seem nasty or brutish—*Woman on
the Edge of Time* still projects a powerful image of human courage and
city madness. Barely removed from our present, it reveals us to
ourselves all the more savagely in the urban mirror of our distortions.

Set only half a century hence, once more in New York, Thomas Disch's *334* (1976) also stands at the threshold of fantasy, revealing us to ourselves implacably. Again, life there seems so close to our own that we scarcely recognize it as alien. Yet violence and hebetude, garishness and despair, mingle easily in this crammed city of the imminent future; everything there seems a grotesque parody of our best hopes. Still, many characters—whether engaged in the cryonics black market or the no less deadening market of sex—strike us as vibrantly human, and their will to endure miraculously endures. As Lottie in Bellevue Hospital broods:

And anyhow the world *doesn't* end. Even though it may try to, even though you wish to hell it would—it can't. There's always some poor jerk who thinks he needs something he hasn't got, and there goes five years, ten years getting it.[34]

That same Lottie, however, in the same year of 2026 says:

The end of the world. Let me tell you about the end of the world. It happened fifty years ago. Maybe a hundred. And since then it's been lovely.[35]

Indeed, the dominant structures and metaphors of the work suggest both perplexity and decadence. Composed of interrelated fragments, vignettes, tableaus, the book is a labyrinth of miseries—smog, lupus, television, eugenics, overcrowding, sado-masochism, artificial foods—each preternaturally vivid, all absurd. Centered on a dismal building at 334 East 11th Street, the various families accept historical decline within their spatial frame. Thus the titular number 334 evokes an address as well as the imaginary "birthdate" of Alexa, a character in the section called "Everyday Life in the Later Roman Empire"; her imaginary "death" in 410, the year Alaric sacked Rome, terminates her "alternate historical existence" under the influence of a drug, Morbihanine. And so Alexa dreams of bloody ritual sacrifices at the Metropolitan Museum, and wakes to wonder, in Spenglerian gloom, if civilization still warrants the human effort. Clearly, the city of Disch, Pynchonesque, emanates a subtle insanity: ourselves.

This theme is brilliantly prefigured in Samuel Delany's trilogy, *The Fall of the Towers* (1977), which includes *Captives of the Flame* (1963), *The Towers of Toron* (1964), and *City of a Thousand Suns* (1965).[36] The city here, at last, realizes its fabulous potential: it emerges as a cosmic frame of mind, an extension of intelligences both terrestrial and extraterrestrial. In fact, the trilogy contains not one but many cities. There is, first, silent Telphar, deserted, with spires and high looping roadways, ruled by a "psychotic" computer, symbolizing mind turned against itself, symbolizing death. There is, next, the island capital, Toron, like "a black gloved hand, ringed with myriad diamonds, amethysts by the score, turquoises, rubies," rising with its towers "above the midnight horizon, each jewel with its internal flame," yet all too human, with kings, ministers, tycoons, circuses, rabble, a city conspiring against itself in a wholly imaginary war that projects its own civic corruptions till all its towers come tumbling down.[37]

There is also that rough, utopic City of a Thousand Suns, salvaged by malcontents from death and rubble, rooted in earth, reaching beyond its forest clearing for the stars. Then, halfway across the universe, there is a nameless city, provisional home of the Triple Being, built twelve million years ago by a vanished civilization, yet so made as to continue recreating itself into time. As the Triple Being, supernal spirit, explains: *"The city responds to the psychic pressures of those near, building itself according to the plans, methods, and techniques of whatever minds press it into activity."*[38]

In that city, beneath a double sun immeasurably distant from our own, a conference of sentient beings convenes. Delany depicts the scene marvelously. "What is a city?" he asks to begin; and the conferees begin thus to answer, each according to "its" nature:

To one group at the meeting, immense thirty-foot worms, the city seemed a web of muddy tunnels and the words came as vibrations through their hides. . . . A metallic cyst received the words telepathically; for him the city was an airless, pitted siding of rock. . . . To the fifty-foot eyestalks of one listener the atmosphere of the city was tinged methane green. . . . To one living crystal in the city the words of the Triple Being came as a significant progression of musical chords. . . . A sentient cactus shifted its tentacles and beheld the city almost as it was in reality, a stretch of pastel sand; but, then, who can say what was the reality of the city.[39]

And so it continues, while the Triple Being unfolds the cosmic conflict centered now on cities of the Earth, a conflict of men engaged in fantasmic wars against themselves, which hence attract the Lord of the Flames: a roaming, curious, amoral force in the universe, negative by human reckoning, strange by the reckoning of all.

But I risk to make trite the exuberant inventions of Delany's work, which raises the question of the city radically—that is, at an imaginative limit. What is upolis? The good city eschews inversions of the (human) will, and turns randomness not into uniformity but choice. "It is a place where the time passes as something other than time"; and the one and the many attain to a harmony that only time can yield.[40] More empathic than telepathic—for Delany's characters know

that communicating minds can jar and clash, and still remain iso-
late—the good city grants its citizens time to touch, "experience and
perception weighed against experience and perception, the music
their minds made free in the double sound of their names."[41] No
wonder then that even the Lord of the Flames finds something to learn
on bungling Earth. Though collective in his consciousness, dispersive
in his influence, reversed in his polarities of love and death, matter
and anti-matter, this everted intergalactic creature realizes at last his
kinship with creation.

Again, what is Delany's upolis? Both arcadian and utopian, in time
and also out of it, at once cosmic, social, and personal, material as
well as immaterial, founded on work and boundless in mind, concrete
no less than universal, this city, unfinished, absorbs cosmic randomness into the ever-widening circles of its awareness, which may also
be called—however shyly—love.[42]

VI

Given the human propensity for endings, what may we conclude
about the city, or fiction, or the city in fiction? Nothing conclusive, I
fear.

Fiction and the city have been complicit, if not from the rise of
Babel, then since Picaresque and *Bildungsroman*. In these early
genres, the novel often portrayed the innocent young man from the
country come to experience urban sins and pleasures. In so doing, the
novel recovered an ancient debate between nature and civilization,
arcadia and polis, earth and fire, two mythic modes of human being in
the world that still strain the sensibiliies of our ironic age.[43] It is as if
the original sin of the race were not only disobedient knowledge
(Adam and Eve in the garden) but also disobedient artifice (Pro-
metheus and his fire, the babbling builders of Babel).

I insist on this old complicity of language, knowledge, and artifice
because I believe that it constitutes the central archetype of the city,
its ambiguous gnosis. For the city has always been a "crime against
nature," against the pleromatic condition of some fabled disaliena-
tion; and it remains the "crime" that consciousness itself perpetrates,
perpetuates, against creation. Mythically, then, and prophetically
too, the city is less city than a moment in that human project realized
by mind, a mind, as Nietzsche knew, which can think only in fictions,
a mind, as so many modern gnostics think, seeking ever-wider—and
more problematic—expression of itself in the universe.[44] Hence the

"dematerialization of metropolis," often associated with the emergence of extraordinary human powers, finally depends on psychic even more than technic resources.[45]

Such "dematerialization," though, can prove horrendous, as the examples of Rotterdam, Coventry, Dresden, Hiroshima—of Auschwitz and Gulag, and all those other cities of night in our land, including Watts—have shown. Can we wonder that the city has become another name for bedlam, slum, prison camp, asphalt jungle, every kind of dystopia we know? Certainly, the contemporary novel provides no reassurance on this score; with rare exceptions, the "city in fiction" embodies an "imagination of disaster," which, as Susan Sontag remarked of science fiction films, responds to "seemingly opposed destinies: unremitting banality and inconceivable terror."[46] Far richer in response to these threats than celluloid, the novel still admits no bright and exacting vision, no luminous trope.

Perhaps our dreams themselves have lost the edge of hope. For the city is itself desire, as I have persistently argued, as well as trope. But perhaps, also, history has begun to veer from the city, swerve. Spengler, we recall, thought that though world history was the history of cities, a time came at the end of a Civilization when, "empty receptacles of an extinguished soul," these doomed world-cities would move on "to final self-destruction."[47] Yet our destiny need not hinge on such dubious exercises in cyclicism and gloom. The city may simply cede the initiative to another organization of human energies, another definition or disposition of what we have hitherto called civilization, and so open new vistas for our earth. Here is Boulding's roseate vision:

> We may very well ask ourselves, therefore, whether we visualize a period in the not very distant future when in postcivilized societies, the city will really have disappeared altogether as an entity. We can even visualize a society in which the population is spread very evenly over the world in almost self-sufficient households, each circulating and processing everlastingly its own water supply through its own algae, each deriving all the power it needs from its own solar batteries, each in communication with anybody it wants to communicate with through its personalized television, each with immediate access to all the cultural resources of the world through channels of communications to libraries and other cultural repositories, each basking in the security of an invisible and cybernetic world state in which each man shall live under his vine and his own fig tree and none shall make him afraid.[48]

Yet the time is neither dusk nor dawn in the West but the present. We stand as ever between history and hope. And standing there I perceive the postmodern city as a place of ecumenism, open to the universe. Nervous, mindful, turbulent, it intensifies alienation as well as planetization. The process derives from no mystic doctrine or Teilhardian intuition, but rather from human interactions that Emerson presaged more than a century ago: "Our civilization and these ideas," he observed, "are reducing the earth to a brain. See how by telegraph and steam the earth is anthropolized."[49] Such "reductions" of the earth seem, at times, to threaten us with homogeneity, if not baleful constraints. But the city is variousness itself inscribed in steel and stone. Terrorism and totalitarianism in it are but extreme revisions of the one and the many, neither of which we can ignore. Thus, we distrust utopic uniformity precisely because each of us needs to quicken the city with some image of his or her dream. Happy Babel: immaterial in its languages, diverse in its desires, projected to some end still obscure to us, which yet menaces the gods!

Notes

1. Lewis Mumford, *The City in History* (New York: Harcourt, Brace, and World, 1961), p. 37. I am also grateful to Samuel R. Delany for many books and suggestions offered with signal generosity while I was writing this essay.

2. Ibid., p. 97.

3. Ibid., p. 113.

4. Some years before Marshall McLuhan, Mumford wrote: "The electric grid, not the stone age container, provides the new image of the invisible city and the many processes it serves and furthers" (ibid., pp. 566f.). But this "electric grid" can also speak and sing; says Italo Calvino: "Your gaze scans the streets as if they were written pages: the city says everything you must think, makes you repeat her discourse, and while you believe you are visiting Tamara you are only recording the names with which she defines herself and all her parts" (*Invisible Cities* [New York: Harcourt, Brace, Jovanovich, 1974], p. 14).

5. For references in this paragraph, see respectively: Max Weber, *The City*, eds. and trans. Don Martindale and Gertrude Neuwirth (New York: Free Press, 1958), pp. 65–81; Robert E. Park, Ernest W. Burgess, and Roderick D. McKenzie, *The City* (Chicago: Chicago University Press, 1925), p. 1; Jane Jacobs, *The Death and Life of American Cities* (New York: Random House, 1961), pp. 14f; Raymond Williams, *The Country and the City* (New York: Oxford University Press, 1973), pp. 295, 278; Marshall McLuhan, *Understanding Media* (New York: McGraw-Hill, 1965), pp. 104f; Charles Jencks, *Architecture 2000* (New York: Praeger Publishers, 1971), pp. 112–114; Nicholas Negroponte, *The Architecture Machine* (Cambridge, Mass.: M.I.T. Press, 1970); Paolo Soleri, *Arcology: The City in the Image of Man* (Cambridge, Mass.: M.I.T. Press, 1969), p. 31; and *The Bridge Between Matter and Spirit is Matter Becoming*

Spirit (Garden City, N.Y.: Doubleday Anchor Books, 1973), p. 250, where, like Toynbee, he says: "On this earth, the most comprehensive structure embodying the becoming of etherealization is the city."

6. Jean-Paul Sartre, "American Cities," in *The City: American Experience*, eds. Alan Trachtenberg, Peter Neill, and Peter C. Bunnell (New York: Oxford University Press, 1971), p. 201.

7. See Kenneth Clark, *Civilization* (London: British Broadcasting Corporation, 1969), chapter 4, especially pp. 94–101; and Ian Todd and Michael Wheeler, *Utopia* (New York: Harmony Books, 1978), pp. 27–43.

8. Jane Jacobs, "Downtown is for People," in *The Exploding Metropolis*, eds. Editors of *Fortune* (Garden City, N.Y.: Doubleday Anchor Books, 1958), p. 168.

9. See Robert Sheckley, *Futuropolis* (New York: A. & W. Publishers, 1978), illustrations 22, 79, 112, among others.

10. Charles Baudelaire, "Le Cygne" and "Les Sept Vieillards," in *Oeuvres*, Bibliothèque de la Pléiade, v. 1 (Paris: Gallimard, 1944), pp. 99–100.

11. Henry Miller, *Black Spring* (Paris: Obelisk Press, 1958), pp. 18–20.

12. Ironically, Miller in this same work cries: "THE GREAT ARTIST IS HE WHO CONQUERS THE ROMANTIC IN HIMSELF." Ibid., p. 245.

13. Ibid., pp. 253, 257.

14. Nathanael West, *The Day of the Locusts* (New York: New Directions, 1950), pp. 165f.

15. Obviously, this proves more true of some novels than others—more, say, of James Purdy's *Malcolm* (1959) than of Bernard Malamud's *The Assistant* (1957)—and provides no index of artistic merit or demerit. Notable postwar fictions set in various American cities include Jean Stafford's *Boston Adventure* (1944), J. D. Salinger's *The Catcher in the Rye* (1951), James Baldwin's *Go Tell It on the Mountain* (1953), Wallace Markfield's *To An Early Grave* (1964), Norman Mailer's *An American Dream* (1965), Mary McCarthy's *The Group* (1965), John A. Williams' *Sons of Darkness, Sons of Light* (1969), Ishmael Reed's *Mumbo Jumbo* (1972), Isaac Bashevis Singer's *Enemies: A Love Story* (1972), Saul Bellow's *Humboldt's Gift* (1975), and William Styron's *Sophie's Choice* (1979).

16. Ralph Ellison, *Invisible Man* (New York: New American Library, 1953), p. 463. See also Ralph Ellison's "Harlem is Nowhere," *Shadow and Act* (New York: Random House, 1964), in which the author comments on the dreamlike qualities of the city.

17. Saul Bellow, *The Adventures of Augie March* (New York: Viking Press, 1959), p. 454.

18. Ibid., p. 159.

19. William Burroughs, *Naked Lunch* (New York: Grove Press, 1959), pp. vif.

20. Antonin Artaud, "Three Letters," *Evergreen Review* 7, no. 28 (1963): 60.

21. *Naked Lunch*, p. xiv.

22. William Burroughs, "Introduction to *Naked Lunch, The Soft Machine*, and *Nova Express*," *Evergreen Review* 6, no. 22 (1962): 100.

23. *Naked Lunch*, p. 229.

24. For a discussion of Burroughs' later fiction, which develops this same theme, see Ihab Hassan, "The Subtracting Machine: The Work of William Burroughs," *Critique* 6, no. 1 (1963): 4–23.

25. Thomas Pynchon, *The Crying of Lot 49* (New York: Bantam Books, 1967), p. 95.

26. Ibid., p. 136.

27. Ibid., pp. 37f.

28. Donald Barthelme, *Snow White* (New York: Bantam Books, 1968), pp. 97f., 106.

29. See Mas'ud Zavarzadeh, *The Mythopoeic Reality* (Urbana: University of Illinois Press, 1976), especially p. 98, where the author accurately notes that Joyce and Eliot use the collage to interpret and totalize experience, while Barthelme uses the same technique to an opposite end.

30. Joe David Bellamy, ed., *The New Fiction: Interviews with Innovative American Writers* (Urbana: University of Illinois Press, 1974), pp. 51f. In that same interview, Barthelme also comments wittily on his aesthetics of fragments (pp. 53f.).

31. Donald Barthelme, *City Life* (New York: Bantam Books, 1971), pp. 178f.

32. Marge Piercy, *Woman on the Edge of Time* (New York: Fawcett Crest Books, 1976), p. 280.

33. Ibid., p. 204. See also José Delgado, *Physical Control of the Mind* (New York: Harper & Row, 1969).

34. Thomas M. Disch, *334* (Boston: Gregg Press, 1976), p. 265.

35. Ibid., p. 198.

36. First collected and published by Ace Books in 1966, revised for the British edition of that same year—*Captives of the Flame* was renamed *Out of the Dead City*. The latest American edition incorporates these revisions.

37. Samel R. Delany, *The Fall of the Towers* (Boston: Gregg Press, 1977), p. 153.

38. Ibid., p. 78.

39. Ibid., pp. 281f.

40. Ibid., p. 297.

41. Ibid., p. 410.

42. Ibid., p. 7. In this book, Delany takes his epigraph from Auden's "Horae Canonicae."

43. Interestingly enough, the archetypal journey from country to town persists in current science fiction, though nearly always reversed. Thus, Connie Ramos, in Piercy's *Woman on the Edge of Time*, flees her city of dreadful night to find refuge in an idyllic future; and Michael Statler, in Robert Silverberg's *The World Inside* (1971), attempts to escape from "urban monads" a thousand floors high, housing a world population of nearly 75 billion people, to the few scattered earth and marine communes. In science fiction, this arcadian motif probably reverts to E. M. Forster's "The Machine Stops" (1909).

44. I have discussed this new gnostic tendency, this presumed immanence and im-mediacy of mind, in *Paracriticisms: Seven Speculations of the Times* (Urbana: University of Illinois Press, 1975), ch. 6, and *The Right Promethean*

Fire: Imagination, Science, and Cultural Change (Urbana: University of Illinois Press, 1980), chs. 3, 4, 5.

45. Clifford Simak's *City* (1952), for instance, ingeniously relocates consciousness, out of cities, back into nature. Animals carry into future evolution the noetic heritage abandoned gradually by man. In this evolutionary task, human mutants—solitary, telepathic creatures endowed with superhuman intelligence, who roam the woods and reflect upon creation—play a crucial role before they vanish into some other dimension of time.

46. Susan Sontag, *Against Interpretation* (New York: Farrar, Straus & Giroux, 1966), p. 224.

47. Oswald Spengler, *The Decline of the West*, abridged edition (New York: Alfred A. Knopf, 1962), pp. 252, 381. See also Mumford, *The City in History*, pp. 558f.

48. Quoted in Trachtenberg, *The City*, p. 537.

49. Quoted by Mumford, *The City in History*, p. 567. Mumford himself elaborates in many places this theme: "There is another side to this reorganization of the metropolitan complex that derives from the de-materialization, or etherealization, of existing institutions: that which has already created the Invisible City. This is itself an expression of the fact that the new world in which we have begun to live is not merely open on the surface, far beyond the visible horizon, but also open internally, penetrated by invisible rays and emanations, responding to stimuli and forces below the threshold of ordinary observation" (p. 563; see also pp. 568–573). Similarly, C. A. Doxiadis and J. G. Popaioannou note: "The changes which are taking place now will end in a completely new system of life, which will be ecumenic in form and will lead us from civilization to ecumenization. Human settlements will have a completely new physical structure, a total global system of linked units of every size" (*Ecumenopolis: the Inevitable City of the Future* [New York: W. W. Norton, 1974], p. 394). For further references to this theme, see Ihab Hassan, "Toward a Transhumanized Earth: Imagination, Science, and Future," *The Georgia Review* 32, no. 4 (1978–79).

Mythicizing the City

Leslie Fiedler

For millennia now mankind has been moving inexorably into cities—streaming from forest clearings and lonely farms, hillside hamlets and island villages to found Athens and Rome, Cairo and Jerusalem, Kiev and Odessa, Shanghai and Tokyo, Sao Paolo and Mexico City, San Francisco and New York—until the whole world promises or threatens (it can be, has been, felt either way) to turn into The City, Metropolis, Megalopolis. But, alas, though we have desired this, we have forgotten why. Once, *once* we knew, and the memory is preserved in the frozen etymology of certain words: "civilization" (the creation of human culture by clustering together in the *civis*, which is to say, the city); and "politics" (the science of living together in large numbers, of creating communities bigger than the family or the tribe in the *polis*, once more the city). "Outside the *polis*," Aristotle taught, "no one is truly human, but either a god or a beast." And for a long time we believed him, or at least acted as if we did.

Moreover, looking around now in what will always be for me the city *par excellence*, in Newark where I was born and my father before me, I can see still the institutions which this city, like all cities, created, institutions for which the city was a necessary pre-condition: the Library, the Museum, the University. Though I did not go to college in Newark, I was—as I have written before—educated in this library, this museum; but also I learned what museums, libraries, and schools cannot teach in Military Park. There in my lunch breaks at the tedious job I started at age thirteen or fourteen, I listened to the political speakers and evangelists on soap boxes, the drifters and hoboes who sat beside me on the benches, and the wino who read aloud from Jack London's *The Iron Heel*. But this, too, is what cities alone make possible: the confluence of many people, preaching and remembering, lying and telling the truth, asking and answering— until not just dialogue happens, but the dialectic is invented. Nor is it invented once and for all in, say, the Agora of ancient Athens, but over

© 1981 by Leslie Fiedler.

113

and over, wherever the traffic of buying and selling turns mysterious-
ly into the traffic of ideas. And what I had begun to learn passively and
in silence, I finished learning by talking to crowds gathered on urban
street corners, where—long before I had stood behind a desk in the
classroom—I first tried to teach over the catcalls of hecklers. "Patiently to explain," Lenin called that art, which he also described as
"the first duty of the revolutionary." But patience is a virtue we all
acquire in cities, a necessity for urban survival.

Yet somehow we grow impatient with cities themselves, that growing majority of us who continue to crowd into them, or who, like me,
return to them after a temporary flight to the boondocks. Nor is that
impatience, that dis-ease the product of a belated discovery (not in my
own case surely, since I have always known it) that the city creates
along with the Agora, the Library, the Museum, and the University
unprecedented human indignities. Squalor and poverty have always
been parts of human existence, but never somehow so visibly. And
though violence and terror are also a part of recorded history from the
very beginning, organized crime is something new under the sun; as is
organized repressive force, the sanctioned counter-terror of the uniformed police.

But the dis-ease, the impatience of which I speak, existed in the
literature bred by our deepest nightmares long before the Industrial
Revolution had radically transformed the more humane *polis* into an
impersonal hub of communications, a center for mass production,
marshalling yards, slaughter houses, and assembly plants. At first,
indeed, that transformation seemed a blessing rather than a curse for
the city poor, since it created more work, more goods, and eventually
lifted more men and women above the subsistence level. But simultaneously it raised expectations even higher, making those still excluded and deprived ever more aware of their suffering, while rich
and poor alike became conscious of the price paid: the growing
alienation of all humankind from the natural world in which we first
become human, and which in turn we have humanized by making it a
part of our essential mythology, the perceptual grid through which we
see and understand our identity and destiny.

But though our poets and storytellers have striven valiantly to
mythicize the city, too; to make it a fact of the imagination as well as of
geography, demography, and sociology—like the Sun, the Moon, the
Desert, the Ocean, the Forest, even the King's Palace and the Peasant's
Hut—it has proved oddly resistant to any mythic images except for
certain negative, dark, infernal ones, which reinforce rather than
neutralize our sense of alienation. Very early on, to be sure, the notion

of a city, one's own city (Babylon, let's say, or Rome or Jerusalem or Byzantium) as the center of the world, the navel of the Universe, was part of the official legends of certain imperial powers. And some of these parochial myths continue to influence our political behavior to this very day. Think, for instance, of how the mythological competition of Jews, Christians, and Muslims over the "Holy City" of Jerusalem helps to determine, even in the face of rational self-interest, war and peace in the Middle East.

But the attempts of Christianity to adapt that myth to its own universalist theology, by making it the model or prototype of the "Heavenly City," has somehow failed to fire the imagination even of its own communicants. The single Christian poem which continues to shape our deep fantasies, whether we are believers or not, follows the opposite strategy, using the City as the model or prototype of Hell: a symbol of absolute alienation rather than total fulfillment, of shared misery rather than communal bliss. In Dante's *Divine Comedy*, Heaven is compared to the boundless ocean and at its heart to a great white rose, while Purgatory is portrayed as a lofty mountain on a lonely island—all three images derived from the world of pre-urban, if not pre-human, nature. But Hell is figured forth as a walled city, much like the poet's own Florence, which had exiled him forever but continued to obsess him to the end of his days. "*Per me si va nella città dolente*" reads the inscription upon its gates. "Through me one goes into the mournful city."

And when some 600 years after the writing of the *Divine Comedy*, T.S. Eliot is evoking, in the major urban poem of the post-World War I era, his—and our—real, unreal city ("Falling towers / Jerusalem Athens Alexandria / Vienna London / Unreal"), it is other lines from Dante's *Inferno* which come inevitably to his mind. "A crowd flowed over London Bridge, so many / I had not thought death had undone so many. . . . " It is, however, not only this reactionary American expatriate, appalled by the Russian Revolution and trembling on the edge of madness ("I think we are in rats' alley / Where the dead men lost their bones") for whom the Dantesque metaphor of Hell as the City becomes the modern metaphor of the City as Hell.

Among Eliot's contemporaries as well as his immediate predecessors and successors that mythological equation is echoed and reechoed: in Baudelaire and Ezra Pound, Stephen Crane and Hart Crane and William Faulkner, Dostoevski and Zola and Samuel Beckett. Politics makes no difference, nor does sex. Leftists as well as rightists are possessed by the image—women (think of the infernal city of *Waiting for Mr. Goodbar* and of Joan Didion's Los Angeles) as well as men. Nor is it confined to Europeans and Americans of European descent. For Afro-Americans like Richard Wright and James Baldwin and Ralph Ellison the streets of the City are the byways of Hell; and Amiri Baraka confesses his debt to Dante openly, calling his most ambitious effort in prose (whose setting is, of course, Newark) *The System of Dante's Hell.*

The instances I have cited all belong to the nineteenth and twentieth centuries; but the Dantesque metaphor did not slumber through the long centuries between the late Middle Ages and the modern world. It appears sporadically throughout the Renaissance; most notably, perhaps, in Shakespeare, whose urban plays—*Coriolanus, Timon of Athens, Measure for Measure, Troilus and Cressida*—tend to be his most horrendous. It scarcely matters whether they are nominally set in Rome or Athens, Vienna or Troy (one suspects he is always thinking of London); he portrays the urban milieu as a culture in which disloyalty and disease thrive, a place where love is sold for gold, and syphilis eats away the human body, once thought to have been created in the image of God. Similarly, in our own mid-nineteenth-century Renaissance, the infernal myth of the City reappears in full force, especially in the fiction of Herman Melville.

Remembering *Moby Dick*, we tend to think of that tormented novelist as exclusively a laureate of the sea; but in *Redburn* and "Bartleby the Scrivener," and especially in *Pierre*, he returns to the land, evoking visions of London, Liverpool, and New York as terrifying as anything in Dante or Shakespeare. The eponymous hero of *Pierre* has, as a matter of fact, been reading in both of those authors even before he leaves the idyllic countryside for New York. And when he enters Manhattan after nightfall, the inscription on the Gates of Inferno is still ringing in his head, so that it seems inevitable for him to describe the city jail where his nightmare journey ends in Dantesque language: "The thieves' quarters, and all the brothels, Lock and Sin hospitals for the incurables, and infirmaries and infernoes of hell seemed to have ... poured out upon earth through the vile vomitory of some unmentionable cellar."

But Melville has also been reading certain utopian socialist novelists of the earlier nineteenth century, authors of best sellers like Eugene Sue's *Mysteries of Paris*, George Reynolds' *Mysteries of London*, and the American George Lippard's *The Monks of Monks Hall*, in which he lubriciously describes the rape and seduction of working-class girls by rich Philadelphia voluptuaries, while preaching that: "Literature merely considered as an ART is a despicable thing. . . . A literature which does not work practically, for the advancement of social reform . . . is just good for nothing at all.''

If critics have failed to notice the influence on Melville of the urban "Mysteries,'' which won a large audience of newly literate working-class readers, largely male, by combining revolutionary doctrine, soft porn and Gothic horror in a city setting, it is because these books have long since lost their mass appeal without ever having won the approval of the critical establishment. But they seemed once to represent a breakthrough in fiction of real political importance (Karl Marx devoted a large part of his first book, *The Holy Family*, to an attack on Eugene Sue) as well as aesthetic interest. And this seems fair enough in light of the fact that they represent the first fully self-conscious attempt to create a new Myth of the City as an arena for class warfare rather than a symbol of infernal horror.

But unfortunately, Sue used as his model James Fenimore Cooper; convinced, perhaps, that even as "the American Sir Walter Scott'' had achieved popularity by mythicizing the virgin Forest of the New World and its "savage'' inhabitants, he could succeed with the mass audience by mythicizing the "wilderness'' of the Old World cities and their "savage'' inhabitants, "the barbarians in our very midst''; which is to say, the *lumpen* poor and the "criminal classes,'' whom he describes as gathering to plot murder and mayhem in a "mysterious language full of dark images and disgusting metaphors.''

The fascination with crime, however, takes Sue and his followers away from the factories and workshops and the daytime streets where workers demonstrated for their rights into the nighttime, nightmare region typically called by one of the traditional names of Hades, "the underworld''; which is to say, the secular Hell which underlies the Earthly Paradise, into which utopian dreamers (some of them the very authors of these books) dreamed the cities of the world could be transformed with the coming of socialism. At the very moment, however, that Eugene Sue was writing about the old, corrupt, fascinating, shadowy Paris, it was being changed in ways he had not foreseen; the Baron Hausmann supervising operations which would break through the old tortuous byways and alleys that had become the refuge of outlaws and revolutionaries, in order to open great boulevards, down which the rich could ride in splendour and the police charge without obstruction to maintain Law and Order.

But even where socialism has triumphed, the more the city has changed, the more it has remained the same; since *essentially*, not accidentally, "it contradicts nature . . . denies all nature . . . [the words are Oswald Spengler's, who for once speaks the truth] the gigantic megalopolis, the city-as-world ... suffers nothing beside itself." And it is a sense of the contradiction implicit in this insight between what our conscious needs demand, i.e., civilization, the city-as-world, and what our instinctive, impulsive undermind yearns for, i.e., nature, the persistence of the pre-human, a world we never made, which nurtures our underground resentment of the City and our image of it as a Hell to which we are self-condemned.

There seems (at least as far as the evidence of literature can be trusted) no way out of this trap. Just as the genre of the "Mysteries," invented at the same moment and out of the same impulse as "The Communist Manifesto," submitted finally to the infernal myth, so too its successor, modern science fiction, which is born with the "New City" and constitutes the storehouse of both its mythology and that of the technology which begot it. For a while in its beginnings, some of its founders, themselves often utopian or "scientific" socialists, did their best to imagine the future in terms of a benign super-city (*Looking Backward* is the earliest example which comes to mind); and occasionally such attempts are made even now. By and large, however, science fiction, on either side of the ideological split which presumably divides our world (it is a genre most of whose truly successful practitioners come either from the Anglo-American world or the immediate orbit of the Soviet Union), when it imagines an urban future, imagines it in grimly, bitterly, blatantly dystopian terms. Indeed, the pattern was set very early with *The Time Machine* of H. G. Wells, the first novelist to leave behind a body of work universally admired and recognized as unequivocal science fiction.

In later life, Wells tended to discount his first romance as the product of youthful pessimism; but he was already at the point when he wrote it a self-declared socialist. It seems therefore significant that the new genre (as if it had a mythic essence, if not a will of its own) imposed on him a vision of the remote future not as a classless society but one even more split along class lines than his own. Moreover, what looks to the Time Traveller at first glance like an Earthly Paradise, in which mankind lives at peace with nature, turns out to be merely a kind of super-garden suburb presided over by effete and sterile consumers, the Eloi. Beneath the sunlit world which they inhabit, lies a hidden industrial city of perpetual darkness, inhabited by bestial workers, the Morlocks—who emerge out of their living hell from time to time under cover of night, and, in the guise of slavering demons, quite literally consume the consumers.

Once invented, this notion of locating the working-class ghetto on which the prosperity of the industrial city depends underground, which is to say, in the very place in which the cosmology of the pre-Death-of-God imagination located Hell, proved very attractive. It appears, for instance, in E. M. Forster's much-anthologized tale of the future, "The Machine Stops," and in the first real science fiction film, Fritz Lang's *Metropolis*. But above ground or below, the city of science fiction remains infernal in key works of science fiction in all media, from dystopian classics like Aldous Huxley's *Brave New World* and George Orwell's *1984* to more recent favorites like Anthony Burgess's *Clockwork Orange* and Samuel Delany's *Falling Towers*, whose title is intended to remind us of Eliot's *Wasteland* and behind that of Dante's *Inferno*, where it all started.

Nor are such extrapolative works confined to the capitalist world, where urban alienation has presumably been exacerbated by shameless profit-seeking and the exploitation of labor. At least equal in horror are visions of the urban future dreamed in the cities of "socialist" eastern Europe. Beginning with Zamyatin's *We*, which appeared in Moscow not long after the Bolshevik Revolution of 1917, such books reach a grim climax in *The Futurological Congress* (1971), of Stanislaw Lem, a Polish writer who was born in Łwow, and has lived since the annexation of his part of Poland by Russia, in Cracow. In the opinion of many (including me), he is the greatest living writer of science fiction; and though his Marxist philosophy is orthodox enough to insure him publication in the Soviet orbit, he seems unable to imagine a post-industrial urban future in which, no matter who owns the basic means of production, humankind will flourish. In *The Futurological Congress*, for instance, he projects the society of 2089, the world as dying city, the city as dying world, in which sixty-nine billion legally registered inhabitants—plus another twenty-six billion in hiding—struggle to survive, though the annual average temperature has dropped four degrees and the return of the glaciers lies only fifteen or twenty years ahead.

The actual inferno these men of the future inhabit is made bearable only by the final invention of the advanced technology which has produced it, i.e., psycho-chemicals, secretly introduced into the water supply, which create shared euphoric hallucinations that everyone takes for the "reality" of their lives. Everyone that is, except for Lem's hero, Ion Tichy, who by dosing himself with an antidote to the hallucinogens is able to see the hideous truth behind the glorious illusion: a world of wrecked machines, rusted robots, collapsed build-

ings, and monstrous mutant humans who tread a perilous way
through frozen accumulations of rubbish, until stumbling over obsta-
cles they never see, they themselves freeze to death—not even knowing it until the last spark of altered consciousness flickers out. But
Tichy, who has read *his* Dante, is scarcely surprised, observing only,
"I thought there would be ice in hell."

Yet though the very pit of Dante's Hell is ice, into which Satan
himself is frozen forever, the walls of his City of Dis are lit by eternal
flames; and, indeed, in the popular imagination of the Christian West,
it is fire which represents the ultimate torment of the damned. So, too,
many writers of modern science fiction and urban fantasy imagine the
end of Megalopolis in terms of fire rather than ice. Think, for instance,
of fire-bombed Dresden in Kurt Vonnegut's *Slaughterhouse Five*, a
book banned in the pious provinces of America for denying the
existence of God, which nonetheless ends in a Dantesque apocalyptic
vision; or the fantasy of "The Burning of Los Angeles" which possesses Tod Hackett at the conclusion of Nathanael West's *Day of the
Locust*. Guilt and terror are the feelings evoked by Vonnegut, by West,
who, like his artist-protagonist, imagines Hollywood in flames with
something more like relish than fear or foreboding.

And reflecting on this, I am led to the final question evoked by this
meditation. Do those who imagine the end of the City, whether in fire
or ice, wish it or dread it—or, like me, dread they wish it, wish they
dreaded it? Certainly, I at least, who have fled the city and returned in
fact, but flee it still in my troubled sleep, am caught in an unresolvable
ambivalence. And I suspect that those others, too, endure fantasies
bred by their love/hate for the City the world threatens/promises to
become. I have been forced to confront this doubleness in myself,
since the last story I have written but not yet published, a kind of
dream-fugue entitled "What Used to be Called Dead," which started
out to be a fairy-tale set in a magical wood, insisted on turning into
science fiction; taking me back at the moment of transition to where I
found myself in an underground cavern (womb or tomb, place or
refuge or simply Hell once more) under the statue of the Wars of
America in Military Park. Above me, the city burned in a fire from
which I an old man grown young again—with a handful of long-dead
shoesalesmen beside whom I worked nearly fifty years ago—had
somehow managed to escape:

No matter. The old man was not there, but lay in the bosom of his boyhood,
grounded in a dark concrete chamber far underground. And before he quite
knew it, he was remembering why. The city had burned for two days and three
nights. But what had started the fire no one could guess. The Blacks, perhaps,

eager to destroy the rat-infested ghettos in which they lived. Or the Whites no longer able to abide the reproach of their misery. Or others, neither Black nor White and more like trees than men, whom no one had ever seen in daylight, though both Black and White dreamed them nightly. Or perhaps it had only been the long hot summer that had dried everything up: sidewalks and plateglass show windows, wood and stucco and brick and the streetside maples in their jackets of wire mesh, cats in back alleys and dogs breathless beside stone lions on the stone stoops—parching everything to a dryness that could grow no longer, only burn under the unremitting assault of the sun.

But notice, please, as I had not noticed until I re-read my little parable for the purposes of this essay, that my city burns not in a future close or remote, but has burned in an irrecoverable past, before my character's, *my* fifteenth birthday; which means I have never left Newark, but have always been there, been *here*: in a womb, a tomb, a place or refuge or a chamber of Hell, far beneath the threatening flames, the city streets and the monument to our futile wars.

Theater and Cities

Richard Eder

The word first is a dangerous one; and the rites at Memphis in the year 3000 B.C. *may* have had some of the character of theater. Still, the first substantial city theater we know of was the fourth in the yearly cycle of Dionysian festivals in Greece. Under the tyrant Pisistratus in the sixth century B.C., it was formalized into a contest of tragedies; Thespis introduced the first actor—impersonating events and not simply narrating them; and over the next century Aeschylus, so the tradition goes, introduced the second, and Sophocles the third. The great stone theater of Dionysus was built—one of the world's abiding used forms. You can see it, remarkably little changed all over this country: at the Mark Taper in Los Angeles, the Long Wharf in New Haven, the Milwaukee Rep. There is no Aeschylus or Sophocles writing for them—leaving aside John Simons' crack that David Mamet, like Aeschylus, still seems to be waiting for Sophocles to introduce the third character for him. It is not whether the theater goes up and down; that makes about as little sense as speculating whether the human race has gone up or down. What the theater has done, remarkably enough if you think about it, is to accompany the human race for a great many centuries. Of all the arts, words and the theater have kept their force intact or nearly so for the longest time.

The great, sustained burst of Greek theater that still, after two and a half millennia, continues to move and govern us was born out of a city. Its themes, its sense of life, were inextricable from the notion of a city which, as it existed then, could be defined as the largest community that men could comprehend. Anything bigger was not a community but a league. Man's fate, the city's fate, and the gods' fate—gods had fates in those days—were all part of an organic destiny. As Poseidon, protector of Troy, says in *The Trojan Women*:

So I must leave my altars and great Ilium since once a city sinks into sad desolation the gods' state sickens also, and their worship fades.[1]

© 1981 by Richard Eder.

Since then, of course, the theater has moved to other places, as well. To the churches, and out on the squares in front of them. To the courts of Europe, to Victorian drawing-rooms, to the suburbs (in point of fact, though hardly of theme, Sophocles was a suburbanite), to the subconscious, and to the artificial, willed landscapes of the avant-garde.

These shifts, of theme as well as setting, have not been casual or without meaning. If theater can be said to have a mainstream—granted, if it does, it can only be seen retrospectively; I would not want to have to say where it lies at this moment—it is its tendency to be in the vicinity of the action; and by action I mean that sphere in which, at any given time, man seems most called on to try to define himself. Hence, if you like: that shift to the churches—the mystery plays; to the courts where the concept of nations was emerging—Moliere, Shakespeare, Calderon; to the drawing-rooms—for that brief optimistic time when nature and society were under firm control and it only remained for man to elevate his finer feelings and self-satisfaction and then, like Ibsen, to find despair under the heavy rugs; and this century's breaking of forms and splintering of consciousness, with the stage set up on a grid of dreams and nerve-endings.

But wherever the city figured as a central part of man's identity—though never as central as with the Greeks—and became his antagonist as well, its themes populated the theater. I will speak briefly about cities in the theater, really for not much more than a survey of the territory. What I would like to get to afterwards is the theater in cities: their presence and their importance.

For Shakespeare the city was generally not a great deal more than a stage set—in many of his comedies, for example. In the history plays they were intervals in a pageant: garrison points for the action, scenes of coronations or assassinations, with an occasional whiff of the crowds mustering behind one faction or other. His tragedies mostly had little to do with cities; although retrospectively we get an urban feeling to *Romeo and Juliet*, thanks partly to Zeffirelli and *West Side Story*. Two plays, however, make the city a very central theme. In *Julius Caesar* and *Coriolanus*, we are dealing in different ways with the city's populace as a dynamic protagonist: the mob swayed alternately by Brutus and Marc Antony; and the more substantial tragedy of governance in *Coriolanus*, with the popular and aristocratic principles clashing in a mutual destructiveness.

Between Shakespeare's time and the nineteenth century the city figured relatively little on the stage—Ben Jonson's *Bartholomew Fair* was something of an exception—except as the name of the place where the drawing room was situated. Restoration plays were essentially indoors; when the theater went outdoors, as with *The Recruiting Officer*, or *She Stoops to Conquer*, or O'Keefe's *Wild Oats*, it went out into country villages and manors. And the major exception was not a play but a musical. The kind of vigorous, unabashed portrayal of urban life, half picaresque, half misery, that Defoe and Smollett were writing burst onstage in *The Beggar's Opera*, set to all the popular tunes of the day. When Brecht took it for his *Threepenny Opera*, he did not invent the sardonic, cynical vitality of London's hellholes; he found them there already—congenial and useful to his own vision.

As long as we are skipping a couple of centuries, it is interesting to note that if, nowadays, what might be called the city play figures relatively little on our stages (except for black theater and a still developing Hispanic theater; and I suppose, in Neil Simon), the city occupies a major role in recent musicals, from *Guys and Dolls* and *Fiorello*, through *West Side Story* and *Runaways*, and on into *Sweeney Todd*.

For most of the nineteenth century the theater stayed away from the city—even if Dickens and Mayhew and Gissing were writing it down in books. Shaw breaks through in a way, if only to make a point. Liza Doolittle's father brings in a bit of London—again, it's curious to note that there is more city in the musical *My Fair Lady* than in the play *Pygmalion*—and there is the Salvation Army outpost in *Major Barbara*. Schnitzler with *La Ronde* gave hints of the solitude of cities; and Wedekind with his Lulu plays had a panoply of urban, profit-making evil that in different ways would be continued by Brecht and Odo von Horvath.

It was Gorki with *Lower Depths*, though, who brought the theme of the city out of a kind of peripheral, adjunct role, and integrated a whole vision of human suffering with a whole sense of the city's pitiless mechanisms. Another fearful and splendid vision—again in a rooming-house, which for the Russians, I suppose, was the equivalent of Thebes—was put forth in Nikolai Erdman's *The Suicide*, discovered last year by the Royal Shakespeare Company in Stratford on Avon, and brought here by the Trinity Company in Providence.

The postwar English theater was largely urban, though in keeping with the splintered and partitioned contemporary sense of reality it rarely, if ever, saw the city whole. It was urban pockets—the seedy aspirations of *Look Back in Anger*, the lunatic lace-curtain slums of Joe Orton, and the urban voodoo of Pinter. In the United States of the thirties there were plenty of urban plays, many with more or less explicit political themes. O'Neill kept away from the city except, spectacularly, in *Iceman*; Tennessee Williams' urban scene is mostly at the end of the trolley line; Arthur Miller gets his city into *View from the Bridge*, and less directly, *Death of a Salesman*. Albee at one stage, and more recently Thomas Babe and David Mamet, have given partial urban views; Neil Simon has too, I suppose, if you define the city as everything on the elevator above the tenth floor. Jean Shepard writes not about cities but about the ruined spaces between them. The most full and open approach to the city in our times, however, comes from the black playwrights—Baraka, Bullins, Hansberry, Wesley, Ward and too many others to mention—for whose characters the city was not a dent on the consciousness but a real country to come to terms with, or be mangled by, or both.

Although this patchy and profoundly incomplete list indicates that the theme of the city came and went in the theater, and that it was strongest when the tie between the city and the human sense of destiny was most pronounced, I think there is another, broader link that goes beyond the subject matter of the theater. It is the link between the life of the theater and the life of the city.

It is obvious that there is a great deal in a city that can nourish the theater, even if the theater is devoted to pastoral comedy or modes of non-verbal performance. Whether the theater pays attention or not, in fact, it is only in cities that it has developed to any advanced degree. The presence of money and audience, a diversity of talents, urbanized free time, intellectual movement and change, and even—this, at worst, is a retrospective partiality—the buzzing of critics: all these make a kind of fertile substratum lacking, say, in Oswego. All this is true and probably not very interesting.

More important, I think, is what the theater nourishes in the city, and here I quickly offer an example: West Forty-second Street between Ninth and Tenth Avenues in New York. Within the last three years or so, more than a half a dozen theaters have opened on the south side of the street. Now you could say that, considering the sleazy and derelict state of the block before, anything would be an improvement. Six antique stores, or six restaurants, or six movie houses. Of course they would be an improvement. But if you stop a moment to think, I believe most spenders will agree that there is a kind of life brought by six theaters that very little else could bring. Just why this should be so is difficult to say directly, so I will try to say it indirectly.

I will start by announcing the general proposition that there is a quality to theater that sets up a very vital and active relationship to the community it reaches. It is a live art not merely in an individual but a communal way, whether it is in tune with its community or at odds with it. When I was writing regularly about the theater, people would ask me from time to time what I thought of the state of the art. It was a mixed answer I gave, and quite as hopelessly general as the question. Whatever the state of the art, however, what I do find healthy is the state of the need. I think our individual and communal needs at this corner of the century make it a particularly propitious time for theater.

For quite a few years of my life I was a foreign correspondent. Apart from Evelyn Waugh's definitive description of the job in *Scoop*, some Waughian disciple has described it as essentially a matter of catching planes. Even that is a bit grand: more likely it is a matter of missing them and getting used to it. Still, there are times that make it worthwhile. These are the odd visions of human life at its heightened moments: looking at the revolutionary society in Cuba in its nascent blend of corruption and promise; seeing the courage and resourcefulness of life under the late dictatorship in Spain; the spectacle of the Greek coup when two all-but-unlettered colonels and one bold brigadier decided to reinvent civilization and got it backwards; and the whole process in Czechoslovakia in 1967 and 1968, when people became artisans of freedom, fabricating it in the basement as if it were moonshine whisky.

In these situations of stress, where one gets a heightened sense of the shape of the world and where it may be heading, and of what nourishes people and what blinds them, the theater has a particularly useful and direct function. It can be a uniquely human vehicle for fighting the prevailing distortions or oppressions. I've seen a production of *Mother Courage* bring tears of recognition to middle-aged Spaniards, who only seemed to have grown away from the starved wanderings of the Civil War, and plunge government officials into a floating sense of alarm, even though they couldn't quite figure out a reason why the production should be stopped. I've seen the Czech theater set up a crossfire of allusion and life against an oxlike dictatorship. I've seen, a couple of seasons ago, one play—*Spokesong*—that said more about the human values submitted to war in Northern Ireland than all I was able to read or write in the course of covering it for three years.

If it were only a matter of words or ideas, books would do it better. The theater is action as well; the message is not merely asserted or represented but acted out. The action may be a facsimile, but it is real action in real time by real people up on that stage. And the impact is not received in privacy, as with a book or in the cocoon of a movie theater. We receive it as a group; it is shared by the audience as well as the actors. We do not simply react; we are seen to react, and we see or feel others react.

This independent reaction is essential: our participation shapes the work onstage and it shapes us as well. In a time of alienation, theater is among the least alienated of the arts. In a time when individual passivity overtakes us, it asserts, it calls out for our response. We work, we contribute at a play in a way we do not in a movie theater or in front of a television screen.

At the same time, theater has what I expect none of those involved would like to call the advantage of poverty—putting aside of course, the crowned fringe theater of Broadway. Many of our arts are in the hands of agents of collective management. Even book publishers are being bought by conglomerates. They tend to move away from that fundamental artistic unit, the individual impulse to express itself, because their machineries cost so much and need so much responsible approval to get them going.

When pressed, the theater has a singular capacity for leanness and resilience, and the world is coming upon lean times. The theater is an art of encounters, not distances; and the comfortable distances of our society—where's Iran? where's Afghanistan?—are about at an end. That blackout of a few years ago was a reminder of a number of things, none of them pleasant, and most of them reinforced since. That the consumption of energy and other things has limits that may be hard to endure. That the part of the world that has lived rich will live poorer. That disasters, economic and social, are more than conceivable and perhaps even close. And that helplessness is part of the American as well as the human condition.

Which of the public arts is made for the blackout? Which is most able to live poor? Not movies, which have become expensive to distribute as well as to make; and not television, which is no medium for bad times except, perhaps, to convince us that bad times are good times. In prisoner-of-war camps, television is on the side of the camp commander; it is the prisoners who set up the theater.

Furthermore, as the times show signs of getting harder, there is less confidence about mass remedies for them. There is some growing feeling for intimacy, for a participation in visible and finite tasks rather than an intoxicating but passive association with large ones. Most people cannot live vicariously when the water is rising in the cellar. Certainly the power of mass culture has not ebbed, but there is less satisfaction with it, and an urge for more direct and participatory cultural forms.

Theater offers this intimacy, this exercise, this concrete and particular life. Each production of a play is different; each performance, from day to day, is different. Plays can be put on anywhere, from elaborate theaters to lofts. Except at certain Broadway shows, perhaps, the audience goes in to take part, to work, even; and its participation shapes what is going on upon the stage. The theater is a magician that needs us to hold its deck of cards. Robert Wilson once said that he wanted an audience that is not particularly attentive; but what is needed for his hallucinatory abstractions is indeed a very strenuous and highly concentrated form of disattention.

It is a roundabout way of explaining the particular civilizing force of six theaters on West Forty-second Street. They are workshops for the life of the city.

Note

1. Richmond Lattimore, trans., *Euripides III, The Complete Greek Tragedies*, eds. David Green and Richmond Lattimore (Chicago: University of Chicago Press, 1958), p. 128.

Part Two

The Language of the Streets

James Baldwin

The subject is vast—that is the only way I can put it. I can't imagine anyone being able to do justice to it. I will improvise, but I have more questions, as I have indicated, than answers because it is a great question and I am a city boy.

For example, I am trying to figure out what I am doing here. I thought—and I suppose this is insignificant, but this is how I began to think about the subject. Many years ago I was out of the city—that is the only way to put it—I was in the country, walking along a country road to go to the store, to do this or that, and a woman passed me—a white woman, by the way—and she said, "Good morning," and I thought, "Who is this nut!" No one in the city, except your immediate family—not always they—says good morning. I thought about it because it meant something, it meant something enormous, that I had grown up or I had become accustomed to such an incredible silence. Or again in New York, when it is immobilized by some natural disaster like snow. New Yorkers don't believe in snow. I have been there during a couple of blizzards when the city is completely immobilized: subways can't go, buses can't go, taxis can't go, people have to walk, and for the first time they talk to each other. They are like children at a fair: delighted by the snow, delighted by the fact the subways aren't moving, buses aren't moving, they can't get to work. All they got is each other. But when the snow melts and things go back to what we call "normal," nobody says a word to nobody.

Now, what does this mean? Obviously, I can't tell you what it means. I can only ask myself what it means, what it has meant for me in the time I have been on earth.

I think of one of our poets, a black poet, who wrote a song called "Living for the City." It was Stevie Wonder, and it contains these lines:

© 1981 by James Baldwin.

> His hair is long, his feet are hard and gritty
> He spends his life walking the streets of New York City
> He's almost dead from breathing in air pollution
> He tried to vote but to him there's no solution

And Stevie says, "Stop giving just enough for the city."[1]

It may be interesting to suggest that, apart from our other addictions, the city is probably the most visible product of the industrial revolution. People left the land to come to the city because they had no choice.

Now, I am not a sociologist, and I am not equipped to discuss in any detail the implications of the creation of the city, but I can say that that creation has had devastating effects on human life everywhere.

I have, for example, a typewriter somewhere else in the country, and I spend a lot of my time living in the country trying to work, trying to write, and in the country there is this: You wake up whenever it is that you wake up, and you look at the sky. It is there, and it gives you some idea what kind of a day you are going to have, and you walk on the ground. It's there. It gives you some sense of yourself, and you go about your duties: You have your lunch, you take a walk, you know that at a certain moment the sun is going to go down, and you prepare yourself to deal with that. Close the shutters, turn on the lights, have a drink, make love, go to sleep. And every day in the country is a little like that.

Every day in the city, on the contrary—and I grew up in the city—involves a subtle divorce from reality. There is something a little terrifying about being forty stories in the air and looking around you, and you see nothing but walls, other skyscrapers, and you don't dare look down. And if you are on the ground, if you want to see the sky, you must make an effort of the will and look up. And if you do that, you are likely to be carried off to Bellevue—but that is another story.

Now, if I am right, the tremendous noise of the city, the tremendous claustrophobia of the city is designed to hide what the city really does, which is to divorce us from a sense of reality and to divorce us from each other. When we are divorced from each other, we have no way back to reality, because even in this democracy people cannot live without each other—something Americans are going to have to discover again.

Now, for example, the European immigrants coming through Ellis Island is a very important matter. They had gone to the cities before I did; and once they had become white Americans, part of their function, part of their action, was to keep me out of the city. When I got to the city, I met slaughter. But more important than that, the reason my father left the land and came to the city was because he was driven by the wave of terror which overtook the South after the First World War when soldiers were being lynched in uniform, slaughtered like flies. So, daddy came to New York—others went to Chicago, others went to Detroit—and we know what happened when we got there. We immediately became, from an economic point of view and from another point of view, a captive population. We immediately were herded into the ghettoes which the immigrants were trying to get out of; and, you see, part of the hidden thing—part of the hidden thing which Americans again are going to have to think about and confront—I know, historically speaking, what drove me to these shores, and I may be the only American who can say, quite candidly, "I know I never meant to come here." Never. A friend of mine, Judge Bruce Wright, says I am the only immigrant who never got a package from home.

Now, if that is so, and that is so, it says something about what I would call the price of the ticket, the price Americans paid for the ticket to cross all that water and to become Americans—and the price of the ticket was high. The price of the ticket was to become white. Americans failed to realize that they were not white before they got here: They were Greek, they were Russian, they were Turks—they were everything under heaven, but they were not white. They were being white because they had to keep me black; and there are economic reasons for that, and the economic reasons have moral repercussions and moral results.

The life of the city, watching it—I watched—well, I grew up in Harlem, and when we were able, when we made a little money, enough to put something aside—and do not underestimate that effort; it is hard for everybody, but, baby, try it if you are black—we began to move across the river to the Bronx. When we started moving across the river to the Bronx, all those people who had lately become white fled in terror, and one of the results of that is the present disaster called the South Bronx where nobody can live. The motion of the white people in this country has been—and it is a terrifying thing to say this, but it is time to face it—a furious attempt to get away from the niggers.

Now, having fled all the way to the suburbs and as a result having created the disaster that we call the inner city, which is an unmitigated disaster—time or courage will not even permit me to begin to talk about the schools—they now are trying to reclaim the land in Harlem and Detroit and Chicago, are moving back into the ghettoes that they drove us into and then drove us out of, are reclaiming the real estate, and nobody knows and nobody cares what is going to happen to the niggers.

Now, the quality of life in all of our cities is a direct result of the American terror. It says something, which I cannot describe, about the American morality. In short, the American panic has made all of our cities virtually unlivable.

What to do about this is more than I can tell you, but I do know that in the attempt to escape black people, for that is what it is, or the non-white person, for that is what it is, Americans have lost their own sense of identity. It is very important I think to suggest that of all the billions of people who came here—this is a paradox, and I want you to think about it—the only people who did not deny their ancestors—let's put it that way, and that is not much of a phrase—were black people. Concretely, for example, there was a moment in the Greek boy's life when he could not talk to his father because he had to speak English and his father only spoke Greek. One has overlooked the meaning of that rupture because it means when you are in trouble, there is nothing behind you, there is nothing to sustain you in the midnight hour when you have to get through somehow to your father and your mother and the people who produced you, who gave you the strength to move from one place to another. And if you give that up—of course, if you give that up, you may—well, you married the boss's daughter. Sooner or later you find a psychiatrist, and, sooner or later, as it is happening now, you go back to witch doctors and become born again.

Black people who were unknown to history, had no written history at all, who came here chained to each other from different tribes, unable to speak to each other, whom it was forbidden, it was forbidden by law, to teach to read or write—and that was a law—and the law also said he was three-fifths of a man and had no rights which the white man was bound to respect. That was law. That was not a thousand years ago. And the effect of that law lives among us till today.

This despised and unknown people, who were given one thing only—they were not given the Bible because it was forbidden to read—they were given the Christian cross. And that is all. And with that they had to forge an identity and discover who they were, whence they came, and bring us to where we are now.

I suggest that that is an unprecedented journey, and it says everything about America; and the question before this country, not only in the cities, is whether you will find in yourselves, whether we will find in ourselves, the courage and the moral passion to accept this miracle, which is really the miracle of our brotherhood, or perish.

Note

1. Stevie Wonder, "Living for the City," from *Innervisions* (New York: Black Bull Music Inc., 1973; and Hollywood, Calif.: Motown Record Corporation, 1973).

Black Literature
and the Afro-American Nation:
The Urban Voice

Amiri Baraka

The history and culture of Black people in this country are steeped in pain and suffering, exploitation and oppression. This is obvious to all but racists and those kept in ignorance by racism. The slave trade, slavery, and national oppression, and their attendant evil—racism— have been the dominant forms of our torture. National oppression and racism are still very much with us, and as we have done since the trade in slaves (which could only have been conducted with the collaboration of an African feudalist elite), our lives are shaped and indeed characterized by struggle.

We were brought to this country as many different African nationalities, from eastern, central, southern, and northern Africa, but mainly West Africa. Our native cultures were attacked and the slavemasters attempted to strip them from us, to reduce us to objects, soulless tools to be worked to death. Culture, as Amilcar Cabral said, is a form of resistance to oppression, since it always preserves history, and if it is the history of oppressed people, it preserves a history the slavers say never existed in the first place.[1] Slavery, colonialism, and imperialism remove the oppressed from history, Cabral pointed out. The oppressors tell us that our only history is as irrelevant footnotes in their history, and only revolution and liberation restores the oppressed fully to their own history, recreates them completely in the world.[2]

Afro-American literature does not come to exist as a genre, that is a *body* of work, until the Slave Narratives that emerge in the early part of the nineteenth century. Frederick Douglass' *Narrative* is a signal work, but there is a fantastic display of the beginnings of Afro-American literature from the very wealth of narratives that emerge

© 1981 by Amiri Baraka.   139

during this same period. Works by Henry Bibb, Linda Brent, Moses Roper, H. Box Brown, the Krafts, Wells Brown, James Pennington, and Solomon Northrup are some of the best known. This is literature that reflects the ideological concerns of the majority of Black people. It is unlike some of the earlier works commonly pushed as the beginnings of Black literature, e.g., Phyllis Wheatley and Jupiter Hammon who were house slaves who wrote apologias, in the main, for slavery. It was against the law for Black people to read or write for two hundred years, and the slave narrators learnt, when they did, against the will of the white slave state, under the threat of beating or death! (For people who want to know why Blacks did not melt in the melting pot, it was against the law!)

But what is very important about this development in the 1840s is the fact that at this point it begins to be clear that what has developed from all the separate African nationalities brought to this country in chains was a *common* nationality, a *new* nationality, the African- or Afro-American. The complete development of this new nationality as part of a nation would wait only a few more decades (and we will come back to this again).

At the same time that the Slave Narratives developed, though somewhat earlier, a group of writings emerged, as a reflection of the struggles of Northern, mostly "free" (ha ha!) Blacks and particularly as a reflection of the Negro Convention Movement, but not limited to it.[3] This movement produced speakers, preachers, and Black militants, who many times wrote their addresses and so created a body of completely functional struggle literature. These were men like Henry Highland Garnett and C. H. Langston and C. L. Redmond. But even before these powerful speaker-writers, there was David Walker, whose *Appeal* (1829) rocked this slave country, caused the southern plantation owners to quarantine Black sailors from coming into Southern ports—such terror did Walker's *Appeal* create. The slavemasters' fears were not at all unfounded either, since eighteen months after Walker's *Appeal*, Nat Turner led a rebellious force of Black slaves to kill at least fifty-five slaveowners and their families. (It should be noted that Nat's raid was completely sanctioned by the Bible—"An eye for an eye," and so forth.)

Walker wrote from Boston, though he had come originally from North Carolina. The conventions were held in Northern cities: Philadelphia (1830, 1831, 1832, 1833, 1835, 1855); Buffalo (1843); Cleveland (1848); Troy (1847); Rochester (1853); and Syracuse (1864). It is clear that most of the Slave Narratives also had to be written from Northern cities or cities in the West, after the slaves had escaped from the "peculiar institution." So even in this early period of the nineteenth century, before the Civil War, the voice of freedom, the outcry against slavery and for liberation could be heard most clearly, in *written* form, from the Northern cities. But the constant uprisings and rebellions not only in the South, but throughout this country where Blacks were held in bondage, were also a voice of freedom. Not only rebellions, but poisoned slavemasters, crop burnings and plantation burnings, and runaway slaves were also the voice and fist of freedom.

The Civil War was the most important event in the nineteenth-century U.S. It determined that the United States government from that moment forward would be controlled by Northern industrialists and bankers, developing monopoly capitalists, headquartered on Wall Street, rather than by the landowner-Slavocrats of the South. This was, of course, determined by a "Northern" victory, spearheaded by white workers who felt slavery encroaching on their jobs and Black slaves who fought to see that slavery would die, who fought for their freedom, for their supposed entrance into America.

After the Civil War, with the creation of the Reconstruction governments in the South and the Freedman's Bureau to handle the distribution of the "forty acres and a mule" that would have to be the basis for the slave entrance into America as citizen, it looked like Black people would at last be admitted into the land of the free as free rather than as chattel. The passage of the Thirteenth, Fourteenth, and Fifteenth Amendments, outlawing slavery, guaranteeing "due process of law" for the ex-slaves, and granting Blacks the right to vote—these were all further evidence that Blacks finally would be integrated into a democratic America, which they helped fight for. But once the Northern capitalists had gained complete control of the country's economic and political power, transforming the Southern landowners into their agents, the Reconstruction was destroyed. The Hayes-Tilden Compromise gave the Southern states back to the Slavocrats to run for Wall Street. Federal troops were pulled out, Black people disarmed. And counter-revolutionary guerilla terrorists like the Ku Klux Klan were set in motion, and even romanticized (even by some white intellectuals) to take all semblances of power and democracy away from Blacks, and drive them back to virtual slavery, with the Black Codes, Jim Crow Laws, lynching, share cropping, and peonage!

The last part of the nineteenth century was one of the most reactionary periods in American life, but certainly cruelest and most destructive for the Afro-American people. But at the same time, in this period Black people had developed all the characteristics of a nation, an oppressed nation. (A nation—an historically constituted stable community of people based on a common language, common territory [the 1800-mile-long, 300-mile-wide Black-Belt region of the Lower South where 53 percent of the Black population still live even today],[4] common economic life—meaning all the classes found in a modern nation had developed [peasants, workers, petty bourgeoisie, and bourgeoisie]—and a common psychological development manifest as a common culture.) So that from the last part of the nineteenth century until this day, there has existed and does exist within the boundaries of the continental United States an Afro-American Nation, whose land base is the Black-Belt South, whose people *cannot* be integrated into the United States, and whose fundamental struggle for democracy can only be realized as *Self-Determination*, i.e., the right to decide what our relationship will be with the U.S., any U.S.

And even outside the Black South, the Afro-American people live in about twenty-odd cities, which are ghetto reproductions of the Black-Belt South, over which until this day "the shadow of the plantation hangs."[5] To talk of democracy to Black people is to talk about Self-Determination. Even in these Northern ghettoes, democracy and equality must be based on the possession of land and power—Black Power; otherwise we are babbling illusory racist unrealities. The powerful and the powerless can *not* be equal, except if the powerless gain power, control over their own political and economic realities.

By the end of the bloody nineteenth century, amidst well-advertised capitulationist philosophy, bought and paid for by the Carnegies and the Mellons (not a little of which came championing out of Booker T. Washington's mouth), millions of Black people left the South, headed North and Midwest and West, but mostly North. They were leaving "the scene of the crime." They were leaving their slave past, many thought; they were getting out from under the boll weevil caused unemployment; they were fleeing the Klan and white Southern fascism. They were heading where they heard there was work. The Northern industrialists needed cheap Black labor to ready their own entrance into the world arena as big-time imperialists. The Spanish-American War (1898), the first modern imperialist war, which "freed" Cuba, Puerto Rico, and the Philippines from the declined Spanish colonizers, had announced the U.S. motion from an early competitive capitalism to imperialism. The First World War "to make the world safe for democracy" would announce that—"Hey, the Yankees are on the scene"—and they sent native labor specialists into the South to bring the Black gold North. Check out the Blues songs of the period and you will see.

> Say, I'm goin' to get me a job now, workin' in Mr. Ford's place
> Say, I'm goin' to get me a job now, workin' in Mr. Ford's place,
> Say, that woman tol' me last night, "Say, you cannot even stand Mr. Ford's ways."[6]

or My home's in Texas, what am I doin' up here?
    My home's in Texas, what am I doin' up here?[7]

or I'm poor ol boy, a long ways from home[8]

or I rather drink muddy water and sleep in a hollow log
    Than go up to New York City and be treated like a dirty dog.[9]

In Richard Wright's *Black Boy*, which appears in 1945, but expresses perhaps some aspects of Black feelings leaving the South in an earlier period—the twenties—the last paragraph of the book states: "With ever watchful eyes and bearing scars, visible and invisible, I headed North, full of a hazy notion that life could be lived with dignity, that the personalities of others should not be violated, that men should be able to confront other men without fear or shame, and that if men were lucky in their living on earth they might win some redeeming meaning for their having struggled and suffered here beneath the stars."[10]

(Importantly, the ending of the book issued as *Black Boy* was not really the ending of the book Wright submitted to Harper's! The entire last section of this manuscript was suppressed by the publishers for thirty-two years, and was finally released in 1977 as *American Hunger*. This book, or the last part of the *Black Boy* manuscript, tells about Wright's move to Chicago, and its harrowing negative tone exposed to the bone the reality of poverty and racism in this Northern "Jordan." By the late sixties, the out-migration of Blacks from the Black Belt was surpassed by Blacks returning to the Black-South homeland. Obviously, by this time there was no more use in creating a false picture of the North, so the rest of Wright's book was finally released.)

But the late nineteenth and early twentieth centuries marked a massive flight by Blacks out of the South, spurred in the main by Northern capitalists' promises of work. It is during this period that the

Black masses are transformed from a largely peasant mass, small farmers, to industrial workers; from rural people to city folks and for many Blacks, from Southerners to Northerners. Even though, even today, eight out of ten Blacks were born in the Black-Belt South!

An initial motion to the large cities from the countryside is first manifested with the appearance of City Blues and Jazz in New Orleans just after the turn of the century. The Black Blues matrix transferred to European instruments, as well as African banjos and drums, in a mix made possible by the incredible cross-fertilization of cultures in New Orleans, could then produce a high level of cultural development in a city of Africans, Afro-Americans, French, English, Spanish, Native Americans, and assorted mulattoes. For this reason, Jazz itself, unlike Blues, is an urban development.

This music "goes up the river," like they say, when the people do; with jump-offs in such places as Memphis and Kansas City, but ultimately with the largest impact first in Chicago—which is right dead up the river—and then later in New York.

By the 1920s, the Harlem Renaissance saw the emergence of an Afro-American urban intelligentsia, centered in Harlem because it was the largest Black city in the world! The twenties are also called the Jazz Age because Black music had reached not only a maturity, clearly shaped by its sophisticated urban surroundings, but also because now this music was communicated across the country and around the world. The Blues came North and connected up with urban Afro-American dance music and slick rags, and the big bands associated with these. The results were impressive, with Fletcher Henderson and Duke Ellington as two startling "for instances."

So too the literature reached a similar sophistication, combining the brash open optimism of the arriving peasant and the sleek *savoir faire* of their soon-to-be-assumed urban identities. But this literature also carried with it an affirmative progressiveness, a willingness to shed useless identities and negative roles, to oppose self-defeating compromises and demeaning labels.

Langston Hughes' important statement, "The Negro Artist and the Racial Mountain" (1926), serves as an open statement of purpose and direction of the advanced elements identified with the Harlem Renaissance: "One of the most promising of the young Negro poets said to me once, 'I want to be a poet—not a Negro poet,' meaning, I believe, 'I want to write like a white poet'; meaning subconsciously, 'I would like to be a white poet'; meaning behind that, 'I would like to be white.' And I was sorry the young man said that, for no great poet has ever been afraid of being himself. And I doubted then that, with his desire to run away spiritually from his race, this boy would ever be a great poet. But this is the mountain standing in the way of any true Negro art in America . . . this urge within the race toward whiteness, the desire to pour racial individuality into the mold of American standardization, and to be as little Negro and as much American as possible.''[11]

Much of the earliest and strongest literature of the Harlem Renaissance can be called "Black Is Beautiful" and "Black Consciousness," calling also for attention to the African heritage and culture of the Afro-American people. Langston Hughes and Claude McKay are among the most impressive writers of the period. And their writing is clearly a continuation of the progressive tradition in Black literature represented by the Slave Narratives, the literature of the Negro Convention Movement, and revolutionary forerunners like David Walker as well as the various writings of W. E. B. DuBois. But the literature of oppressed peoples in its early stages of *national consciousness* always reflects the need the people have to first defend themselves against their oppressors and then to attack them!

Imperialism, for instance, in attacking Third-World peoples, in order to exploit them, must also transform large sections of small farmers into industrial workers. In so doing, it also creates the conditions for the emergence of a national intelligentsia who announce their appearance by celebrating the oppressed people in the face of their enemies who not only exploit and oppress them, but attack them with cultural aggression, telling the oppressed they have no history, no culture, and that they're ugly and should be glad imperialism is even exploiting them so they can finally be a part of something great!

The writings of Hughes and McKay as well as DuBois (who in this period was also living in Harlem and editing *The Crisis* magazine) are clearly part of the national democratic struggles of the Black masses. DuBois is actually the link between the nineteenth-century anti-slavery writers and the Harlem Renaissance, which voices and implies struggle at a higher stage for democratic rights and self-determination. It is interesting that the crest of DuBois' earlier works, *The Souls of Black Folks* (1903), suggests Atlanta, perhaps as capital city of the Black South, as a seat of learning and culture and the activist contemplation of history! DuBois, in this sense, was the first major Black writer to come into his own after the formation of the Afro-American Nation. Atlanta was (and is) the focal point of sophisticated urban life in the Black Nation. And again, it shows the city as a fusion point of a culture—where older elements and materials come together with newer elements under newer conditions, to pro-

vide a more mature synthesis, a higher and more advanced understanding. DuBois leaving Atlanta in 1910 is more than symbolic of the
people themselves headed North for a new life, a higher synthesis.

That higher synthesis the Northern Black city of Harlem allowed to
emerge was a more pronounced *national consciousness*. Certainly it
was not the first appearance of such a consciousness. David Walker,
Henry Highland Garnett, and C. H. Langston express such a consciousness, even in advance of the actual coming-together of all of the
elements necessary for the existence of a Black Nation. DuBois' work,
and its development, is measurable by means of its deepening national consciousness, i.e., the sense and expression of the presence,
struggle to exist, and needs of a particular nationality, based on its
own designs and ideological constructs, independent of any other
entity—not necessarily in a hostile sense, but clearly as a *national*
expression—its history, conditions of existence, with strategy and
tactics for its *own* advancement. DuBois expresses this in contradistinction to Booker T. Washington in the exercise of their debate,
though even here DuBois makes repeated reference to overall American needs. Booker T. Washington *submits* to American "needs,"
which were that Blacks submit and be submissive.

Even the writers who were less advanced socio-politically than
Hughes, McKay, and the middle-period DuBois expressed new Black
stances in contradiction to the slave image of Blacks the white rulers
demanded—Rudolph Fisher, Wallace Thurman, Zora Neale Hurston,
Countee Cullen, Sterling Brown, Eric Walrond, Arna Bontemps,
Frank Horne, Anne Spencer, Georgia Douglas Johnson, among many
others. Jean Toomer was able to utilize the most advanced techniques
to proclaim the presence of Black life, though ultimately he could not
come to grips with it in real life. Toomer and Hurston drew on the
peasant experience to express a more sophisticated consciousness in
urban reflection.

The whole of Black urban life during the renaissance was undergoing deep change, and the literature of this period reflects it. The
Garvey Movement, which saw the leadership of the Black Liberation
Movement pass from the hands of the Black bourgeoisie to the Black
petty bourgeoisie, was composed largely of the Black peasant masses
newly arrived in the city. Garvey's emergence clearly signalled the
further development of a Black national consciousness, articulated by
his calls for "Black Pride" and "Black Power," and by his identification with Africa. DuBois' organization of a Pan-African Conference in
1900 also demonstrates that the national sector of the Black
bourgeoisie had developed an international consciousness: a national

consciousness *aware of its own interests, domestically and interna-*
tionally.

The Garvey years were one high point of mass action and struggle in
the Black Liberation Movement, and this helps shape and is reflected
in the literature of the period. Not only the Garvey movement, but also
movements like the African Blood Brotherhood, a left-wing break-
away faction of Garvey's Universal Negro Improvement Association
(UNIA) also had considerable influence, and whose demands, including land in the Black South, were more militant than the UNIA.
Harlem, during this period, was intensely political, producing political writers like Cyril Briggs and W. A. Domingo, and hosts of political and literary journals, sometimes under the same cover. *The Crisis,*
The Messenger, The Crusader, The Liberator, Opportunity, and *Fire*
are a few of the more notable examples. Not only was the struggle of
the Black Liberation Movement in a period of extreme activism, but
international political events were reflected inside Harlem as well.
Whether it was Garveyites marching to support Ethiopia or A. Philip
Randolph siding with reformist and chauvinist Social Democrats,
reflecting the international split in world socialism over what should
be the Socialists' stance toward the First World War and over support
of the liberation movements of the colonial countries.

The Harlem Renaissance had a very large influence on Black writing the world over. Leopold Senghor, Aimé Césaire, and Leon Damas,
who were the leaders of the Negritude Movement originating in Paris,
all cite Hughes and McKay as their principal influences. The *Negriss-*
mo Movement of Cuba and Puerto Rico, the *Indigisme* Movement of
Haiti (all terms meaning *Blackness* or "*Roots*") also claimed the
Harlem Renaissance as critical in their own development. Important
Caribbean writers like Jacques Roumain of Haiti (*Masters of the Dew*)
and Nicolás Guillén of Cuba spoke directly of Hughes and McKay and
the Harlem Renaissance as inspirations. These movements occurred
generally during the same period, and demonstrate the entire colonial
world in upheaval against imperialism and its cultural aggression. In
each case, the urban consciousness is clearly in evidence.

The thirties saw an even sharper upsurge of struggle in the Black
Liberation Movement because the bottom dropped out of U.S.
monopoly capitalism with the 1929 crash, indeed out of world capi-
talism. This, and the fact of a successful socialist revolution in the
USSR, the revolutionary socialist ideas pushed by Lenin's Third
International and reflected in the United States by the Communist
Party–U.S.A. in this its most progressive period, sharply influenced
all struggles in the U.S. and around the world. Where Harlem had

been a site of both genuine artistic and political renaissance, it now became more directly a staging ground for Black protest. The more exotic aspects of the Harlem Renaissance are cited by Hughes, "When Black Folks Were in Vogue," e.g., white-only Cotton Club explorers entertained by Duke Ellington's "Jungle Music"; a sudden smattering of Black authors being published signalled by the appearance of Alain Locke's anthology *The New Negro* (which tried to portray the renaissance, though with flawed political understanding); Black musical theater like *Shuffle Along*, erupting on Broadway to raise the level of all American musical comedy; and well-meaning zany travelogues like Van Vechten's *Nigger Heaven*. All these things suddenly dried up. As Langston Hughes said in *My Early Days in Harlem*, "Before it was over—our New Negro Renaissance poems became placards: Don't Buy Where You Can't Work!"[12] As he suggests, the cities now were inflamed centers of social uproar in response to the depression. Blacks, already at the bottom of U.S. society, were hit hardest by the depression. And so some of the most impressive literature of the period would reflect the desperation and anxiety, the social calamity the Great Depression brought about.

In *American Hunger*, Wright is walking along and sees on a news-stand: "STOCKS CRASH—BILLIONS FADE." At the post office where he is working, he records the following dialogue:

"The cops beat up some demonstrators today." "The Reds had a picket line around the City Hall." "Wall Street's cracking down on the country." "Surplus production's throwing millions out of work." "They're more than two million unemployed." "They don't count. They're always out of work." "Read Karl Marx and get the answer, boys." "There'll be a revolution if this keeps up." "Hell, naw, Americans are too dumb to make a revolution."[13]

Langston Hughes' work in the thirties developed a marked internationalist and socialist character. Hughes wrote perhaps his most intensely political work during the thirties and the early forties, though it has in the main been suppressed. But some of it is collected in the book *Good Morning, Revolution*. His plays, like *Dont You Want to Be Free* (1937) and *Scottsboro Limited* (1932), speak of this period with great force. Hughes' Harlem and Richard Wright's Chicago, evoked so savagely in *Native Son*, speak of the urban consciousness grown objectively or consciously revolutionary in the thirties. Hughes' "Advertisement for the Waldorf Astoria," which lost him his rich Park Avenue patron, or "Air Raid Over Harlem" or "Goodbye, Christ" or the title poem, "Good Morning, Revolution," are memorable examples of how high up into revolution that Black urban consciousness had risen in the thirties. And this was a consciousness that existed not only among Black writers, but was widespread among all sectors of U.S. intellectuals and, of course, the people themselves. For Black writers like Wright and Hughes, the thirties were an expansion of the national consciousness into revolutionary consciousness, from revolutionary nationalism to internationalism and socialism. But the thirties' literature, because it was drawn more directly from revolutionary and proletarian themes, was not made as accessible by publishers as was the literature of the twenties.

The Federal Theater Project, established in 1935, was an attempt to control and co-opt the spread of progressive and revolutionary ideas among cultural workers, specifically in the theater. Like the WPA and CCC or the anti-poverty programs of the sixties, the Federal Theater Project was created to pretend that the government could really deal with the needs of different sectors of the American people, but it was like an aspirin prescribed for a cancer. Still, a great many progressive works did come out of the Federal Theater Project before the bourgeoisie closed it down in 1939, alarmed that a really progressive American theater was being created. The project allowed quite a few plays by Black playwrights to be done in the thirties, but quite a number were also suppressed by the government censors. But Hughes Allison, William DuBois, Lester Fuller, Theodore Browne, J. A. Smith, Rudolf Fisher, Frank Wilson, Gus Smith, and Theodore Ward were among the Black playwrights whose works were performed. Hughes' *Mulatto* actually reached Broadway in a "sexed up version." There were also several Black theater companies that opened during this period, like Hughes' Harlem Suitcase Theater, Negro People's Theater, and The Rose McClendon Players. Early in the forties, with the same heavy impact of progressive ideas and radical energy, the American Negro Theater and the Negro Playwright's Company opened. Earlier, the Krigwa Theater Movement was initiated by DuBois when he was at *The Crisis*, and it saw to many small Black theaters and performance centers opening across the country in various cities.

There were sixteen "Negro Units" of the theater project scattered across this country—in cities like Boston, L.A., Seattle, Atlanta, Buffalo, Hartford, New York's celebrated Lafayette Theater, Newark, and Philadelphia. These Black units functioned for a time, but even at their most functional they all had white directors. The only exception was in Boston, where Ralf Coleman was director. Theodore Ward's *Big White Fog* (1938) came out of the project, and it is one of the finest plays written in this country! Not only does it give us a contemporary relationship to a Black family in motion from the nationalist twenties into the depression-radical thirties, but it also describes this family in searing ideological diversity and conflict, with various family members being Garveyite, Black capitalist, hedonist, culturally aggressed and Socialist. It is also the story of the impact of urban life, again in the Hog Butcher—Chicago—on a Black family moved up from the South. It shows the depressing poverty of Black Chicago, the loss of Southern roots, the hideous absence of social alternatives, the terror of Black national oppression.

It contains the same environmental social madness as Wright's more celebrated *Native Son*, but *Fog* is a more progressive, more focused, and more aesthetically realized work. *Fog* was suppressed as too hot to handle by the Federal Theatre Project, and though Ward's work was done briefly on Broadway in the 1940s (*Our Land*, 1947), his vision is too complete, too revolutionary, conceived with such an amazingly tragic yet heroic—not martyred, *heroic!*—beauty, that white racist bourgeois theater, which is *most* big-time American theater, refuses to touch his work, even today!

The forties allowed some of the radical, even revolutionary, ideas that erupted in the thirties to continue. Black literature, urban-shaped, raising up repeatedly the contemporary questions of Black life distorted and smashed by national oppression, continued to expand in the forties—not only Ward and Richard Wright, but Margaret Walker and Gwendolyn Brooks. Brooks speaks the Chicago tongue, moving from an early relationship to mainstream academic American literature to the 1960s where she developed a full and sharp Black tongue full of the eyes and ears and souls of Black folks. Margaret Walker's *For My People* is a classic work celebrating and advancing the Afro-American sensibility, raising our level of perception. Walker is always, finally, revolutionary. She still lives in Jackson, Mississippi—the only real city in that heartland of the Black Belt and seat of Black repression. And even though Margaret Walker lived for a time in Chicago, when Richard Wright was writing his most powerful works, her writings even then reflected the yearning for land and power that the Black masses feel, especially there in their own nation, the Black-Belt South, where they are denied even the basics of human existence. For even in these Northern cities our deepest understanding tells us that we labor in the shadow of the plantation, and without land and power, *somewhere*, our dream of equality and democracy remains just that, a dream!

The rise of fascism and the Second World War, in which the U.S. had to make alliance with the Soviet Union, set conditions for the continuance of many of the revolutionary ideas of the 1930s. But after the Second World War, the United States, unscathed and world powerful, was in a position not only to press for a Cold War with the Soviets in the late 1940s and 1950s, but to unleash a domestic inquisition designed to squash the most celebrated radical and revolutionary intellectuals inside this country. By 1947, Richard Wright had left this country, after having broken with the Communist Party–U.S.A. and moving toward one variation of existentialist thought, opting for a more subjectivist prose rather than the powerful revolutionary writing of say, *Uncle Tom's Children.*

In the fifties the McCarthy plague rose more intensely and succeeded in wrecking many peoples' lives, sending some, like the Hollywood Ten, to jail for having had revolutionary thoughts! The Cold War turned into a hot war, with the United States trying to blockade China and ending up with the Korean War, which it lost. For Black writers as well, these same cities of development and protest now became courtrooms of the inquisition and places where they could be placed in virtual house arrest. Langston Hughes was made to go to the House Un-American Activities Committee (HUAC) and copout before great humanitarians like the fascist Senator Eastland, that he was sorry about his thirties' works, and that America really was democracy for all.[14] This was the only way Hughes thought he could save his career—a tragic flaw created by the determination he had all his adult life to try to make a living as a writer. For most Black or oppressed nationalities or even progressive white writers, it is best you get a job, so that your writing can be what you and the rest of the people need it to be, and so you will not have to answer to the demands of the white racist power structure, to kneel before their filth!

W. E. B. DuBois was indicted as an agent of a foreign power, and forced also to travel abroad. Paul Robeson was exiled in his own country, kept out of concert halls and refused parts in plays and films, denounced by house negroes in the halls of Congress, and finally hounded to his death! But Robeson had spat defiance at the HUAC, calling them fascists and semi-literate racists, and so he had to pay the price!

During this same period, the so-called New Criticism also arose, which was the aesthetic companion of McCarthyism. It babbled that art could only be understood removed from its social context, so that this provided the aesthetic justification to say then that the great works of social consciousness were not really art in the first place! Interestingly, these New Critics were inspired and led by a core of

Southern white writers, like Robert Penn Warren and Allen Tate, who even upheld slave society, saying it had created a great culture, despite the minor flaw of slavery!! If you can get to that! They even opposed modern industrial society, upheld the southern agrarian (read plantation) culture, and were called the Southern Agrarians.

Black writers were now assailed for writing about Black people. Many essays appeared saying that the trouble with Black writers is that they always wrote about Black people and not just people. Some Black writers who emerged in the 1950s actually got their fame by denouncing Black writing, especially denouncing Richard Wright, and all literature that was characterized by a high level of social consciousness. But if you cannot stand the Irishness of James Joyce and O'Casey or the Russianness of Dostoevsky and Gorky and Chekov or the Chinese essence of Lu Hsun or Cervantes' Spanishness or the American sweep of Melville and Twain, you are in deep trouble. Though I can understand the British imperialists having trouble with some parts of O'Casey or Shaw and Joyce for that matter, just as white racists have problems with the real-life analysis and commentary that must be found in the most important works to come out of the Afro-American people. The reality of Irish life challenges English oppression, just as the reality of Black life challenges the white racist monopoly capitalist system we live in. If one was a slavemaster, admittedly, it would be hard to read Frederick Douglass or David Walker. Nat Turner would get you mad—later; scared, first!

The fifties was a reactionary period, certainly, with young people being called a "Silent Generation," and the standard intellectual's joke being about what brand of baby food the president of the United States must eat—the Eisenhower years. On the surface, some of the most sophisticated of the urban voices were now backing away from the traditional socially committed Black literary expression. Happily, Baldwin's early denunciation of a socially committed literature was reversed by the sixties. By that time he had walked in the activist's tracks and knew the terror and beauty of struggle, and his eloquent essays spoke about this. Ralph Ellison, on the other hand, was the Academy's dream. His much-touted *The Invisible Man* denounced both nationalism and Marxism, and held up individualism as the way. But Ellison showed the Black experience was as complex and "psychological" as Dostoevsky or Kafka. (But hell! only racists and those made ignorant by racists believed otherwise!)

The so-called integrated voice of the late forties and fifties did want to show that Blacks were like everybody else (i.e., middle-class white Americans). But that is not true. Black people suffer not only as workers under capitalism, but they suffer from national oppression and racism. Black women are triply whipped by class, nationality, and because they are women. All this makes us different, and it is not a difference we saved up box tops and sent away for.

As the Civil Rights Movement came into being in the middle fifties, a companion literature also developed. A Chicago voice transported to New York in the person of a Black woman—Lorraine Hansberry— gave utterance to the classic Civil Rights work, *A Raisin in the Sun*, the first play by a Black woman to make it up the river to Broadway. It is a play about struggle, but it is struggle largely from a petty bourgeois perspective. And even though the family is made up like they are part of the Black working class, what comes out of their mouths, and their concerns, are obviously those of the Black middle class. But like the Civil Rights Movement, which itself was a Black mass movement led by Black bourgeoisie and petty bourgeoisie, whose most articulate spokesman was Dr. Martin Luther King, so too the concerns of the Civil Rights literature were most linked to these forces.

As the Civil Rights Movement was transformed by the fact that the reformist and idealist thrust of "Turn the Other Cheek" and "We Shall Overcome . . . Someday" and "non-violent struggle" all were revealed as futile most clearly by the reaction of the killer state, whether in blue suits or white robes, there emerged a figure whose powerful articulation of America's corruption and abuse of Black people touched millions—Malcolm X. Malcolm signified the Black majority's struggle to provide progressive leadership to the Black Liberation Movement instead of reformist leadership. Malcolm's line of Self-Determination, Self-Respect, and Self-Defense gave revolutionary guidance to the movement, and it gave expression of its real essence—a militant anti-imperialist movement.

The young Black writers of the 1960s were giving voice to the same passions as Malcolm X, and most were influenced directly by him, as well as the overall struggle of the movement against white racist monopoly capitalist America!

Like Malcolm, these young writers were also reacting to the domination of white imperialist and Black bourgeois political and aesthetic criteria over Black life and art in the 1950s. Just as the Harlem Renaissance literature had reflected the lives and struggle of the people, so the young Afro-American writers who were part of the Black Arts Movement of the 1960s consciously wanted to create a contemporary Black art that was: (1) *Black* (an art that utilized the forms and content of Black life); (2) *revolutionary* (an art that would transform America, that would help Black people transform it); (3)

mass-oriented (a literature that would reach and educate and mobilize and even organize the masses of Black people); and (4) *oral* (a literature that would be spoken and public, not an academic literature conceived and received and read in deadly silence).

Erupting out of New York, the Black Arts literary stance came to be taken up by Black writers all over the country, with centers in Chicago, Detroit, San Francisco, and later hundreds of other cities. At their most expressive, these works were revolutionary-nationalist and, therefore, anti-imperialist. At their most negative, they veered off into metaphysics and idealism and cultural nationalism. Some took up Islam because Malcolm had come out of the Nation of Islam; hence Islam seemed revolutionary in contrast to the obvious social control that Christianity represented to the Black masses. These writings also took up Africa, which was also a reflection of Malcolm's teachings. But after Malcolm's death, sometimes this concern with Africa (which is positive and necessary for Afro-American people) became not only in literature but in various forms of political organization an atavism, a useless concern with the past as artifact. In the main, however, the concern with Africa was healthy and revolutionary.

The Umbra workshop of the Lower East Side of Manhattan was a signal effort at organizing Black writers around a collective urban expression in the early sixties. This group split because of controversy concerning John Kennedy's death, where the right-wing elements in the group wanted to suppress a poem critical of Kennedy, and the left-wing elements wanted this poem to appear, even though Kennedy had been assassinated.

The Black Arts Repertory Theater School formed also in Harlem in 1965 a month after Malcolm's murder, but it too had originated on the Lower East Side in 1964. Early in 1964 Malcolm had predicted that young Blacks would no longer turn the other cheek to America's brutal oppression. In February of that year, James Baldwin's *Blues For Mr. Charlie* opened in New York on Broadway and shocked the establishment with its frank questioning of the non-violent philosophy of the Black bourgeoisie and the revisionists of the Communist Party–U.S.A. who were now telling us that even socialism could be brought non-violently via the ballot. In March, LeRoi Jones' *Dutchman* opened off-Broadway and dismissed non-violence as a form of social pathology. By summer the Harlem rebellion broke out, not only confirming Malcolm X's vision, but announcing that the struggle had risen to another level. Malcolm X influenced the entire Black Liberation Movement, and his ouster from the Nation of Islam really demonstrated the sharp contradiction between revolutionary nationalism and anti-imperialism on one hand and Black capitalism and cultural or religious nationalism on the other.

The Black Arts Theater in Harlem brought poetry, drama, art, and music into the streets of Harlem in 1965, and held forums and other programs that gave voice to a new consciousness. It was revolutionary Black nationalist, and it was violently anti-white. For many young Blacks, Malcolm's murder had been the final open declaration of war without quarter to the end. Many Black artists left their integrated Bohemias and began to try to utilize their art as a weapon in the struggle for Black liberation! Writers like Clarence Reed, Charles and William Patterson, Clarence Franklin, Steve Young, and LeRoi Jones formed the core of the BARTS, but associated with that institution and involved deeply in the new Black Arts Movement in the East were Askia Toure (Roland Snellings), Larry Neal, Sonia Sanchez, Yusef Iman, Sun Ra, Keorapetse Kgositsile, Ed Spriggs, Sam Anderson, Welton Smith, Harold Cruse, painters Joe Overstreet and William White, pianist Andrew Hill, and musicians Albert Ayler, Sonny Murray, Archie Shepp, Milford Graves, and Pharoah Sanders, adding yet another aspect of that urban voice that was now given freely in the streets of Harlem.

In Detroit, Woody King and playwright Ron Milner took up the challenge, opening theaters and producing new works. In San Francisco, Ed Bullins and Marvin X opened Black Arts West, and by 1967 we were bringing Black plays up and down the West Coast, in conjunction with the Black Student Union of San Francisco State, whose president was playwright Jimmy Garrett, as part of a Black communications project. Many of these students later joined the Black Panther Party, because that was the same spring that Huey Newton and Bobby Seale and the newly formed Panthers had marched into the Sacramento legislature with their weapons to demonstrate forcefully that Black people had the right to armed self-defense. Many young poets flocked to that company as well, and Ben Caldwell's one-act play *The First Militant Minister* was seen that spring by thousands of Black people up and down the West Coast. Plays were also done of Bullins, LeRoi Jones, Marvin X, Dorothy Ahmad, and Jimmy Garrett, all headquartered in Black House—an institution much like the BARTS—in San Francisco, but shared with the Black Panther Party, who pulled security for the poetry readings. These artists collaborated with the Black Panthers on many occasions, until this unity was split by the traitor Eldridge Cleaver who got the Panthers to drive the artists out of Black House because they were Cultural Nationalists.

But clearly, in the late sixties and early seventies, the urban voice of Black literature was a revolutionary nationalist one—a voice that wanted to openly combine its politics and its aesthetics, that reflected the still intensifying militancy of the Black Liberation Movement. The Black Arts Movement was widespread and very influential. Later, writers like Haki Mahabuti, Carolyn Rogers, and the Last Poets expanded its influence even further. To a great extent the movement remains so today. There are many parallels between the twenties' Harlem Renaissance and the sixties' Black Arts Movement. They were both essentially aesthetic and social/political movements that were Black nationalist in character. Though the Black Arts Movement was more nationalist and more militant, it was also a later, higher stage of struggle.

Another parallel is that in the mid-seventies a similar motion toward internationalism and more pronounced leftist ideology, even Marxist ideology, could be seen in some elements of the Black Arts Movement, much like the thirties in relationship to the nationalist twenties. This is a process that is still very evident today. But the bourgeoisie tries to pretend that because the strong nationalist tone is not present to the same extent in contemporary Black literature as it was in the sixties, Black artists have been cooled out, or can be cooled out. This is the same faulty logic the rulers apply to the Black masses themselves, since the fire-rebellions of the sixties have momentarily subsided.

But this momentary seeming lull in the Black Liberation Movement is already disintegrating, and the eighties promises nothing but flame at an even higher intensity. The assault on the movement by the FBI's Cointelpro and other undercover and overt agents of the U.S. imperialist state (Operation Chaos, the CIA, and so forth) are what basically turned the movement around, with assassinations and espionage. But even more important, there was no scientific revolutionary party, no genuine Communist Party to transform rebellion into revolution! There was also the Black political pimp syndrome where a few middle-class and bourgeois negroes got big off the people's struggles, and then nutted out completely, joining forces with our enemies, as agents, messengers, sophisticated stool pigeons, or professional confusers. Certainly, we here in Newark, New Jersey, could write the book on this kind of negative development, where our city hall has become an especially unattractive whore house! These kinds of developments caused widespread disillusion, just as the destruction by the state of our various organizations nationally and locally caused widespread disorientation even among the most advanced elements of the Black community.

Even though we are now in a period of deep reaction and sharp movement toward the right (toward a narrower, and more repressive society), the struggle against this kind of repression is also intensifying, and the literature of the period is beginning now to show this. By "move to the right," I mean, for instance, the Baake decision, eliminating affirmative action, which we struggled so hard for in the sixties. Opposition to the Equal Rights Amendment is another certain sign of the rightward trend the bourgeoisie is trying to force us into. The reappearance of the Klan and Nazis (probably from out of the basement of the FBI Building!), the restoration of the death penalty, and the marked increase of police murders of Blacks and Latinos are more ominous signs—plus former President Jimmy Carter's anti-Iranian jingoism and sword-rattling to protect the Middle-Eastern Hitler, the late Shah of Iran!

More and more books by Black writers are simply out of print, and it is more and more difficult for young Black writers to get published. As in the thirties, the fad of publishing Black writers is over. In literature, and in the media generally, the same disgusting evidence of such a rightward motion is obvious. Publishers make certain negroes famous for putting down the Black Liberation Movement and the sixties, and one well-known backward colored writer came out putting down Malcolm X in his most recent book of essays.[15] In films, once militant-spouting actors play homosexual pimps and normal sick policemen by the dozens. TV gives us Huggie Bear and Rooster, pimps and sidekicks, and more cops. Tarzan is coming back, with Bo Drek as Jane. An entire anti-struggle literature is being mashed on us as real art (remember the late forties and fifties?).

Racist institutions like this one (Rutgers University) are making it more and more difficult for Blacks and other oppressed nationalities to be admitted, and they block the tenure and hiring of Black and Latino faculty. The U.S. itself is caught between a rock and a hard place, i.e., revolution in Asia, Africa, and Latin America—the Third World; and its growing contention with the other imperialist super-power, the Soviet Union, for control of the world. This contention could very well lead to the Third World War. So that now with Third-World revolution, which the urban voice of Gil Scott Heron reminds us of, cutting super-profits away from U.S. imperialism, and the U.S. rulers' preparations to ready for war with the Soviet Union making it necessary to spend billions and billions of dollars for

Neutron Bombs and B–1 Bombers, the imperialists then want to put the weight directly onto our backs, with budget cuts, elimination of social programs, closing hospitals, and destroying school systems, as in Newark, where they cut art, music, recreation, and library service in the elementary schools.

At the same time, a sharpening economic crisis, of inflation and recession at the same time, causes auto plants to close all over the country, sends Chrysler on the Welfare line, and ensures us that the quality of life in this country is worsening every day. The crime rate naturally rises—since most crime is economic—and our cities are clearly more and more each day, *jungles*, where people made wild by capitalism roam destroying themselves and each other, and those of us with families and jobs struggle to make ends meet, being whipped down with crazy taxes, while Reagan and Carter pay no taxes at all!

So that today, the urban voice, the most sophisticated vector of the Black Nation and oppressed nationality, is being reorganized by objective conditions and its own history and experience to raise yet another cry—and that cry is a song, but that song says Fight! That song says Struggle! For if the cities represent higher levels of perception and sophistication for us in America, they must be the focal points of yet more advanced levels of struggle. And the majority of Black writers, like the majority of Black people, are *patriots*, i.e., motivated in some part by a desire to see their people and their own Black selves free! And all the negativity in their lives eliminated. Which means continuing the struggle for Self-Determination and Democratic Rights, the right of Black people to decide what our relationship will be with the U.S., any kind of U.S., and conceiving of a literature that will carry that struggle yet further towards its victorious resolution!

Mao Zedong in *Problems of War and Strategy* points out that in the capitalist countries, "when the time comes to launch such an insurrection and war" (meaning the civil war between the working class and its allies on the one hand and the tiny bourgeoisie and its lackeys on the other, to end capitalism and thus end national oppression, racism, and women's oppression), "the first step will be to seize the cities, and then advance into the countryside."[16] And at that time the cities will speak once again, at the highest level of our epoch, and that will be the most advanced and the most beautiful literature that we can conceive of, at least right now!

Notes

1. Amilcar Cabral, "The Weapon of Theory," in *Revolution in Guinea* (New York: Monthly Review Press, 1969), pp. 90–111.

2. Ibid.

3. William McAdoo, *Pre–Civil War Black Nationalism* (California: Unity Newspaper, 1968), p. 44. (Reprint.)

4. *Number of Negro Persons by Counties of the U.S.: 1970* (Washington: U.S. Government Printing Office, 1973), Map number 0-492-493.

5. Harry Haywood, *Negro Liberation* (New York: International Publications, 1975), p. 66.

6. Blues lyrics quoted from LeRoi Jones, *Blues People* (New York: William Morrow and Company, 1963), p. 98.

7. Ibid., p. 106.

8. Ibid., p. 105.

9. Ibid., pp. 105–106.

10. Richard Wright, *Black Boy* (New York: Harper & Row, 1945), p. 285.

11. Langston Hughes, "The Negro Artist and the Racial Mountain," *The Nation* 122 (1926): 692.

12. Langston Hughes, "My Early Days in Harlem," *Freedomways* 3 (1963): 314.

13. Richard Wright, *American Hunger* (New York: Harper & Row, 1977), pp. 29–30.

14. Langston Hughes, "Langston Hughes Speaks," *Good Morning, Revolution*, ed. Faith Berry (Connecticut: Lawrence Hill & Company, 1973), pp. 143–145.

15. Ishmael Reed, *Shrovetide in Old New Orleans* (New York: Doubleday, 1978), p. 204.

16. Mao Zedong, *Selected Military Writings of Mao Tse Tung* (Peking: Foreign Languages Press, 1967), p. 270.

Culture Confrontation
in Urban America:
A Writer's Beginnings

Chaim Potok

The Bronx of the Thirties and Forties was my Mississippi River Valley. Yes, I saw poverty and despair, and I remember to this day the ashen pallor on my father's face that night in the late Thirties when he told us we would have to go on welfare. And, yes, the streets were on occasion dark with gang violence and with the hate that had made the sea journey from the anti-Semitic underbelly of Europe. But there were books and classes and teachers; there were friends with whom I invented street games limited only by the boundaries of the imagination. And alone, on a concrete and asphalt Mississippi, I journeyed repeatedly through the crowded sidewalks and paved-over backyards, the hallways of the brick apartment houses, the hushed public libraries, dark movie houses, candy stores, grocery stores, Chinese laundries, Italian shoe-repair shops, the neighborhoods of Irish, Italians, blacks, Poles—journeys impelled by eager curiosity and a hunger to discover my sense of self, my place in the tumult of the world. I was an urban sailor on the raft of my own two feet.

I had little quarrel with my Jewish world. I was deep inside it, with a child's slowly increasing awareness of his own culture's richness and shortcomings. But beyond the tiny Hannibal of our apartment, there was an echoing world that I longed to embrace; it streamed in upon me, its books, movies, music, appealing not only to the mind but also to the senses. Faintly redolent of potential corruptions of the flesh, dark with the specter of conquest by assimilation, it seemed to hold out at the same time the promise of wordly wisdom, of tolerance, of reward for merit and achievement, and—the most precious promise of all—the creations of the great minds of man.

© 1981 by Chaim Potok.

I was one of millions, millions, making that concrete Mississippi journey. We were the children and grandchildren of the last great tribal migration of our species on this planet, the east-west wandering of the frightened, the persecuted, the hungry, the poor, the seekers after new wealth and power—the movement around the turn of the century from Europe that inundated this land. The immigrant generation crashed into urban America. Often I think that our parents and grandparents, watching the world of urban America work its beguiling charms upon us, must have wondered if they had acted wisely in leaving their land, desolate and oppressive as it no doubt had been. To lose a child to an alien culture is to suffer a lifetime of anguish and pain.

Wandering through the urban world of my early years, I encountered almost everywhere the umbrella civilization in which all of us live today, the culture we call western secular humanism. It is western because it functions pretty much only on this side of our planet; the eastern side is off on a tack all its own. It is secular because it makes no fundamental appeal to the supernatural; it is committed to the notion that man will either make it alone or he will not make it at all. No gods, no God, no comforting Truths and Absolutes; only stumbling, fumbling man, provisional truths, and an indifferent cosmos in which man, though a trifling speck in the totality of things, commits himself to life and dreams and to pumping meaning into the universe. It is humanist because of its concept of the individual, the self, not as a member of a community, but as a separate entity hungering to fulfill his or her own potentialities the one time around each of us has on this planet.

I encountered many of the cultures embedded beneath this umbrella civilization, varieties of Judaism and Christianity, ethnic groups, interest groups. I saw how each of these sub-cultures rubs up against the other and also against the umbrella civilization. In the world of urban America these rub-ups are intense, grating, relentless. Ideally, the umbrella acts as a protective cover that keeps all the sub-groups in check and prevents any of them from becoming so powerful that it can threaten the existence of the others. The umbrella is tenuous, fragile. When it fails—and it fails too often—there are riots in the streets, as there were in my teens when the city grew dark with the rage of one of its suffering people.

In the libraries of urban America I learned that a culture is the still mysterious creation on the part of members of our species who have somehow clustered together—whether for reasons of geography, tribal loyalty, cataclysm, and the like—and have worked out their own unique responses to the questions we normally conceal from ourselves during the busy day, the four-o'clock-in-the-morning questions that sometimes snap us awake in the night. We lie in the darkness and listen to the questions swarm around us. What is all this really about? Does anything that I do mean anything? How can I ever hope to comprehend this awesome universe in which I live? I barely understand myself, how can I ever understand another human being? What is this narrow river of light I wander upon between the darkness from which I came and the darkness toward which I am inexorably headed? Cultures work out hard responses to these questions, responses which adherents are at times asked to defend with their lives. Often different sets of responses collide—as a result of armies in the field, merchants at fairs, scholars in libraries, or a youngster's urban wanderings. The collision generates questions and tension: Why are my answers better than those of another culture? Sometimes the tension gets out of hand, and there is bloodshed. Sometimes it results in creativity—books, music, art—and gold is given us to mine forever. Sumerians and Akkadians, Israelites and Canaanites, Judaism and Hellenism, Christianity and Rome, Islam and ancient Greek thought, Christianity and Judaism—and ancient Greek thought: these collisions of great thought systems and styles of life were culture confrontations.

I learned as I grew up that culture confrontation has been one of the ongoing dynamics of our species for the five thousand years that we can track ourselves through writing. Today, in the western world, the dynamic is umbrella and sub-culture in confrontation. The rhythm of confrontation has accelerated in this century. The culture highways are wide open. The traffic is dense, especially in cities. The word "civilization"—it cannot hurt to remind ourselves—comes from the Latin *civitas*, which means city or city-state.

Those who made that urban journey confronted other cultures in a variety of ways. Let me briefly describe one such confrontation—my own.

In the Jewish tradition, writing stories occupies no point of any significance in the hierarchy of values by which one measures achievement. Scholarship—especially Talmudic scholarship—is the measure of an individual. Fiction, even serious fiction—as far as the religious Jewish tradition is concerned—is at best a frivolity, at worst a menace.

When I was about fourteen or fifteen years old, I read *Brideshead Revisited* by Evelyn Waugh. That was the first serious adult novel I ever read. In high school English classes in those days you read works like *Treasure Island* and *Ivanhoe*. I was overwhelmed by that book. Somehow Evelyn Waugh reached across the chasm that separated my tight New York Jewish world from that of the upper-class British Catholics in his book. I remember finishing the book and marveling at the power of this kind of creativity. We each have our own beginnings with the hot madness called writing fiction.

From that time on, I not only read works of literature for enjoyment but also studied them with Talmudic intensity in order to teach myself how to create worlds out of words on paper. During the mornings in my school I studied the sacred subjects of my religious tradition; during the afternoons I studied the secular subjects of our umbrella civilization; at night and during weekends I read and wrote fiction. The great writers who created modern literature became my teachers.

The years went by.

In time I discovered that I had entered a tradition—modern literature. Fundamental to that tradition was a certain way of thinking the world; and basic to that was the binocular vision of the iconoclast, the individual who grows up inside inherited systems of value and, while growing, begins to recoil from the games, masks, and hypocrisies he sees all around him. About three hundred years ago, on this side of the planet, certain writers began to use one of the oldest instrumentalities of communication known to our species—story-telling—as a means of exploring the taut lines of relationship between individuals on the one hand and societies on the other, the small or large coherent worlds with which those individuals had entered into tension. Individual and society in polarization—that is one of the mighty rivers in the geography of modern literature. Sometimes the world of that individual is tiny and benign, as in Jane Austen; sometimes it is cruel and sentimental, as in Dickens; sometimes it is stagnant and decadent, as in James Joyce and Thomas Mann; sometimes it is icy and brutal, as in the early Hemingway. That is what I saw in the novels I read during my high school and college years in the teeming urban world of New York.

It was not difficult for me to realize that nothing was sacred to the serious novelist; nothing was so sacrosanct an inheritance from the past that it could not be opened up and poked into by the pen of the novelist. Someone born into an ancient tradition enters the world with baggage on his shoulders. If, in your growing up, no one messed up your particular world in an irreversible way—parents and teachers brought patience and love to your problems—you might come out of your sub-culture appreciating its richness, its echoing history, and eager to cope with its shortcomings. And if, at the same time, you have stumbled upon modern literature during the years of your growing loyalty to your private past, you find by the time you are nineteen or twenty years old that you have become a battleground for a culture confrontation of a certain kind. I call it a core-to-core culture confrontation. From the heart of your sub-culture, trained in its best schools, able to maneuver through its system of thought, its language, its way of structuring the world, you have come upon literature, an element from the core of the umbrella civilization in which all of us live today. Literature is a core endeavor of western secular man; it is one of the ways western secular man gives configuration to his experience—through the faculty of the imagination and a certain aesthetic form. In the history of our species, core-to-core culture confrontations have often resulted in explosions of creativity. An encounter with soaring alien ideas often sets us soaring toward new ideas of our own; or we enter into a process of selective affinity, finding in the alien thought system elements with which we feel the need to fuse. Few experiences are more extraordinary in the history of our species than that sort of culture confrontation in which one culture will spark another into seminal creativity.

I do not intend to write a novel about my encounter with the novel. But some who grew up with me might have encountered other elements from the core of western secular humanism. And that is what my work has been about so far. In *The Chosen*, Danny Saunders encounters Freudian psychoanalytic theory; in *The Promise*, Reuven Malter encounters text criticism; in *My Name Is Asher Lev*, a young man encounters western art; in *In the Beginning*, David Lurie encounters modern Bible scholarship. All these disciplines are located in the core of western culture. And all my people are located in the core of their sub-culture.

You can grow up along the periphery of your sub-culture and enter the rich heart of western secular humanism—say, by going to a university, the generating plant of western secular civilization. You will experience a periphery-to-core culture confrontation. Saul Bellow's *Herzog* is about such a culture confrontation: Herzog at the heart of western secular humanism experiencing the crises of our world and his life through his peripheral emotive connection to his sub-culture, his memories of an ethnic past.

You can grow up along the periphery of your sub-culture and experience only the periphery of western civilization. That is a periphery-to-periphery culture confrontation. The early stories of

Philip Roth are accounts of that kind of collision of cultures. Almost always, that sort of culture confrontation gives rise to cultural aberrations, awkward misunderstandings, bizarre fusions.

At the core of a culture is its world view, its literature, art, and music, its special ways of thinking the world. The more difficult it becomes to move inside an alien culture, the closer you are to its core. Peripheries of culture—street language, foods, clothes, fad music, superstitions—are almost always the easiest elements to understand, imitate, absorb.

I am writing about a particular sub-culture, about people and events that were of special concern to me as I grew up and began my own Mississippi journey into this world. The compression of urban existence, the living mix of peoples and cultures in my Bronx world, made possible for me a rich variety of culture confrontations. I chose to write about core-to-core confrontation because that is the world I know best.

What happens when two ultimate commitments—one from your sub-culture, the other from the umbrella culture—meet in you and you love them both and they are antithetical one to the other? There is a dimension of Greek tragedy in this collision of two equally valid systems of values. How do you maneuver? How do you talk on the phone, go to school, ride a train, cross a street, attend class, relate to others, talk to your parents and friends, go out on a date, read texts? What are your dreams? What are your loves, your hates? I am writing about the feelings involved in the experience of core-to-core culture confrontation.

Urban wanderings that result in core-culture confrontations often shape a certain kind of individual. I call that individual a *Zwischenmensch*, a between-person. Such an individual will cross the boundaries of his or her own culture and embrace life-enhancing elements from alien worlds. I remember the pink-faced, bald-headed Italian shoemaker who sang in his tenor voice as he pounded away at my torn shoes. He taught me the word "opera." That was the birth of that passion for me. I always listened carefully from then on to the classical radio station. Can you conceive of how distant the tumultuous world of opera is from the mind-centered ambience of Talmudic disputation?

Late one spring day a seedy-looking man wandered into my parochial school. He was an artist, he said, and was willing to teach a summer course in art for a pittance. It would keep the children off the street, he said; give them something to do. He was in his late forties, a tired man reeking of tobacco, his eyes watery, the cuffs of his shirtsleeves frayed, his jacket and trousers creased. He looked weary, worn. Inexplicably, he was taken on. There were sixteen of us in that class. I was about ten years old. He watched me move colors across a canvas board one day and took me aside. "How old are you, kid?" he asked. "Who've you studied with?" That was my first step into the world of western art. In my childhood, what Joyce was to Jesuits, painting was to Talmud.

To be a *Zwischenmensch* is to feel at home everywhere and nowhere simultaneously, to be regarded with suspicion by those along the banks as they watch you float by on your raft.

My Mississippi has no Delta ending. It runs on and on. We are most human when we communicate creatively across the Hannibals we make for ourselves. Yes, the raft is frail. Anything made and experienced by man seems frail—anything. Each new day of sun and sky is frail, frail. Still we remember the journeys begun a long time ago on the cement rivers of urban America. Different cities boil within each of us. There is so much we hate—the dirt, the poverty, the prejudice; there is so much we love—the one or two friendships that somehow crossed boundaries, the libraries where we joined ourselves to the dreams of others, the places where we composed dreams of our own, the museums where we learned how to defeat time, certain streets, alleys, staircases, apartment-house roofs, certain radio stations we would listen to deep into the night, certain newspapers we read as if they were a testament to the ages. We remember the terrors and joys of our early urban wanderings. We write, and continue the journey.

A Double Life:
The Fate of the Urban Ethnic

Jerre Mangione

The question of dual identity is an ancient one that persists throughout the human experience. Yet relatively little attention has been paid to the dual personality thrust upon millions of American immigrants who upon arrival were separated at once from the rest of society by the fact that they spoke a foreign language. The problem of duality, with all of its negative nuances, became ingrained in the offspring of the immigrants, and it keeps surfacing as a basic difficulty of the American ethnic experience. "Alienation," a word which has the philological advantage of incorporating "alien," the true status of the arriving immigrant, is the more familiar term for the same problem.

Who are the Americans mostly affected by it? When Oscar Handlin wrote that "the history of immigration is the history of alienation and its consequences," he was referring to the American immigrants who had "uprooted" themselves from their native European heath in the nineteenth century and the early decades of the twentieth.[1] One would suppose that the Germans, Irish, and Scandinavians, who constituted the bulk of nineteenth-century immigration, would have by now lost their Old World identity and become indistinguishable from the descendants of the nation's earliest settlers. But the sociologists tell us otherwise; symbolically at least, and sometimes for political reasons, millions of them still retain their Old World identity.

Yet they cannot be said to have the same identification problems as the offspring of the immigrants from Southern and Eastern European countries. The latter have become part of a powerful ethnic movement that is far from symbolic. Indeed, during the past decade the movement has taken on the character of a crusade, the thrust of which is to transform duality into a social force that will being each nationality

© 1981 by Jerre Mangione.

group into closer participation with the Old World culture of its immigrant forebears.

Those were the so-called "new immigrants," who in the period between 1880 and 1920 numbered more than 27 million men, women, and children. In less than forty years they provided the bulk of the working force in the nation's key industries; by 1920 they accounted for two-thirds of our urban populations, despite the fact that the large majority of them, particularly the Italians (the largest of all the twentieth-century immigrant groups), had been farmers living in small villages.

The legacy of this demographic phenomenon, though it has affected every segment of American society and continues to be conspicuously evident, has engaged the attention of a number of American novelists, but it is still to be adequately explored by sociologists and historians. One of the difficulties has been that, until the early sixties, most of the scholars were locked into the "melting pot" syndrome, which misled them into believing that the immigrants and their children were gradually but gladly liberating themselves from the immigrant way of life in order to merge into the dominant Anglo-Saxon culture. In my youth, when the melting pot concept was still being strongly championed, I would fascinate myself with the image of a giant, bubbling cauldron, some three thousand miles wide in which Italian immigrants (my own relatives among them), impervious to its boiling temperature, dived and swam about until they spoke English with almost no accent and developed a marked preference for potatoes to spaghetti.

Yet the melting pot concept, which, incidentally, got its name from the title of a 1914 play by an English-born Zionist, Israel Zangwill, was far less presumptuous than the nineteenth-century nativist attitude toward immigrants (defined as "assimilationism" by the sociologists) which held that it was the American duty of every immigrant, if he wanted to become a legitimate member of this nation, to be "Anglo-Saxonized" as quickly as possible. Quite accurately, the immigrants, particularly the foreign-speaking ones from Southern and Eastern Europe, were generally regarded as a serious threat to the established Anglo-American Protestant tradition.

Not until the sixties, when the American Blacks forcibly asserted their right to be culturally different, was the melting pot concept relegated to the junkpile of history. Propelled by the Blacks, the Chicanos, and the Puerto Ricans, the concept of "cultural pluralism," which encourages ethnic groups to maintain whatever is unique about their cultural identity, began making rapid headway. The rest of the ethnic groups, chiefly the offspring of the early-century immigrants, were quick to adopt the concept.

Cultural pluralism means, of course, a quest for identity, a way of resolving problems of duality. But it also has economic implications—that is, the effort of the poor trying to get their fair share of the capitalistic pie. While it is reasonable to assume that most of the ethnic poor have middle-class aspirations, we know that millions of them live in a state of poverty. The fact that many ethnics have been assimilated into American society and are considered successful has, in effect, obscured the economic and social insecurity prevalent among all ethnic groups, be they Browns, Blacks, or Whites.[2]

Among White ethnics, the poorest are the ones most likely to have retained the Old World attitudes and customs of their immigrant forebears, cultural pluralism or not. In the ongoing debate among scholars as to what degree it is possible for ethnic groups to maintain their own cultural identity, Herbert J. Gans points out that "poorer ethnics have been less touched by acculturation and assimilation than middle-class ethnics and have in some cases used ethnicity and ethnic organizations as psychological and political defenses against the injustices which they suffer in an unequal society." "In other words," he concludes, "ethnicity is largely a working class style."[3]

This is a significant point since it is from the working class that we derive the novels, plays, short stories, and poems that establish our impressions of the urban ethnic's attitudes toward himself and toward American society. Such works of literature, usually written by the offspring of the immigrants, often reveal that fundamental aspect of ethnic life which is either glossed over or ignored by scholars—that is, the psychological dilemma of the ethnic as he or she tries to cope with the conflicts of a dualistic existence.

They also reveal the duality in the life of the immigrants who came to the United States with high expectations of being welcomed, only to find themselves mired in the marshes of poverty and prejudice. But what ethnic literature seldom indicates is that the psychological problems of the immigrants themselves were not nearly as serious as those of their offspring. Whatever their difficulties in the New World, the immigrants had no personal identity problems. As individuals, they invariably knew who they were and were prepared, psychologically at least, for the experience of living among foreigners with foreign customs and values. To a greater degree than their parents, the children of the immigrants were truly victims of circumstances, born to live a double life, caught between two sharply differing cultures— that which their parents had brought with them from the Old World and that which was thrust upon them outside the home, particularly in classrooms where teachers repeatedly emphasized philosophical values that were frequently at odds with those of the parents.

The children of the immigrants from southern Italy, for example, constantly heard their teachers speak of freedom, free enterprise and free will; but at home they encountered a fatalistic view of life ingrained into the ancient south Italian soul by centuries of oppression, poverty, and resignation. The differences between the two cultures were further aggravated by parents, such as mine, who forbade the use of English in the home out of their fear that they would lose communication with their children. Torn between the need to conform to American customs and values and the obligation to be loyal to their parents, the children lived in a state of emotional insecurity—a condition which was bound to generate identity problems that often persisted in adulthood.[4]

In the opening pages of *Mount Allegro* (1943) which describes the experience of growing up among scores of Sicilian immigrant relatives in Rochester, New York, I report a childhood conversation with my brother and sisters which sounds the keynote to the duality of our lives:

> "When I grow up I want to be an American," Giustina said. We looked at our sister; it was something none of us had ever said.
>
> "Me too," my younger sister echoed.
>
> "Aw you don't even know what an American is," my brother scoffed.
>
> "I do so," Giustina said.
>
> It was more than the rest of us knew. "We're Americans right now," I said. "Miss Zimmerman (my grade teacher) says if you're born here you're an American."
>
> "She's nuts," my brother said. He had no use for most teachers. "We're Italians. If you don't believe me, ask Pop."
>
> But my father was not very helpful. "Your children will be *Americani*," he said. "But you, my son, are half and half. Now stop asking me foolish questions. You should know those things from going to school. What do they teach you in school anyway?"

We were urban ethnics in every sense of the word, yet our neighborhood could hardly be called a ghetto. There were Austrian, Russian, and German Jews, Poles, Italians, and a few Anglo-Saxon families that had chosen not to escape the neighborhood after the new immigrants began moving in. Although the Jews outnumbered everyone else, no single group dominated the neighborhood. There were street gangs, but their membership was based on territorial considerations rather than nationality. At all times the street was our playground. On the street we were Americans, though not sure what that meant; inside the home, we were Sicilians, and there was never any mistaking of what that meant.

As I tried to bridge my life at home with that on the street and the classroom, I felt resentful of my Sicilian relatives for being foreign. My fondness for privacy, which my relatives considered a symptom of illness, added to my feeling of incompatibility. I was offended by their incessant need to be with one another. Only the families of my Jewish playmates approached their gregariousness, but they were recluses by comparison. I was constantly tormented by the worry that they were making a bad impression on the Americans around us. The most excruciating moments came when the Sicilian mothers during family picnics in the park, not caring how many Americans might be watching, bared their breasts to feed their infants. A mindless conformist like most children, I was incapable of appreciating my relatives' compulsion to be themselves as a way of coping with an alien world that was generally hostile.

Not all children were consciously aware of the tug of war in progress between their Old World influences and those of the New World. The majority of them eventually succumbed to the pressures of their parents, especially if their education did not extend beyond high school, as was frequently the case. Often as not, they retained many of the distinctive values and attitudes of their immigrant forebears, such as the authoritarian status of the father, deep involvement with relatives, and suspicion of outsiders.

Not all of the children were willing to accept the values imposed by their immigrant parents. Some escaped into the American mainstream, anxious to find some resolution to the duality of their lives. Among them were the men and women who were to write the novels and short stories which provide us with insights into the ethnic experience usually missing from the writings of the historians and sociologists. How did it happen that such persons, who were brought up in households where English was spoken brokenly or not at all and where books were seldom seen, except schoolbooks, became good American writers? To attempt to answer that question, one would have to examine the question of why people write fiction. Some authors believe that it is a way of "getting back" at an unfriendly world which in childhood had given them a sense of rejection. It has been claimed also that novel writing, involving as it does so many disparate elements, comes from the compulsion of making order out of chaos. Freud may well have been thinking of the fiction writer when he said: "If the individual who is displeased with reality is in possession of that artistic talent, which is still a psychological riddle, he can transform his fantasies into artistic creations, and in that way escape the fate of a neurosis." In effect, Freud seems to be suggesting what every serious writer of fiction must surely know—that writing a novel, a short story, or a play can be a method of self-analysis, a means by which a writer can discover himself and at the same time cope with personal feelings of conflict and guilt.[6]

All such reasons have undoubtedly fostered the writing of novels about American immigrants by their children. Certainly no future fiction writer could have felt more rejected and more displeased with reality or more fearful of neurosis than a sensitive second-generation Italian American growing up in a bi-cultural situation that inevitably created feelings of conflict and guilt. To be American—that is, to conform to the value system imposed by the classroom and movies—seemed to signify happiness and prestige, a condition that appeared to be missing in the lives of their immigrant relatives. Although they may have observed a great deal of love in their families, there was not happiness, at least not the kind portrayed on the screen.

As for the classroom teachers, one could not rely on them for genuine understanding. Whether it was in a parochial school or a public one, there was little or no consideration of the foreign customs and values imposed on the student by his parents. What little consideration was shown was often based on cliché generalizations—as, for example, the assumption that if your parents were Italians you, as a student, were bound to excel in such subjects as art and music. If one proved to be a dud in such subjects, he or she would be accused of being contrary. The only whipping I ever received was from a public grade-school principal who refused to believe, despite clear and repeated evidence, that I was incapable of painting a landscape that could be recognized as a landscape.

If there was little understanding of the child's cultural dilemma on the part of teachers, there was even less from the parents. Especially in the early decades of the century, many of them imposed on their children their own stereotyped notions of what they should believe and how they should behave. For all of their Old World wisdom, they were unaware of the extent to which they were compounding the problems of identity in their children and contributing to their psychic distress.

In the process of leading a double life, a few of the more sensitive children eventually developed enough objectivity to understand their situation and to try to express it in some distinctive fashion that would provide a catharsis as well as a means of gaining a toehold in the American mainstream, in the hope of reducing their sense of ethnic isolation. From a sociological point of view, the most illuminating of these writers emerged in the thirties and forties, about the time when the children of the early-century immigrants were becoming adults.

One of them was Garibaldi Marto Lapolla, a public school principal in Brooklyn who grew up in a typical, urban Little Italy. Actually, he was born in southern Italy and was brought to Harlem's Little Italy by his immigrant parents at the age of two. *Grand Gennaro* (1935) is the best of the three novels he published. Gennaro, the central character, is an ambitious Italian immigrant who becomes a ruthless opportunist, clawing his way to wealth and power until he is murdered by a former friend and business partner whom he has cheated. The murderer, ordinarily a gentle soul who symbolizes the gracious quality of Old World personal relationships, had once told Gennaro:

> The touch of gold in your hands has been too much. We are not used to it. It does queer things to us—the good it makes mad, the mean it makes brutal. Give me the money that is mine and you can have the business. You stay here. I'll go back to the old country.[7]

The first step in the alienation of the immigrants, the novel implies, is the realization that the expectations of social acceptance and economic security which had lured them to America were delusions. The old country meant poverty, but it did not erase self-respect; here materialistic values seemed to supersede all others.

Lapolla's younger contemporary, John Fante, who was publishing novels and short stories about Italian-American life during the same period, concentrated on the point of view of the second-generation Italian American. In one of his most effective short stories, "Odyssey of a Wop," Fante, writing out of his experience as an urban ethnic in Denver, Colorado, dramatizes the feelings of shame that overcame children of immigrants for having foreign parents. Told in the first person, the narrator's embarrassment and anger are accentuated by his own mother, the daughter of Italian immigrants, who pelts him with anti-Italian epitaphs:

> From the beginning I hear my mother use the words Wop and Dago with such vigor as to denote violent disrepute. She spits them out. They leap from her lips. To her, they contain the essence of poverty, squalor, filth. If I don't wash my teeth or hang up my cap, my mother says, "Don't be like that. Don't be like a Wop." Thus, as I begin to acquire her values, Wop and Dago become synonymous with things evil.

The narrator goes on to tell how, as a student in parochial school, he pretends that his name "Fante" is French and even enjoys being nicknamed "Frenchy."

Thus, I begin to loathe my heritage. I avoid Italian boys and girls who try to be friendly. I thank God for my light skin and hair, and choose my companions by the Anglo-Saxon ring of their names. If a boy's name is Brown, Whitey or Smythe, then he's my pal; but I'm always a little breathless when I'm with him; he may find me out.[8]

The most powerful of the Italian-American novels, *Christ in Concrete*, published in 1939, pits the immigrants of another urban Little Italy against the forces of American society that keep them isolated and exploited. The narrator is the son of an immigrant, but he successfully merges the two dominant points of view—his own and that of the Italian immigrant construction workers with whom he works. The novel begins with the horrifying death of the narrator's father Geremio, who is suffocated under an avalanche of cement, the victim of a builder who, in his zeal for profiteering, cuts corners that ignore the safety of the construction workers. Paul, the narrator, at the age of twelve, undertakes the burden of supporting seven orphaned children and his mother. As the youngest of bricklayers, Paul shares the emotions and perils of the exploited construction workers, but he becomes sufficiently American, through his reading of books and his association with a neighboring Jewish boy, to break with his relatives' fatalistic view of life, particularly with their faith in life-after-death heavenly rewards. When his intensely devout mother thrusts a crucifix upon him in an effort to comfort her son who has just seen his godfather—a fellow worker—smashed to death in another job accident, he crushes "the plaster man wooden cross" in her presence.[9]

Paul, in his role as his father's substitute, experiences no identity problem; except for his break from the philosophy of the immigrant workers, he becomes one of them. But, unlike his fellow workers who accept the duality of what they expected in America and what they actually got, Paul, symbolically at least, develops into a revolutionist.

As in *Christ in Concrete*, the interaction of Italians and Jews in the pages of ethnic fiction is frequently presented in a positive manner. The interaction in Michael Gold's novel *Jews Without Money* (1930) is mainly negative: although the Jewish and Italian immigrants live in the same slum area, they have a low opinion of one another. Yet even in that novel the narrator's Jewish mother, who regards all gentiles as "the great enemy to be hated, feared and cursed," is drawn by compassion to the misfortunes of an Italian mother living in the next

tenement; they become close friends.[10] Usually the interaction between Jews and Italians is depicted between the children of the
immigrants rather than between parents. In Ben Morreale's novel
monday tuesday . . . never come sunday (1977), a strong friendship
develops between a Sicilian-American family and a neighboring Jewish one, especially between the young boys in the families.[11] For the
Sicilian-American boy, his somewhat older friend Iggy, like the Jewish boy in *Christ in Concrete*, represents intellectual leadership and
militant idealism. Iggy winds up being killed in Spain fighting against
the fascists.

In the memoir, *An Ethnic at Large* (1978), I wrote about a less
militant Iggy of my own boyhood. Mitch Rappaport and I were kin-
dred spirits, but there was one essential difference. Mitch had no
identity problem; he knew who he was long before I knew who I was.
His parents were Russian immigrants with as little education as mine;
they spoke Yiddish to each other and broken English to their children.
Yet Mitch accepted his parents' foreign mannerisms with no embarrassment and, unlike myself, had no difficulty bridging the gap between the world of his immigrant relatives and the American world
we knew on the streets and in the classroom. There was far more
discrimination in our city against the Jews than there was against the
Italians—two of its leading factories barred both from employment—
yet, unlike my relatives, the Jews I knew seemed to take it in their
stride. It was their ethnic self-confidence as much as our mutual
passion for reading books that made me gravitate to Jewish playmates
as a child. At one time, I found myself the member of a settlement-
house boys' club which consisted of fourteen Jews and myself.

As we know from history and literature, the Jewish and Italian-
American immigrant experience had a great deal in common. The two
groups, arriving at about the same period of mass immigration, were
among the largest and the most visible of the immigrant groups. They
lived in the same or in adjoining slum areas, sent their children to the
same public schools, and became part of the same trade unions,
especially in the garment industry. They each placed great emphasis
on the sanctity of the family. There were, however, a number of
significant differences, other than those of religion and language—
differences which produced quicker upward mobility for the Jews. As
a people who had long been disenfranchised by anti-Semitic nations,
the Jewish immigrants were better equipped to cope with the hostility
that they and their fellow immigrants encountered from the time of
their arrival and for several ensuing decades. There was also the fact
that the Jews, unlike the Italians, who chiefly hailed from peasant

villages, were already an urban people when they arrived, more qualified to develop into entrepreneurs and step into white-collar jobs, and also more alert to the advantages of eduating their children.[12] Moreover, unlike the Italians, the Jews were able to transcend their strong family ties and develop effective community organizations that would promote and protect their interests in an alien land.

That there was—and is—a potentially strong affinity between the two groups, differences notwithstanding, is suggested by the fact that some of our leading Jewish-American writers have produced works that have Italian Americans as their major characters. Paddy Chayevsky's popular television play *Marty* (1955) immediately comes to mind. Clifford Odets was one of the first Jewish-American writers to write about Italian Americans. In his play *Golden Boy* (1937), the central character is a young Italian American who shocks his immigrant father, Mr. Bonaparte, by forsaking his talent as a violinist to become a prize fighter bent on rapid fame and fortune. The ensuing tragedy is played against a Jewish-American background: Mr. Bonaparte's best friend is a Jewish intellectual, and Mr. Bonaparte's daughter is married to a Jewish cab driver, but the emphasis is on the cleavage between the Old World values of Mr. Bonaparte and the son's compulsion to make his life an American success story.

A more pointed example of Italian-Jewish interaction is Bernard Malamud's novel, *The Assistant* (1957). The title of the novel refers to a young Italian American who, out of a feeling of guilt, works in a grocery story owned by a poor Jewish-American family whom, unknown to them, he had previously robbed. Despite his good intentions, he cannot keep his hands out of the till, and is fired. But by that time he has become so involved with the family's problems that when the father, depressed by the failure of his store, tries to commit suicide, the ex-assistant saves his life and runs the store while the old man is recuperating. Gradually, his association with the family changes his attitude toward Jews as well as toward himself. He achieves a sense of moral responsibility and with it self-awareness. In the end, he converts to Judaism, able to turn his back on the culture of his forebears, which in urban America had become eroded, and embraces a culture which had remained more or less intact.

In Mario Puzo's *Godfather Papers and Other Confessions* (1972), the erosion that often develops in the relationships between Italian immigrant parents and their children is described in explicit nonfictional language:

As a child and in my adolescence, living in the heart of New York's Neopolitan ghetto, I never heard an Italian singing. None of the grown-ups I knew were charming or loving or understanding. Rather they seemed coarse, vulgar, and insulting. And so later in life when I was exposed to all the cliches of lovable Italians, singing Italians, happy-go-lucky Italians, I wondered where the hell the movies and the storywriters got all their ideas from.

In his childhood Puzo dreaded "growing up to be like the adults around me." As a youth he was "contemptuous" of them and felt a "condescending pity" for them, for their illiteracy and their lack of economic security and for their willingness to settle for very little in life. "And so," he writes, "with my father gone, my mother the family chief, I, like all the children in all the ghettos of America, became locked in a bitter struggle with the adults responsible for me. It was inevitable that my mother and I became enemies." He resented the fact that her highest ambition for him was to become a railroad clerk: He who wanted to become rich, famous, and happy, either as an artist or, in his more sophisticated moments, as a great criminal, would hear his mother say to him: "Never mind about being happy. Be glad you're alive."

Unlike most of the children who either accepted this kind of duality or rebelled against it in one way or another, Puzo matured into an adult with perspective and compassion. Although he was still bitter about his Italian relatives when he began writing *The Fortunate Pilgrim* (1964), and had every intention of portraying himself as "the sensitive, misunderstood hero, much put upon by his parent and family," much to his astonishment, his mother soon took over the novel and became its heroine. Not only that—all other Italians of his youth whom he had regarded with contempt "turned out to be heroes." What struck Puzo most, in retrospect, was their courage. "How," he asks, "did they ever get the balls to get married, have kids, go out to earn a living in a strange land, with no skills, not even knowing the language? . . . Heroes all around me. I never saw them. But how could I?"[13]

If this confession smacks a little of sentimentality, there is an admirable lack of it in *The Fortunate Pilgrim*,[14] the novel which Puzo acknowledges to be his best. Lucia Santa, the immigrant woman who is compelled by circumstances to become the head of her family, is one of the most memorable characters in ethnic literature. Another outstanding feature of the novel is that a woman is its pivotal character, a rare occurrence in Italian-American fiction. One of the first Italian-American novels to have centered on a woman may have been the 1943 work of Michael DeCapite, *Maria*. Its central figure is a second-generation Italian American who becomes trapped into a disastrous marriage when, in an effort to identify with the Old World policies of her parents, she marries the man they have selected for her. In this present era of feminist assertion, there is increasing emphasis on the point of view of Italian-American women. Helen Barolini's recent novel, *Umbertina* (1979), explores the lives of three women: Umbertina, the illiterate goat tender who migrates with her husband during the 1880s first to the dreadful slums of Manhattan, then to a more congenial rural area where she prospers and establishes a large family. The second part of the novel is devoted to her granddaughter, college educated and at odds with the middle-class views of her second-generation Italian-American parents, who tries to find sustenance in her roots by marrying a native Italian and living in Italy. The final section deals with the great-granddaughter, who is both Italian and American and is torn between the two heritages.

That the problems of identity persist for generations is borne out by Tina De Rosa, a third-generation Italian-American writer whose Chicago childhood was spent in a closely knit Italian-American neighborhood. She poses a question that becomes a poignant conundrum for many ethnic Americans:

> What happens to a person who is raised in a passionate, furious, comic and tragic emotional climate, where the ghost of one's grandmother is as real as the food on one's plate . . . what happens to a person who is raised in this environment, and then finds herself in a world where the highest emotional charge comes with the falling of the Dow Jones average, or yet another rise in the price of gold?

Such a person, replies De Rosa to her own question, often winds up alienated from both worlds—the one in which she grew up and the one into which she has been forced and has chosen. Alienation came from her parents' insistence that she become educated. But education changed everything. Her relatives and her father began to regard her differently. She no longer had their approval, nor did she have the approval of the world they had thrust her into. "I belonged nowhere," she writes. "That is the price you pay for growing up in one culture and entering another."[15]

Babette Ingleheart points out that the price the offspring of the immigrants paid was a cultural vacuum that could not be filled by any amount of success gained in the American mainstream, as well as the frustrating awareness that America had substituted very little for whatever cultural tradition it took from their parents.[16] Their dualism was further heightened by the pejorative impressions of the immigrant experience generally held by the American public. The maligning of the immigrants began on their arrival. With a few notable exceptions, such as Upton Sinclair, Jacob Riis, and Frank Norris, whose writings reveal deep empathy for the ordeal that urban ethnics endured, American writers of the early twentieth century were more concerned with emphasizing the foreignness of the arriving immigrants than they were in conveying the devastating aspects of their American experience. Journalists and politicians denounced them as inferior creatures and characterized them as breeders of crime and disease. Henry James saw little future for them. In his book *The American Scene* (1907), he was appalled to find in the Lower East Side of Manhattan "a great swarming" of Italians and Jews; he doubted that "they may really be extinguished in an hour"; then asked: "And, if they are not extinguished, into what pathless tracts of the native atmosphere do they virtually and so undistinguishably melt?" He could perceive "no claim to brotherhood with aliens in the first grossness of their alienism."[17]

The psychological damage inflicted on the offspring of the immigrants by such attitudes could not be repaired. A child who assumes that his parents are not as good as anyone else's often becomes a victim of self-hatred, Andre Rolle observes. "To feel uniquely cut off, isolated and alone, even within one's community, is to court lifelong disorganization, destructive behavior, or feelings of rejection," he adds, characterizing the children of immigrants as "spoiled identities."[18] The "spoilage" was more evident in the first three decades of the century than it is now when it is no longer considered disgraceful to be an ethnic. In those early years, the fear of job discrimination and the need to assimilate into American society as quickly as possible promoted the concealment of one's true identity. In and out of literature, foreign names became "Anglo-Saxonized" in great numbers. An old *New Yorker* cartoon shows a gravestone dedicated to the memory of "our father, David Cohen," and is followed by the names of Mr. Cohen's numerous sons, all of which have an Anglo-Saxon ring to them. The same cartoon could have been drawn of any nationality group with a recent foreign-language background. In his novel *The Family on Vendetta Street* (1968), Lucas Longo describes the tribulations of an immigrant named Bentolinardo who had worked hard and lived the life of a miser so as to pay for his son's medical education only to have the son change his name from Bentolinardo to Bentley. When the old man saw the gold-lettered shingle with the name "Dr. Bentley" on it, he went to pieces. "He couldn't read English but that betrayal he could read."[19]

But if their characters sometimes Anglo-Saxonized their names, the Italian-American authors who dealt with the ethnic experience did

not. For them, writing their novels about the Italian-American experience was an act of self-examination and self-redemption, an assertion
of identity. By reflecting the soul and sociology of a people who have
long been misunderstood, they gained a firmer sense of their own
soul, a truer perspective on their evolution as ethnic Americans.

Actually, of course, all thinking Americans, ethnics or not, are
constantly confronted by problems of duality and identification. For
we are all subject to forces in our society which promote alienation,
insecurity, and loss of individual identity through increasing
homogenization. Particularly cogent to survival with dignity is the
development of one's sense of identity. But in order to acquire a
desirable degree of self-awareness and assurance, one must first
understand that the individual is never merely a creature of the
present. In varying degrees each of us is the product of a culture other
than that we call American; that is, the culture, or cultures, of our
forebears. That is a reality which nothing can change.

Horace Kallen, in 1915, put it more explicitly: "Men may change
their clothes, their politics, their wives, their religions, their philo-
sophies, to a greater or lesser extent, but they cannot change their
grandfathers." He added: "Jews or Poles or Anglo-Saxons in order to
cease being Jews or Poles or Anglo-Saxons would have to cease to
be."[20]

A true appreciation of those blunt truths is a primary step in the
search for identity.

Notes

1. Oscar Handlin, The Uprooted (Boston: Little, Brown, 1951), p. 4.

2. William V. D'Antonio, "Ethnicity and Assimilation: A Reconsidera-
tion," in Studies in Italian American Social History, ed. Francesco Cordasco
(Totowa, N.J.: Rowman and Littlefield, 1975), p. 23.

3. Herbert J. Gans, "Symbolic Ethnicity: The Future of Ethnic Groups and
Cultures in America," Ethnic and Racial Studies 2 (1979): 3.

4. Jerre Mangione, "On Being an Italian American," in Studies in Italian
American Social History, p. 49.

5. Jerre Mangione, Mount Allegro (Boston: Houghton Mifflin, 1943), p. 1.

6. Jerre Mangione, "The Writer's Secret Collaborator," in Psi Factor in
Creativity, eds. Allan Angoff and Betty Shapin (New York: Parapsychology
Foundation, Inc., 1970), pp. 51–63.

7. Garibaldi Marto Lapolla, Grand Gennaro (New York: Vanguard Press,
1935), p. 18.

8. John Fante, "The Odyssey of a Wop," American Mercury 30 (1933):
89–97.

9. Pietro di Donato, *Christ in Concrete* (Indianapolis: Bobbs-Merrill, 1939), p. 296.

10. Michael Gold, *Jews Without Money* (New York: Liveright, 1930), p. 164.

11. Ben Morreale, *monday tuesday . . . never come sunday* (Plattsburgh, N.Y.: Tundra Books, 1977), pp. 182–189.

12. Selma Berrol, "Turning Little Aliens into Little Citizens: Italians and Jews in New York City Public Schools, 1900–16," in *The Interaction of Italians and Jews in America*, ed. Jean Scarpaci (Staten Island, N.Y.: American Italian Historical Association, 1975), p. 3.

13. Mario Puzo, *Godfather Papers and Other Confessions* (New York: Fawcett, 1972), pp. 13–15, 26–27.

14. Mario Puzo, *The Fortunate Pilgrim* (New York: Atheneum, 1964).

15. Tina De Rosa, "An Italian-American Woman Speaks Out," *Attenzione* 2 (1980): 38–39.

16. Babette Inglehart, "The Immigrant Child and the American School: A Literary View," *Ethnicity* 3 (1976): 34.

17. Henry James, *The American Scene* (New York: Scribner's, 1946), p. 12.

18. Andre Rolle, "The American Italians: Psychological and Social Adjustments," in *Studies in Italian American Social History*, p. 112.

19. Lucas Longo, *The Family on Vendetta Street* (New York: Doubleday, 1968), p. 63.

20. Horace M. Kallen, "Democracy Versus the Melting Pot," *The Nation* 100 (1915): 219–220.

The City and I*

Pedro Juan Soto

In 1930, there appeared in Puerto Rico the first novel to explore the theme of Puerto Rican migration to New York. *En babia* (*In Limbo*) by J. I. de Diego Padró (1896–1974) was published as a weekly serial by the daily newspaper *La Correspondencia de Puerto Rico*. Given the difficulties of publishing in Puerto Rico at the time (difficulties which have yet to be resolved), *En babia* took ten years to be printed in book form. The first edition, 767 pages long, tries to distill the New York Puerto Rican vision of a middle-class writer who lived in New York for three years, in 1916–17 and 1927–29.[1]

It is a novel filled with adventures and analysis, since the author is as attentive to the need for a good plot as he is to theorization concerning the genre of the novel. (He communicates this theorization by means of extensive intellectual discussions between his characters.) *En babia* makes use of a technique that was quite innovative in 1930: direct and indirect interior monologue, contrasts between ego and alter ego, reality versus illusion, and sub-plots within the main plot. Jorge Luis Borges, Julio Cortázar, Ralph Barth, and Saul Bellow—to mention only a few internationally known authors—would have been proud to create such a work, because De Diego Padró was, in a sense, in the vanguard of a technique which would later earn them prestige. His novel also instructs the reader with respect to the earliest phase of Puerto Rican migration to a city which, for various reasons, continues to fascinate us.

Jerónimo Ruiz is the narrator of *En babia*. He was born in Vega Ancha, on the island of Caoyara, in 1896. He suffers from a receding hairline and what he describes as "medium" height, although he admits to being 5 feet 4 inches tall, which is actually on the short side. He is a poet, and works as an invoice clerk in a New York firm that deals in commerce with Latin America. He has never married, and

*This article was translated from the Spanish by Kal Wagenheim.

© 1981 by Pedro Juan Soto.

when we run into him in New York towards the end of 1932, he is interested in writing a novel. The span of the novel lasts only a few months, since Jerónimo Ruiz leaves the city in May of 1933, heading for his "Caribbean native soil."

What adventures does this character experience in the New York metropolis? He meets and repudiates the bisexual Sebastián Guenard, but their relationship is never fully severed. Guenard, a Cuban, is not only bisexual; he is also a sadist, a man with a good heart, an epileptic, a member of the idle rich, a collector of art objects, and the author of the beginnings of a novel which he prompts Ruiz to read. Ruiz himself, in thinking about the novel that he wishes to write, has said, concerning the character he hopes to create: "He must be complex, paradoxical. A clinical case. A being, in sum, who is not run of the mill: quite unbalanced."[2]

If Guenard lives in comfortable solitude, thanks to an allowance from his father, Ruiz is unable to do the same. He lives in an apartment with other tenants, rented from a Puerto Rican woman—Clarita Aviñó de Quesada. They all comprise a family of strangers. The landlady, separated from her husband, is seduced by Jerónimo Ruiz, but later returns to the arms of her mate.

After a beating with a cane, administered by the Cuban Guenard, Ruiz is hospitalized and requires surgery, which causes him to live from then on with a silver plate beneath his forehead.

An uncle helps Jerónimo Ruiz to recuperate from his physical and spiritual ailments, since his absence from the office causes his firing. The uncle finds new lodgings for him and promises to help him financially until passage can be booked for a return to his native island.

At this time, Guenard and Ruiz meet again. The Cuban apologizes for the beating of his friend. With their friendship renewed, Ruiz makes a brief visit to the apartment of Guenard, and moments later, after the Cuban has excused himself and gone into another room, he finds Guenard hanging by the neck—dead. Ruiz escapes in a frenzy and lives the rest of his days in New York fearful that the police might detain him for questioning about the apparent suicide of Guenard.

Ruiz is delighted to be aboard the steamer *San Blas* as it leaves New York harbor, despite a severe storm. As the ship heads south, he daydreams of the country life he will enjoy on the hacienda of one of his uncles. But then he is gripped by terror when, among the ship's passengers, he spies the "dead man"—Sebastián Guenard.

Guenard explains the trick he employed to make his apparent suicide credible, and the two of them, friends once more, enjoy the rest of the voyage, in the company of certain women they have just met.

Happy ending? Apparently. Nevertheless, within the picaresque life that Ruiz leads, so as not to lose sight of the "clinical case" that he has managed to discover, certain objections are raised concerning the isolation which he suffered, observations concerning the marijuana he decides to smoke, and comments concerning the city in which he lived. On the latter, I quote the opinion he offers to the woman in whose apartment he lived as a boarder prior to returning to his homeland. Ruiz says: "I assure you that I'll do anything to avoid returning ever again to this city. Here is where you find, to a degree what is worse than in any other part of the world—the exhausting struggle for existence. New York is the world's biggest cheap bazaar of *bluff*. On the surface you find many skyscrapers, many cars, many charitable and religious institutions, lots of noise and movement of gold on Wall Street; but beneath the surface there is only vulgarity, hypocrisy, fraud, competition, boredom, misery, pain. . . . That's the impression I have of the famous city by the Hudson."[3]

This is the novel written by Jerónimo Ruiz, with a prologue by an author who, even with a pseudonym, is none other than J. I. de Diego Padró (another game of mirrors, and an additional game of ego and alter ego). The novel demonstrates irony, humor, bitterness, and various misfortunes whose ups and downs recall the tradition of the picaresque Spanish novel. *En babia* contains violence and humor, dependence between the New York Puerto Ricans and those who remained on the island, the dreams of the migrant with respect to returning home to the island, and love and hate concerning life in New York. *En babia* also reflects a certain disdain for Puerto Rico by not mentioning its name, and using instead the fictitious name of Caoyara, or the picturesque phrase, "Caribbean native soil" (*terruño del Caribe*).

Love and hate for New York, humor and violence, links between relatives and friends who live apart in Puerto Rico and New York, dreams by the migrants of a paradisiacal life in Puerto Rico—all of this is offered in *En babia* and also figures in later works that deal with the lives of New York Puerto Ricans. This is not due to the influence of De Diego Padró upon these other writers, but to the impact of a segregationist city upon the Puerto Rican mentality.

Aside from what I have mentioned about *En babia*, what does De Diego Padró tell us about the life of poor Puerto Ricans who lived in New York between 1932 and 1933, the span of his novel? He tells us nothing about the majority of the 45,000 Puerto Ricans who were already suffering the misery of East Harlem, Brooklyn, and the Bronx. After reading all of his works, this question gnawed at me, and I went directly to J. I. de Diego Padró a few months before his death. When I cited the figures from the 1930 census, with respect to the number of Puerto Ricans in New York, he shook his head and said: "No, I didn't want to focus upon the poor. Nevertheless, there are allusions to poverty (in the boarding-house episodes), where the social stratum is a bit lower than the bourgeoisie. That is a terrible poverty. It's a conscious poverty, while the other kind, due to the force of habit, is almost an unconscious poverty, wouldn't you say? One *feels* poor."[4] I will never agree with that statement. And when I said so, several weeks went by before I was able to renew my dialogue with the novelist De Diego Padró. He wouldn't see me for a while.

En babia, the first literary work about Puerto Ricans in New York, represents, then, the novel of a middle-class Puerto Rican who arrives in New York during the decade of the 1930s. With relation to that, I should cite the following: "On the whole the [1920s and 1930s] migrants were better educated than the average Puerto Rican; they had a somewhat higher level of skill; they tended to come from the urban area [in Puerto Rico]."[5]

Our case was different. I was part of a conglomerate of 187,000 Puerto Ricans who came to New York during the 1940s. The majority were poor, like myself. Other members of this impoverished group who were then living in New York are Piri Thomas, author of *Down These Mean Streets* (1967) and *Savior, Savior, Hold My Hand* (1972), among other works; Pedro Pietri, author of *Puerto Rican Obituary* (1974), and Roberto Rodríguez Suárez, author of the play *Ave sin Rumbo* (1977). Without knowing each other, without there being any conscious agreement between us, we delivered ourselves to the task of illustrating, in our writings, the anguish, the discrimination, and the abandonment suffered by the Puerto Rican in New York.

I came to that city with a strong desire to work and study. When one is eighteen years old, one knows that one is rehearsing to be an adult. I spent a lot of time studying how to find jobs, and worked hard at getting past the front gate of a university for an education. I don't regret having lived in New York for nine years (1946–1954). There, I acquired a stern disposition, and a mask of aloofness, which protects me from hypocrites and people with trivial sob stories.

Three of my works reflect the love and hate that I feel for New York: *El huésped (The Guest)*, a play which opened in Puerto Rico in 1956; *Spiks*, a book of short stories that appeared the same year; and

Ardiente suelo, fría estación (*Hot Sand, Cold Season*), a novel which was published in 1961.

I did not read De Diego Padró's novel, *En babia*, until many years after my return to Puerto Rico. Nevertheless, I find a certain resemblance between his novel and my works, which I attribute to the critical experience in New York which affected members of different social classes.

The anguish of isolation suffered by the tenants who live together with Jerónimo Ruiz, for example, greatly resembles the feelings reflected in the characters of *Spiks*. At the same time, the father and daughters in *El huésped*, strangers among themselves, are somewhat similar to the family of strangers in the boardinghouse in *En babia*. In the same way that there is a dependence between Jerónimo Ruiz and the uncle on whose hacienda he will live upon his return from New York, there is a dependence between the New York Puerto Ricans and island Puerto Ricans whose lives I dramatize. I confess, further, that I, too, have written of the paradisiacal vision of the New York Puerto Rican, something which J. I. de Diego Padró did before me.

The main characters in *En babia* leave the city. No one in *Spiks* leaves New York. In *El huésped*, the daughters remain, although the father commits suicide. In *Ardiente suelo, fría estación*, Eduardo Marín returns to New York, obviously to struggle. I believe I have shown in such works that, despite the pain, despite all the vicissitudes, Puerto Ricans have many roles to play in New York.

I hate the city of New York intensely, and I love it with equal intensity. It is, to me, like a stepmother. A stepmother that has been naïve, cruel, and kind. Its naïveté stems from the fact that it expected to become my mother, something it never achieved.

I still love the city for the access that it gave me to innumerable cultural centers: movies, museums, theatres, bookstores, and I deeply detest the feeling of inferiority that it always tried to impose upon me. This anecdote will serve to illustrate what I mean.

After sixteen years of absence, I visited New York one weekend in 1970, while I held the post of Visiting Professor at the Puerto Rican Studies Center of the State University of New York at Buffalo. I had decided to meet with the editors of *Poetry* magazine, whose offices were then located near Forty-second Street in Manhattan. I entered the building quite discreetly, dressed in the respectable apparel expected of any university professor, and I began to scan the directory in the lobby. Before I finished, I heard someone behind me ask, "Can I help you?" I turned and saw a uniformed employee standing behind a long counter. "I'm looking for the office number of *Poetry* magazine," I said. The man looked me up and down and said, "Well, there's nobody up there right now. If you have any mail to deliver, leave it here." "Mail to deliver?" I thought. "I'm not wearing a mailman's uniform." Then I realized that if I'm not a mailman, and I've got this Puerto Rican face, I must, obviously, be a messenger. Without saying a word, I stared at the man. He didn't blink. Then I turned and left the building, never to return.

I love New York's mixture of races, and I detest its ghettos. In each ghetto I am confronted by the degeneration of William Dean Howells' romantic idea, that the division of the city into villages and hamlets would make it livable. Urban life, according to Howells, would be nourished by the friendship of the newcomers, would be strengthened by the mutual aid displayed by such people, and the characteristic coldness of the city would be changed by basic human warmth. But instead of this planned brotherhood, what do we have? We have the mere crowding together of immigrants in neighborhoods and slums, hating anyone who lives just a few blocks away. There may be things to say in favor of and against romantics; as for planners, I won't make any comment either.

I also hated, for all the years of its life, the sociological superstition of the "melting pot," which tried to impose itself here and elsewhere. It was expected that the immigrant, once in New York, would deny his own culture—which was merely a set of quaint regional customs, according to the people in power—to adopt and defend to the death an urban culture that never managed to define itself. The uprisings in black and Puerto Rican neighborhoods during the end of the decade of the 1960s made the political and educational authorities realize that it's not possible to cut away the roots of any human being, and that it is only logical and sensible to take advantage of the cultural diversity offered by the immigrants who join U.S. society.

I am an optimist. I continue to see serious disorders in the culture and politics of the United States, but I don't lose heart. I believe that the change of attitude with respect to the cultural dignity of each group within this nation has put the country on a positive path towards the kind of equal treatment that many nations are demanding. If the government of the United States ever manages to shed its chauvinism, and its obvious disdain for much of the rest of the world, we will have to be grateful to several of the unyielding ethnic groups that form part of this nation.

Notes

1. J. I. de Diego Padró, *En babia* (San Juan, Puerto Rico: Biblioteca de Autores Puertorriqueños, 1940).

2. J. I. de Diego Padró, *En babia*, 2d ed. (Mexico: Gráfica Panamericana, 1961), pp. 37–38.

3. Ibid, p. 613.

4. Pedro Juan Soto, Alicia de Diego, Carmen Lugo Filippi, and J. I. de Diego Padró, *En busca de J. I. de Diego Padró*. Unpublished manuscript, 1975.

5. Nathan Glazer and Daniel P. Moynihan, *Beyond the Melting Pot*, 2d ed. (Cambridge: M.I.T. Press, 1970), p. 96.

Living with Change

David Ignatow

Early in the forties, feeling desperate about my lack of literary success, feeling totally unworthy of the title "poet," in fact, feeling unworthy as a man and participant in the world because of my continued failure to be recognized as a poet, I fell in love with a beautiful black woman who was then working with me in my father's bindery. The love lifted me out of my self-pity. I knew well enough of what my love consisted, but here was a black woman, who though beautiful and young, was already condemned to a life of drudgery as an unskilled laborer in a factory, never to emerge from it into the light of pleasure and self-regard. We had a fate in common, I then believed, but I had something else which made me happy, yet with a sense of guilt about myself: I was able in my paltry position as my father's assistant in the shop to attract a woman who, like me, was looking for a life that would lift her out of her misery. In short, we saw in each other the means with which to relieve unhappiness with ourselves, she through attaching herself to the son of the boss, and I through acquiring a lovely mistress as a symbol of my power. The color difference between us did not matter to either of us; we both were suffering from a loss of status in our own eyes. We both were among the outcasts of society, and had found a way to enhance each other's image by falling in love. If this sounds crude and self-serving of each of us, it is true to what I have just described, but that it was intentionally so was not the fact. We were acting out of a deep need that was not in our control. We were acting out a compulsion that demanded to be fulfilled within the very society that had shaped us.

Of course, I see all this in hindsight; yet at the time I was conscious of my feelings towards myself, as I looked out on the world of literary recognition from which I was excluded, just as she felt herself excluded from the world of material wealth and status. I speak of all this openly because it represents my first experience with a black person and has remained for me the touchstone of my future experiences.

© 1981 by David Ignatow.   193

Eventually, she became acutely self-conscious of her blackness in relation to me, as we began to find it more and more difficult to keep our relationship secret. Secret it had to be, we thought, if she were not to be fired by my father who, we felt, would not tolerate such a relationship in the shop, once it became known. Besides, there were other men in his shop who would take it as a signal to make their own advances to her—I, the boss's son, having shown the way. Because she was black, went their thinking, she was vulnerable in her inferior social position to the power and blandishments of the whites. Finally, when our relationship became obvious, the predictable followed quickly, and my father, who I thought surely would fire us both, also became involved in reaching for her out of some secret envy of and competitiveness with me in the world of business. He was the one who had the final and absolute power over everyone, including me, to do with as he wished in the workings of the bindery—a power apparently that did not exclude attempting to seduce a woman in his employ through the threat of losing favor in his eyes, no matter how gently put, and so, inferentially, making her feel unwelcome in the shop, if he were refused. I too became nervous in his presence, since I too depended on him for my livelihood. Later in life, as my experiences in the business world grew, I came to realize that he was typical of such men in power.

We were then living through the Great Depression. And so, in the slim hope of retrieving the original secrecy between Sara and me, I began to assume an impersonal manner towards her and tried to keep a distance between us as we worked. To the men, it was a signal that I had abandoned her to them. My father, when she happened to arrive earlier than usual for work, would be alone in the shop waiting for just such an opportunity to press himself upon her. She understood it all. She saw herself as being placed by me in the role of a sacrifice, an offering to their power, and so when I approached her with orders for a particular job, she would deliberately banter about us in front of the others to embarrass me as she was being embarrassed and humiliated too. And she would turn scornfully to flirt with the other men, as I stood there, to show that she knew what was happening and meant to defy it. One morning, before entering the shop for work, she confronted me in the corridor to accuse me bitterly of having used her as a convenience, like any white man would, and then dumping her. The next morning she was gone.

My guilt towards her was deep. I had no excuse but my own cowardice. To have continued to associate myself with her in the open against the wishes and rivalry of my father; to have found myself bound with her in exile from society as I knew it then, with both of us fired and with no jobs; to have my need to write frustrated by desperate poverty; to find myself with her and her people, abused, insulted, trampled on, ignored, and forgotten, as they were in their sufferings; in effect, obliterated from society—all this I could not take and did not dare risk. Frightened and repelled, I suddenly awakened to the significance of my attachment to her, and was profoundly sad at being unable to face the consequence of my attachment. Many years had to go by before I could come to terms with myself, years in which I finally knew that never again would I let myself be drawn into such cowardly behavior towards anyone. With this sorely gained knowledge of myself, I could become reconciled to my wish to live well and write my poems as a balance to my deep, pervasive sense of defeat and self-hatred. Time and events were to test my resolve to remain steadfast in a crisis, and that test would come about in an unexpected and, again, a frightening way.

As my reputation grew among poets, critics, and readers, I received invitations to tour colleges to teach and read from my poems, until one day I settled upon a permanent posititon at York College of the City University of New York. At my father's death in the early sixties, I sold everything of value in the shop—machinery and tools—to pay off the debts incurred by his long illness. I gave up all business contacts and accounts, leaving myself with only a week's salary to start on the adventure of my life as a poet. York College in the late sixties was planned as an institute of innovative programs and teaching, and I was delighted to be chosen, not only for the position of poet-in-residence, but also as a teacher. It was going to be a life exactly opposite, emotionally and intellectually, of what I had led for years in the family business.

In the meantime, I had taken an apartment in a building just around the corner from the school in order to avoid traveling from home on the East End of Long Island, a distance of more than one hundred miles. I was renting an apartment at the recommendation of one of the secretaries in our school; however, she, without telling me in advance, was leaving to take an apartment out of the area where, she finally confided, she would feel much safer than in Jamaica. The school had only recently moved from predominantly white Bayside to South Jamaica, one of the concentrations of black population in Queens County. The student body already was reflecting the change, a shift I had not noticed until she had conveyed to me her decision to move.

Her decision alarmed me. Had I placed myself in a dangerous position? From various neighbors in the building I had gotten reports of handbag snatching in the very courtyard of the building and of break-ins into apartments and of vending machines in the laundry room being smashed open for their coins. These incidents and others, I was told, were all the work of men and women also of the immediate area. The police took notes, looked over the damage or inspected the loss, and left silently. With the departure of the secretary from the building and the area, what was I to think, in view of the stories told me? I felt again that old fear that had its roots in my relationship to Sara. This time I was in her world where it could do as it wished, and in its wrath could force me to live in that abject fear and humiliation which had been its lot for so many years among the whites. I sensed my past had caught up with me, my life had come full circle with a vengeance, and this time there was no escape.

New York was the place where I chose to earn my living, where I wished to stay. I could, if I wished, accept a position in a school elsewhere. I had turned down Berkeley and Wisconsin, each having invited me. New York was my home. I had been raised here. All its streets, avenues, its people, its speech were as familiar to me as my own features and, in a manner of speaking, my own features—emotional, intellectual, and creative—were made up of those with which I was familiar and had grown with in New York. I had tried teaching in schools out of town, only to find myself missing the sounds, the movements, the variety of life and events, and the intellectual ferment of New York. I missed it all, as I had missed my parents at their deaths. In New York I felt at ease with life. There was no leaving New York for me. I would have to work out my destiny as a poet and man here among the sights and people with whom I had grown up, and that included the people of Sara of my father's shop. I still had not forgotten my grief.

But I had to face my fears. There were many young black men at school from the area, South Jamaica, as one result of our college's move. These youths carried themselves aggressively and, as if deliberately in defiance of what they were being taught, spoke the language of their streets to their professors and to one another in the presence of their professors. Their behavior seemed to be a show of anger for all the years of exclusion from the mainstream of American life for which they intended to avenge themselves in the very citadel of American aspiration by converting it into the image of their own debased lives. A civil war seemed to be in the making. The time was the mid-sixties, and these black youths were on the crest of the student rebellions that were overwhelming schools throughout the country. They were taking over the very halls of the university from which, formerly, they had been shut out.

In anguish as to how to deal with them personally, dangerous as they appeared to me and to the functioning of the school, I thought back to my relationship with Charley Johnson, who had worked under my supervision in my father's shop. He had been our main mechanic for one section of the shop. Charley was black. We had struck up a guarded camaraderie between us, guarded as it would have to be between boss and worker. By that time, Sara had been gone for several years. One day Charley quit, without giving notice, and some months later, as I was walking through the corridor of a huge printing plant on the way to its main office to solicit bindery business, who should I see emerging from a side door of the plant but Charley, apparently on the way to the john. He recognized me at once; I was in a kind of absorbed state about the business prospects ahead of me. With a shout of joy and surprise, Charley came charging towards me and embracing me by the shoulders, and grinning into my startled face with a wondrous excited look that I had gotten to know him by, and that stamped him for me as Charley. At first, staggered by his flying embrace, shocked out of my absorption to find him in front of me, I was overwhelmed, finding it hard to speak, to discover that he still thought of me with affection. Months before, because we had had to refuse him his justified raise, he had quit his job in our bindery.

We earned our profit solely on cheap labor. Cheap labor was the one product we had to sell, and it had to be cheap for us to stay in business. We were nonunion and had to compete with union shops. The workers we drew on came mainly from among the poor, uneducated blacks, all of whom had been excluded from training for the better jobs, which the union withheld from them by excluding them from membership in the union that controlled the jobs. So these poor blacks came to us to accept what we could offer—training in the rudiments of elementary routines that they would work at for the rest of their stay with us, with barely a raise beyond a dollar or two each year in recognition of their reliability.

But Charley was not of their kind; he was not silent and accepting. Before coming to us, he had managed to bluff and bluster his way into better jobs in nonunion shops and, through a succession of skilled jobs from which he had been fired after revealing himself to be incompetent, he had learned enough to do a little better at the succeeding one until eventually when he came to us, he was at least familiar with his trade, though with much yet to learn. The tension between us would become high, as he felt himself threatened once again with firing, and sometimes his language would turn threatening too, as if he were defending his very life, but we kept him on because it was difficult, if not impossible, to find a white man for the wages we were paying him. In the meantime, however, growing more skilled on the job, he began to grasp many of its details and relax and even invite conversation. And so we counted on his staying on and, because of his newly found sense of belonging, were planning to increase his salary, needing to keep it below the union scale. But we had not counted on his native drive and temperament, his restlessness to improve himself, and his wonderful swagger—so sure of himself. And now I was meeting him in the corridor of his new and obviously better-paying position in a much larger nonunion shop. He had made it on his own again.

As we stood together, I was grateful to him for remembering me with so much affection as to embrace me warmly. A week before he had stopped working for us, we had had a muted but tense discussion in the office where he justifiably demanded a further increase in salary corresponding to his increasing efficiency. I had to turn him down. During his last months, he and I had broken through the usual worker-employer tension to a relationship in which we came to recognize and accept each other as individuals. Working together every day over difficult problems during his training period, we had grown to understand each other's language and point of view, which led to a corresponding mutual respect and exchange of confidences that reflected our understanding and mutual acceptance. It was a relationship that both of us were happy with, and so the talk between us concerning his deserved raise was difficult for us both, with grimaces of pain and long stretches of silence, at last causing us to part with a foreboding of what was to follow.

But as we stood in the corridor at his new job, both of us talking excitedly, it was time to part again. Suddenly he grabbed me by the shoulders again. It was the old Charley in high spirits. After hasty exchanges of news and promises between us to meet again somehow, we went our separate ways, but not before he had managed to tell me quickly about his new job, about how much more it paid than what I had been able to offer. He spoke with no show of bitterness toward me. He was simply filled with joy and pride in himself.

And so, to him, I had not simply been the manager of exploited labor. I was still the one with whom he had shared confidences. This meeting with him in the corridor became a turning point in my own self-regard as man and poet, depressed as I had been in my key role in an exploitative industry.

And so, as I sat in my office at college remembering Charley, I knew I could and would find a way to reach the students there. Their sense of me was identical with what Charley had originally brought into the shop. Besides, it was a challenge to be accepted on my own terms, as it had been to him to be accepted on his terms. We had formed a relationship that no economic necessity alone could have brought about. But the great difference between the past and the present was that I had nothing to withhold from my students, as I had had to with Charley. I had everything to offer now, but I was troubled by one student in particular. Tall and broad-shouldered like Charley, he was not as high spirited and jovial as Charley could be. A student in my remedial class in English, he represented in acute angry form all the others.

They would come and go as they pleased, sometimes showing up in class, however late, and then sauntering out in the middle of the writing exercise, and sometimes not bothering even to attend class for a whole week. I knew that none of them had had the kind of family life, upbringing, and regard for learning which would have made for a dedication to learning. They came from families in which mothers and fathers toiled at manual labor to come home exhausted, too angry and despairing of their lives to oversee or wish to oversee the education of their children. They were of the same people we had employed in my father's shop. Given their circumstances, they could feel no hope for their futures, much less those of their children, and so this attitude had conveyed itself to the children who, like their parents, kept their anger within, expressing it only in their desultory manner inside and outside the classroom. To receive repeated failing grades in their classwork meant to them only that they could expect nothing else from a white teacher. Failure was what they had been led to expect at the hands of white persons in power and so, except for this one student among them about whom I was worried, they preferred to ignore those failing grades.

But that student had other reactions to his grades. Openly and scornfully, he demanded an explanation for them. He would stride up to my desk to point out on the paper that there was nothing wrong with a particular sentence. He had meant to use the right tense but inadvertently had written the wrong one, and so was entitled to a passing grade. He argued loudly, for the benefit of everyone else in class, and his voice would rise to a threatening climax, which I had to accept as nothing less than a threat to my person. The others would look on in silence, amused and grinning, watching the powerfully built youth tower above me, trying to bully me into submission. Scenes such as this were to repeat themselves after every grading of homework or class exam. In the silence in which I would sit, the bullying youth would return to his seat, swaggering through his defeat, feeling himself compensated by having battered me emotionally.

He was like Charley at his worst, except that Charley would have quickly shifted from this threatening manner, recognizing the danger in it, that is, in getting himself fired. At school, however, no one could be fired, especially not for talking loudly. We had an open-admissions policy, and we were accepting students as they were, not as we expected them to be. Nevertheless, through my fear, I could perceive his fear deep beneath his threatening tone. Like Charley, he did not relish the prospect of failing, and it was worrying him. However, it was only weeks later in the quiet of my apartment, after the first shock of his behavior had passed, that I could make the connection between him and Charley.

In class, after a few moments of silence in which I would find the strength to go on, I would raise my head to look at the two exceptions among the students, two I had already at the start of the term singled out as earnest and hardworking, one a girl, the other a young man, both quiet and with ready smiles for the others, though they had no real camaraderie with them. At the end of the period, the two would walk out of the room separately and unaccompanied. It was clear to me that they were from families where learning was respected or appreciated as a step upwards, and so were determined to emerge from their ghettoes through education. With the bullying youth and the others, they shared the same faults of grammar and word usage. All came from the same depressed and deprived neighborhoods.

One day, as I gathered myself together again, I called on the girl to read aloud from her paper, and the class, as usual, proceeded to settle down in silence to listen. She received my oral comments with nods and quickly offered to rewrite the paper correctly, which offer I accepted. As she spoke, I suddenly became aware that the others in class, including the bullying youth, were gazing at her almost with jealousy, as if they were realizing the pathos of their situation. I was moved. They appeared so helpless at that moment. How, I asked myself, was I going to bridge the gap between myself and these pathetic youths who yearned to know but were somewhere trapped in their hostilities, their angers and hatreds, all directed at me as surrogate for the repressive forces in their lives? What did I need to do to help them come into their own? As with Charley, they came from an alienated culture, and so were their origins so different from mine, I asked myself at that moment. I was born of a family of Jewish immigrants from Russia where they had been bitterly persecuted; yet with never an opportunity in this country to learn the English language correctly, because they had to work twelve and fourteen hours a day, six days a week, simply to survive. Neither did they ever rise to a position in life where they could be accepted among native Americans as Americans themselves, but were scorned, often laughed at, for their ignorance of American customs and speech.

I would often think these thoughts in my office and in my apartment as I sat grading student papers, remembering the struggle of my parents to achieve, by eventually purchasing a home and car, a modicum of respectability in the community. In the bindery, which my father had managed to buy with his earnings as a bindery worker himself, he remained throughout his life the hardest worker in the shop, arriving just after dawn and staying late into the night, long after everyone else had gone home, to continue working at the machines to earn that extra profit that he needed to keep the shop afloat. I always understood his obsession with ownership—it was his particular distinction in a competitive society—but I could not sympathize with his use of cheap labor, nor the arrogance and blindness towards others that was bred in him by his belief in, and obsession with, ownership. He too had suffered his exile in this country. He too had been ruthlessly exploited by those in power above him, the printers in control of their bindery jobs that, withheld from my father, could have bankrupted him and sent him and the rest of the family to the welfare lines during the Great Depression. He too had to bend by accepting prices they forced on him and on which, by working those hours from dawn until past dinner time, he managed to break even, by his own labor, then in turn forcing his employees to accept a low wage to help keep the shop solvent.

I used to share these thoughts with Charley in the privacy of my office when he would wander in during lunchtime to sit down and chat with me about his problems of keeping an apartment and family together. His record player, which he brought in for entertainment during lunch hour, would be blaring out his favorite jazz tunes as we talked of our backgrounds, our upbringing, our responsibilities. As I thought back, I saw in those episodes with Charley the solution to my problem with that unhappy, explosive young man in class, and with the others too, but I decided to concentrate only on him, as the key to the solution. Everything else would follow easily if I could ease the conflict with this student. I knew I did not need to develop any special technique of teaching to bring about the miracle of correct grammar in my students. In a university dedicated to the open-admissions policy and swamped by the illiteracy of its students, no such miracle existed anywhere, but it was my first duty to get the student to feel that I understood, wished the best for him, and would work with him to the utmost of my abilities, for as a person he was my peer. I would make that feeling clear to him to help rid him of his fears, but in turn he would have to treat me as a person so that I could help him in my person.

In a few weeks, after persuading him to stay after class to discuss our differences, I was able to induce him to visit me at my office where we could discuss more at length and in detail those differences between us. At first, our discussions focused on problems with English, particularly his ambivalence about learning it correctly. He was not stupid by any standard. He understood himself well, especially in relation to the English language, which he saw as the instrument of white power whereby he would be made even more subservient by adopting the language of white power and all it stood for. We talked about these feelings.

It was not as if he was unalterably opposed to learning the language, but that he needed to be reassured that learning it would actually give him the tool with which to climb out of his condition. He could manage it, we concluded, with the very means which he feared meant his continued subjugation. He could manage it by his strength of will, backed by strength of purpose and appreciation of the paradox of learning what he had to learn. He had no difficulty in grasping these insights but, since we spoke different languages, it took us some time to arrive at a formulation of these insights which both of us could accept. In the process, we became at ease with each other, observing and gaining confidence from the effort we saw each was putting into the process. Much of his life-style came to the surface, and this life-style, as we both recognized, was centered on his deep frustrations in an impoverished home life with angry, tired, poorly paid working parents who could give him neither financial nor emotional help. It was a relief to me to hear him out patiently and respond, as I had not been able to do with Charley. The situation here in my office was exactly the opposite of the earlier one. I passionately demanded that this husky young man make a life for himself that he could respect, offering to help him in every possible way both in my office and in the classroom. At one time, we leaned back in our chairs, amazed at the leap we had made from our first tense confrontations in class to this open, free give-and-take between us. If, in his case, it was because he felt me reaching out to him, it was only because I had no choice but to do it for the sake of us both. Through circumstances, through history, through the nature of human bondage, we were together, in need of one another for our lives' sakes.

But what of my role as poet during all these years and experiences? When I left New York to take a position as Visiting Lecturer at the University of Kentucky, I was leaving simply for a lark, taking to the hinterlands, and it was not to be for long. Everything outside New York was simply camping ground, as the saying goes in Manhattan. In New York I could spend endless hours seated in coffee houses chatting and discussing with poet friends, then leave to stroll the sidestreets of brownstones, apartment houses, parks, theatres, restaurants, bookshops, antique stores. Even Lower Manhattan fascinated me, with its ancient factory lofts where I had first learned to sweat at manual labor to earn my first pay. Nevertheless, it fascinated me because it was yet so mysterious to me—its swift, ruthless, industrial, and commercial pace, alien to my idealized conception of a city and, much as I wrote of that area's savage, relentless search for gain, its indifference to humans, its power to destroy equally with its power to create, I felt myself belong to it. I felt I should belong at this center of an American vortex of enterprise and culture.

When I left to teach in Kentucky I promised myself to return. New York was my native ground, and I knew I could not exist as a poet without returning to it to become once more infused with its mad energy, its multiple conflicting interests and issues. New York was for me the world intensified, and I had a seat in its midst from which to watch and join in. I would come back to it with renewed appreciation of its unique character, its strengths, its variety, its marvelous confusions. It was because of my reputation as a poet of the city that I was being invited to the hinterlands to teach the ways of the city, its thinking, its literature, its people. My presence would be the presence of the city itself in the classroom at the university, and I was proud to have been so chosen.

From the University of Kentucky I went on to the University of Kansas for a year and then to Vassar College. By that time, my family had settled on the East End of Long Island. We had given up our New York apartment, finding it much cheaper to settle on the Island. And so after my three years of living in open territory of trees, meadows, lakes, and mountains in the Southwest and West, I would continue by living in the countryside of Long Island. I felt a change coming over me. I was learning to relax, to study the trees, the grass, the sky, and the birds, and to write of them with affection and wonder, asking myself how I could have missed it all. Had I simply ignored it while living in Manhattan, even when strolling through a park in the city, because for me city life meant being able to concentrate on ideas, issues, people? Nature, where it showed itself on the sidewalks and in parks, was merely the background for my intense inner life. I had paid little attention to nature.

But it was in the Midwest and in the South and in the Far West where I gave extended readings and workshops that I felt myself becoming a different being, open to senses that I had not thought existed in me, open to sights and sounds, to hours of solitude amid trees, before meadows and lakes, and in view of snow-covered peaks. Still, when it was time to return to New York, to accept an appointment at York College, I came gladly. I felt myself back home. Everything else that I had seen and lived with outside New York had been beautiful but not my way, for it had all served to make the intellectual excitement, the emotional variety, the vast panoply of diverse lives in New York that much more precious to me.

It was the secretary who had recommended me to the Jamaica apartment, who herself had left out of fright to live elsewhere, who brought to consciousness in me a change in New York I had not been fully aware of in my excitement at returning. I began to notice more closely a change in the composition of the population from what I remembered of it before my departure for Kentucky. The year was 1969. In the subway where I had been used to seeing mostly the faces of white men and women, I seemed now to see mostly men and women with black faces, Asiatic faces, and dark Mediterranean complexions. For such a short space of time—four years' absence from New York— the change was baffling. The subways now were full of the loud chatter of Spanish-speaking voices and the drawl of Southern voices, all mingled together with the raucous radios that were being played in the trains by the youths—black and white.

On nearly every ride, I would see men tippling bottles hidden in brown paper bags while leaning drunkenly against the train doors. After a long swig, they would leer defiantly at the passengers. The atmosphere was tense, and the minority of whites that were seated quietly either would stare straight ahead at their reflections in the windows opposite them, or else bury their heads in their newspapers to take them away from the scene and allow them to pretend that they were not present and listening. They were the tense ones in the train. Sometimes a group of young blacks would come charging into the train at a station, stop, and begin staring hostilely at passengers— black and white. They would break into derisive laughter at some joke among them or at a comment about the passengers. They enjoyed acting menacing together. The tension in the train would become unbearable, and many passengers seemed to be leaving at the next stop, if simply to leave these youths behind. New York certainly had become strange to me. I did not feel at home.

My writing in the past about the city had concentrated on other facts and situations—the commercial pace and atmosphere of New York that was so pervasive and dominated with its indifference to anything that could not satisfy its grasp for gain. I was writing out of my own experience with it in offices and factories and in the streets, much as I saw my own life resemble those of the vast majority of people in the same circumstances as myself. I had not given much thought to minorities in particular, but now that I was teaching in a school that was predominantly black and filled with youths who were from families even more deprived than I had experienced, many of the youths on the train reminded me of my students in their tough manner and talk. There but for the grace of chance were my students with brown paper bags wrapped around wine bottles shouting and gesticulating menacingly in subway trains. They were my new experience in New York.

And what did this new experience have in common with my past? That was the question I had to ask myself in my office while grading student papers, or in my apartment alone in a mostly black neighborhood. I needed to know the answer or answers to that question, and I began to see the answers more clearly with time and experience with these youths in and out of class. I was growing more and more adjusted to the change that earlier in my arrival in New York had been so strange to me and so alienating to my idea of New York.

My answer came to this: If my parents had had to suffer exile in the American society itself, which I too had had to suffer, yet were able eventually to gain a foothold on mainland, so to speak, how much worse was it for these youths who felt in their very bones an exile that went to the root of being—rejected outright for their humanity as blacks. It was a far more threatening experience than the one my parents and I had had to face. These youths were literally being threatened in their lives by being rejected in their humanity. They were being murdered by being ostracized. Was it any wonder that, feeling in their nerves this calculated rebuff to their claim as humans, they should throw themselves recklessly into self-destructive acts out of despair with their rejected selves?

From time to time, just such a neighborhood youth, waving his bottle overhead, would stagger into the lobby of the school, shouting obscenities and jeering at the guards. Those black students who were present would laugh self-consciously but move off to their classes sadly, while the guards, themselves black, would gently guide the young man out into the street again, closing the door behind him. The white students witnessing the incident would remain silent and attentive until it was over and then leave for their classes too—but silent throughout. Perhaps they were considering leaving the school for another less frightening, as I myself had been. I had no choice but to stay. One doesn't simply sit down and write about changed conditions in one's life, as if they were simply matters for statistics and expect those changes to come about automatically because of their having been written about. I knew I had not been prepared for such a change as I first witnessed on my return to New York. What I needed was to be able to see these despairing youths as my own people in need of help.

I had begun teaching night classes at the school in order to save my day hours for writing and reading. But teaching at night meant walking home alone through the dark in an area with a high crime rate, one that was well known for drug peddling during the daytime. Each night I had to negotiate the streets by myself to and from classes. I was prepared for injury, robbery, or even death. One night I discovered, as I was speaking with one of my black students after class about his writing problems, that we had to walk the same route on the way home, he to the subway and I to my apartment. We left together and said goodnight to each other at the courtyard of my building, while he continued briskly up the street to the subway entrance around the corner. Eventually, it turned out that several more students, also black, were using the same route on their way home, and we managed each night after class to form a group and walk together, discussing class work and related problems. I was rid of my fears. Youths who were standing on the street corners would look from a distance at one white man surrounded by three or four blacks. It might have looked strange to them, but they must have known we were coming from school. Among ourselves, we grew close enough over the fourteen weeks of the semester to speak candidly with one another. The two women who walked with us spoke of their relief at being with us. They did not have to say more. The black male student with us, a former navy sailor and a powerfully built man, nodded in approval. The fear was not a matter of blacks against whites. It was the desperate against the more fortunate.

Slowly I came to feel that I was back home in New York again. No, the situation in New York had not changed very much in all this time. The cast of characters had changed, but the theme remained what it had been before my departure for the University of Kansas but had grown more intense. I could again distinguish what I and others would have to do, without thought to or consciousness of race or color. What finally mattered was the motive for living, and those of us who wished to make a life for ourselves worthwhile were together as always, as in our small group walking together through the dark street. This was always the way in this city, as we looked out upon the miserable, often driven to crime, with guarded compassion to help where we could, to make of our own lives such a model that could be accepted by others on which to build their own, if they could be counted on to help themselves.

I am back to writing about New York and about myself in it, directly and indirectly. New York is again the source from which I affirm myself and my neighbors and the whole of the city's multiplex meaning.

Epilogue

Sadly, since writing this essay while living in Jamaica, I have moved back to my family house in East Hampton. One afternoon, while standing in the lobby of my apartment house waiting for the elevator to descend to take me up to my sixth-floor apartment, a young man came swiftly up from behind me, threw an arm around my neck, totally immobilizing me, and demanded my money, as he began searching through my pockets with his free hand. To be brief about this horrifying experience, I quietly indicated where my wallet was located, in my breast pocket. He allowed me to remove it, sensing I was not planning to draw a gun. I had managed to keep a slight smile so as to let him know I had no such weapon on me, nor was I planning any violence, but that I wished to get this over with as quickly and peaceably as possible. With my slight smile as a signal between us, he opened the door to the elevator for me to enter. I stepped into it, but not before searching his face for his motive in opening the door for me. Nevertheless, I stepped in with some hope that he had no intention of stepping in with me to do me harm. The elevator door closed behind me, with him looking through the porthole window to watch me as the elevator began its ascent. I was totally traumatized with fear, and I knew I could no longer live in this building or neighborhood if I valued my life and peace of mind. The apartment building entrance was never guarded, and the streets were vacant of people at night, in their apartments, too frightened to emerge. My students were no longer accompanying me to the door of my building. They had moved on to other courses. The option of moving into another neighborhood in Queens or Manhattan was not mine either. The rents were skyrocketing. Significantly, the rents in Jamaica remained depressed, and so the choice was narrowed down to East Hampton where at least my expenses could be stabilized. Perhaps I could have asked my present students to accompany me to the door of my Jamaica apartment building, but how was I to know that another young man would not be lurking in the lobby or the courtyard waiting for just such a person as myself arriving in the silent night alone?

After moving from Jamaica, I switched the courses I was teaching from evening to daytime, at the sacrifice of my leisure time for the sake of safety. Teaching at night had been one of my true pleasures in my relationship with students, most of whom were working men and women with a strong dedication to improve their lot through education, and we had enjoyed each other for the benefits we were deriving from one another—they the knowledge and know-how I could convey to them, and I the eagerness and sincerity of their ambition. I will miss them, but the issue for me in New York still remains what it has been through the years, that of poverty versus opportunity, with the tragedy that is in it for numberless people who are mired in hatred and self-hatred and self-doubt as poverty sinks into them to poison their well-being and sense of life. I remain the writer who must record this and other facts about New York, not simply for the record, but to make it known, felt, and acted upon before it's too late.

The City as Battleground:
The Novelist as Combatant

Marge Piercy

Why do ordinary people read fiction? The most primitive answer is the most real: to get to the next page. To find out what happens next and then what happens after that; to find out how it all comes out.

That desire for finding a pattern in events—for not all happenings will satisfy us, not nearly, only the "right" ending, the proper disaster, or the proper suspension, or the proper reward—still functions as a major hunger we bring to the novel. We want stories that help us make sense out of our lives. We want to see all this mess mean something, even if what we discover is a shape perhaps beautiful but not necessarily comforting. After all, the shape of a spiral nebula when I get into the country and can actually see it does not make me more comfortable—or more self-important.

We want to know when we read a story what happens when somebody makes one choice rather than another: speaks to a wolf in the woods, runs over an old man on the road to Thebes. Sometimes the pattern a novel traces on our mind is overt in the book, and sometimes the most important pattern is covert—the kind of hidden myths that Sandra Gilbert and Susan Gubar have traced in *The Madwoman in the Attic* in nineteenth-century women's fiction. Of course, we can experience resonance, counterpoint, conflict between the overt and covert patterns of a novel.

Fiction builds us alternative cities superimposed on the city whose streets we walk or drive. Some of these paper cities seem close to our own, evoking the pleasure of reading a story set in a Boston you remember, or an Upper West Side of a Manhattan you live in. But some of these cities are exotic, threatening, enticing—cities of the dead and cities of the unborn.

Since our cities are grids of Them-and-Us experiences, fiction is a way of inducting you into the cities other people know: people who

© 1981 by Marge Piercy.

are poorer or richer than you are; people who speak another language; people who construct the world of different forces and different necessities and different desires; people who live down streets you fear or streets who fear you. Broadway is one street in songs and another to a bag lady.

As a woman I experience a city as a minefield. I am always potential quarry or target or victim. The first questions that will be asked of me if something happens are: What were you doing there? Why were you alone? How were you dressed? In parts of some cities at night the police will stop any woman and question her as a prostitute, for she is presumed not to belong on the streets by virtue of biology. The expectation of violence constricts our lives. We don't go where we should be able to go when we should be able to. The expectation of insult also harries us. We walk carefully and often more quickly than we desire to. We may not be able to look around freely or exercise curiosity.

The city of the old who are not wealthy—the ordinary aged whose lives have been passed in useful work—is a web of dangers the young pass through without imagining.

A novel can make us enter those other streets and corridors and hallways and alleys. A novel can reconstruct cities of 1840 and 1890. A novel can take us through cities that may be built in 2137. A novel can put up alternate cities of Atlantis to float like highly colored slick on the bubbles of the imagination. These cities of the past and the future and the never-was can also help us to grasp our own experiences in our cities. A past that leads to us validates us. A past that has created the problems we wallow in can help us to understand and to endure or attack our problems. A future we long for can draw us into activity that might help it happen. A future we fear can galvanize us to prevent it.

Actually few writers of science fiction or speculative fiction have created believable future cities. They tend toward creating simpler societies (after the holocaust novels), or they project capitalism usually in a more primitive stage than today or—somebody help us— feudalism as it existed in France, say around A.D. 1200 and add some laser guns and rocket ships. Samuel Delany is one of the few whose imagination can take us in directions that feel more sophisticated, more complex, more likely in sexual arrangements, families, socialization, pleasure, work, defense, intrigue and art forms.

For an increasing number of us, the city as it is organized now doesn't work. That's why, when I wrote *Woman on the Edge of Time*, I decided to break with the urban tradition in utopian fiction and depict a society that used smaller units spread more uniformly through the landscape. I make no particular brief for the device; it was convenient in enabling me to deal with the changes in people and in the economic, social and familial arrangements I wanted to depict. But I do stand by the statement that for most people, life in cities is getting more difficult. Usually we feel we cannot influence or control the institutions we inhabit like goldfish in a small and poisoned tank—our schools, streets, courts, transportation systems, parks.

The city formed and deformed me. Growing up in Detroit made me a novelist. I have a lot of early childhood memories about my mother and my father and my brother and my Uncle Danny, but I also have in my earliest memories company violence against the unions at Ford, where a large percentage of the men in the neighborhood worked, and the Detroit race riots. I was in day care and we were painting plaster plaques of grapes when the mothers began coming. All the Black children gathered on one side of the room and whispered that the whites had knives and all the white children gathered on the other side of the room and whispered that the Blacks had knives. The mothers came one by one and took their children home.

I belonged among the white children, but not quite. In my age group there were only two Jews, myself and Emily, who was Black, and even many years later we were put on hall guard together and got the same kinds of roles in the school plays (the storyteller, usually, unless there was an Oriental part, which I would play).

What impressed me most was that each side said the same thing with desperate fear, and nobody had any knives—not us children. The next thing that impressed me was witnessing a Black man beaten by a group of whites on Tireman, which was just ceasing to be a dividing line between Black and white working-class blocks then. I recognized him, although I did not know his name, as he worked in the drugstore where I sometimes was taken by my brother to buy ice cream cones on summer nights. I did not know the whites, and I would have nightmares about that beating.

Detroit was a violent place to grow up. Certainly as a child there seemed to me an excessive amount of cruelty from adults to adults, adults to children, children to children, and children to animals. As a child the latter most upset me. I preferred animals, and would have liked to live surrounded by cats and dogs and rabbits and cows and almost anything—short of tigers. Tigers I didn't need.

At the same time, my area was a functioning working-class neighborhood, which meant that people helped each other through trouble and crisis. Women went in and out of each other's houses all day through the back doors, and what you did not know about anyone on your block was simply too uninteresting to repeat. Every operation and drunken spree and lost son and marital squabble and letter from abroad was spoken in every other kitchen on the block before sunset the next day. There was no television—only your neighbor's soap operas to follow. My mother as a gifted palm reader knew everyone's secret troubles besides. She was gossiped to, but she never passed on gossip. Except to me.

The busses were my instrument of class education. Whether you took the Joy Road or the Tireman busses, in one direction they ran downtown (where you still went to shop or for official things when you had to pay on a mortgage or delay paying it, when you had to deal with City Hall in some fearful negotiation, or where you waited all day in a clinic for some cheap Dr. Yankum). As you took the bus downtown, the neighborhoods changed from tough but stable working-class neighborhoods like my own with their Black blocks and white blocks like a checkerboard of turfs, their Irish gangs, their Polish gangs, the parochial school kids versus the public school kids, to ever Blacker streets and shakier housing. As the bus passed the ring of decaying grandeur—Victorian mansions now rooming houses, dog and cat hospitals, chiropractors—you entered the oldest and rankest part of Detroit: low-to-the-ground, huddled-together ramshackle buildings of falling-down slums.

If you took the bus in the other direction, the houses became single-family homes. At first they'd be pastel cupcakes turned out in rows. Then they became what were called Colonials, meaning they had two stories and maybe a perfunctory pilaster on either side of the front door. Finally, the houses were brick. Nobody from the old-brick, rowhouse East can understand how substantial brick houses appear in the Midwest. Brick houses were where rich people lived. Now I know they weren't rich, just upper middle class. We all make fine class distinctions near us and cruder ones farther away.

If you left the city altogether—not possible on public transportation—you found the palaces of those who lived off what burned up the air we tried to breathe.

The difference between what we were taught in school and what I saw bothered me and got under my skin. My mother taught me to respect what it said in books. She had not gotten to finish the tenth grade before being sent to work, but the house was always full of books she brought home from the library. But nothing—including relationships between the sexes, the races, adults and kids—was the way it was supposed to be.

What I saw was a place where people who had little enough devoted their best energy to fighting each other in small groups. My friends were outcastes. I was beaten up a great deal by the other whites for being a Jew, then I went home to a father who told me I wasn't Jewish and a mother who would wait till he went to work to tell me of course I was.

I also had a lot of good friends who died in prison, on the streets, on drugs, from botched abortions, from getting pregnant at fifteen and drunk when it was time to deliver, in car accidents, of hypertension and bleeding ulcers in their twenties and thirties. The love I got kept me alive, so I have tried to carry those friends and relatives in me and birth them again in my work. All the love I ever took in I feel I owe back in work that speaks for all the buried lives that want to be said through me. Detroit is a great place to come from, but it wasn't so easy on those friends who didn't leave their class to make it. I have the guilt of the one who got away.

I went to college on a scholarship—the first person in my family to do so—where I learned that politics was over, and we lived in a classless society. I learned that poetry must be ironic and ambiguous and full of Christian imagery and that the proper novel was one of manners—meaning interior to the world of the affluent and excluding the rest of us. I learned I ought to write like a British gentleman. I learned that a few misguided pinko writers had fiddled with something called the proletarian novel in the thirties, but that had been a mistake, and you didn't have to read them. You had to read a great deal of Henry James.

You also read essays and wrote them on whether it was possible to have real tragedy anymore in the age they called in the textbooks that of the common man or whether only kings and dukes could be truly tragic. Obviously a king was more real than a regular peasant or factory worker and suffered more and certainly louder. Kings suffered in blank verse, while the peasants suffered in prose or silently in piles. Women had clearly been a nineteenth-century invention, since we never read of any women before then. We hardly read any after that, but it's not easy to teach the nineteenth-century novel without reading a couple of women, and women to tend to write about women—one of the factors that trivializes our output, we were taught.

I got a fellowship to Northwestern and went on in graduate school for about nine months, but instead of living in Evanston, I lived on Wilson Avenue in Chicago. It was a gamy neighborhood full of single-room occupancy hotels, old people, recent migrants from Appalachia, Spanish-speaking people—both Puerto Rican and Chicano—nightclubs and dim bars and the El that I travelled every day to suburban dry Evanston where in the imitation Gothic towers of the university we studied textual variants in Keats' "Endymion." Keats was another word-drunk working-class kid with lung problems, and one afternoon when I was getting ready to flee the university permanently, I hallucinated a whole conversation with him up in the stacks of the library about loyalty and stress.

I found that while the university offered the only security I could imagine and certainly would ever know, that class mobility was killing something in me I valued more highly than my busy and certainly necessary intelligence. I wanted to be a writer and had been turning out both poetry and prose since I was fifteen and got a room of my own with a door that shut. I thought that if I did not leave the university I would never write the novels I felt I was supposed to write.

The next four years I lived on the South Side of Chicago doing part-time jobs and learning to write from scratch, for I found I had to unlearn much in order to get at where I came from. I am driven, and one force that impels me is the demand that I speak for those largely unspoken for. Art validates experience.

In college I had observed that whenever people like those I had grown up with, like me, appeared in fiction we read, they represented death or the flesh or simple folk wisdom or simple folk stupidity. When women appeared in fiction we read—and almost all the twentieth-century literature we read was written by men—we were objects granting or refusing sex or nurturing to men. That's all we were, unless we too represented mortality or the flesh or the earth or temptation or redemption or anything else other than ourselves.

I was taught in school, and I still hear statements all of the time that suggest people with less money are simpler than those with more money. This is an idea some writers of the Left have shared with right-wing writers. The notion prevails that people who cannot express reactions in the vocabulary educated people learn to use have fewer reactions worth bothering with.

The conviction that those who talk differently or look different feel less is exceedingly popular. "They don't know the value of human life in the Orient," you say, dropping bombs on them. Or the Middle East. Or Latin America. Or Africa. Or wherever you are doing business. One of the effects of the novel can be to induce the reader to empathize with different people. We may identify with a character who resembles us or whom we wish we resembled. As a novelist, you can use that transference to get the reader to change her or his mind at least momentarily, as the character does. But you can also seduce the reader into identifying with characters whom the reader would refuse to know in ordinary life. Very few people who read *Woman on the Edge of Time* would talk willingly with its heroine, a middle-aged, overweight Chicana woman defined as crazy, shabbily dressed and lucky to get off welfare into any mop-woman job. Nor will many readers of *Vida* ever have met a political fugitive, at least knowingly.

I called cities grids of Them-and-Us experiences, and I consider fiction one way of persuading people to cross those borders of alienation and mistrust into the existence of someone in whose mind and body they may find it enlightening to spend some time. Fiction works no miracles of conversion, but I guess I believe any white reader who spends a reasonable proportion of time consuming Black novels and poetry is less likely to be as comfortably racist in large and small ways; and any man who reads enough of current women's literature is less likely to be ignorant of what women want and need and don't want and don't need, and what patriarchy costs us in blood and energy day and night.

Basically all novels have a political dimension. That is, novels embody in their characters and what happens to them, as well as in the language with which those characters—major and minor—are embodied and described, ideas about what's feminine and what's masculine, who's good and who's bad, who has and who deserves to have it, what behavior's on the side of the angels, who are those angels and what do they want. What's good sexually and economically? Who's allowed to get who and how? And will they die for it? Are uppity women heroes or bitches or upstarts? Whose pain is more real than other people's? What's pretty and what's ugly and who are we made to care about?

Now if the notions embedded in the novel are congruent with those the reviewer or the editor or the grantsgiver is used to hearing over dinner or at cocktail parties he (and I do mean he) attends, then he does not treat the novel as political. It's just a novel about how things are, so it is reviewed or judged in terms of its literary merit or its entertainment potential. Reviewers generally demand the work coincide with the categories and obsessions they were taught were characteristic of "serious literature" when they went to college, based generally on the work of a few men whose childhoods were passed in the nineteenth century; or else they demand the work excite their fantasies.

But when a reviewer or a professor or an editor or a grantsgiver reads a novel that embodies different standards of right and wrong, of masculine or feminine, of the good guys and the bad guys and the haves and have-nots in the brains and virtue and lovability departments, then the reviewer says "polemical." He will then explain to you that political fiction is bad fiction; which means that art is never supposed to embody political ideas different from those the contemporary powerful hold. The notion that literature has nothing to do in the world but is to be consumed in a vacuum is a recent heresy. Go on, sit down with Aristophanes, with Euripides, with Catullus, with Horace, with Alexander Pope and Dryden, with Dickens and George Eliot and George Sand and Tolstoi and explain to them that art has nothing to do with our morals, our politics and our behavior.

In truth, every work of art changes our world a tiny bit simply because it uses up resources—trees died that this book might live— and it will take time from those who read it. Every work of art possesses some infinitesimal capacity to move us and affect our emotional and mental state. It occupies our mind and our attention and alters them as it goes into our memory. In that respect novels are like dreams. If you remember them, and sometimes even if you don't, they never happened and yet they will influence the way you expect things to be, even what you will long for or dread or fear.

In a stratified society, almost all urban literature is engaged politically and morally, whether it is perceived so by the author or not: It will be so perceived by the readers it validates and the readers it affronts. That I speak of the effects novels have upon us and their uses does not mean I believe a novel should be judged by some utilitarian criteria. Art is only partially rational. It operates on all the levels of our brain and influences us through sounds and silences, through identification and imagery, through rhythms and chemistry. But as writers and readers, the novels we read make us more or less sensitive to each other. They tell us how we may expect to experience love and hatred, violence and peace, birth and death. They deeply influence what we expect to find as our love object, and what we expect to enjoy in bed, and what we think it's okay others should enjoy. They help us decide what war is like—boring hell or a necessary masculine maturation experience in a jolly peer group—and therefore whether we are willing to be drafted to fight one. They cause us to expect that rape is a shattering experience of violence, like being struck by a hit-and-run truck or a titillating escapade all women generally desire. Novels tell us how piggy we have a right to expect to be with each other. They influence our daydreams and our fantasies and therefore what we believe other people offer us or are withholding from us.

When the dismembered bodies of women are used decoratively as part of an aesthetic of cool violence that has characterized a lot of American fiction, something is deeply wrong in the heart of that fiction. It stinks.

What I am tired of is the pretense that when we write and when we publish, we don't understand what we're doing, and what we're saying for and against others, like ourselves and different from ourselves, clothed in similar or dissimilar bodies, and with more or less of the goodies we have or hope to have. I believe we are accountable for what we write just as we are for what we say to people we meet on the street. We are engaged in the wars of our violent times whether we wish we lived—as I surely do—in less interesting times, or not. We are responsible for our choices the same as plumbers and politicians and bureaucrats, and our novels embody our values and our choices.

The Child's Perception
of the City

Bruno Bettelheim

The only reason I can think of why I, a child psychologist, was honored by an invitation to speak at this conference, and why I dared to accept, is that the child is father of the man. I know little about how the urban experience is related to literature in any general or specific ways, but I am familiar with how children experience the world, and how strongly their early experiences determine all later ones. The manner in which we respond to our living in a city, and with it what our urban experience will be, is conditioned by the ideas of what city life is all about which we developed in and around our home, long before we had much direct experience with the city's wider aspects, or any ability to evaluate them objectively. These early impressions which are partly vague and disconnected, and partly highly idiosyncratic, nevertheless are decisive for the impact the child permits the urban experience to make on him, and with it how it will shape his life.

The persons who form the child's immediate human environment, the relations they establish with him and he with them, what transpires between parent and child in the home and when together they go out into the city, the places they frequent there and what these mean to each of them—all these shape the child's experience of the world, and of himself as part of it. These experiences also are decisive for whether he will tend to open himself gladly to the urban experience, or shrink away from it. Much depends there on how his parents mediate it, and this, in turn, is determined by what they themselves make of it: whether they feel it enriches their lives, or threatens their existence. Whether and how they see and use, or avoid and reject the urban experience—this creates the framework within which the child views the city and what he encounters in it.

The child's present urban experience, and with it his future one, depends on whether those close to him—most of all his parents—

© 1981 by Bruno Bettelheim.

219

experience urban life as uniquely enriching, or as severely depriving; whether to them the streets of the city are friendly expanses, and what goes on in the city is a source of rewarding experiences and ever new and fascinating challenges to their own growth; or whether, to the contrary, these persons impress him overtly or covertly with their anxious conviction that the city is horrid, its streets murderous jungles where dog eats dog, and that whatever meaningful activities may go on in the city are closed to them, and hence will be also to him.

Thus my thesis is that it is people who condition the urban experience, not buildings, streets, public places, parks, monuments, institutions, or means of transportation, although they all enter our visual image of what makes a city. It is hard to imagine an urban existence that does not involve a large number and a wide variety of people, living rather closely crowded together, each of them enjoying meaningful contacts with a few individuals, and anonymity as far as the multitude of others is concerned. The urban experience requires a large agglomeration of people, but what counts for us most is a very limited number of them. To the young child they are the members of his family, a few close neighbors and friends, and some other persons with whom he has frequent contact. Later, teachers and schoolmates are added to them. From an early age what is read to us and what we read also influence our views of what a city is all about. But whether face-to-face contacts, or more indirect influences, such as what we read, shape our urban experience, it is always people who determine what city life means to us.

What forms the urban experience, what makes it so valuable, are a large number and a wide variety of people living in proximity and hence in potentially close contact. Compared with this fact all other aspects of the city recede in importance. It makes a great difference to the people who live in a city whether they are housed comfortably or poorly, whether or not the city provides for the amenities of life, where the city is located, and how it is governed. These factors determine whether living in a city is pleasant or difficult, whether the life of the inhabitants will be short or long, secure or brutish. But even the citizens of the most tyrannically ruled city, existing in the most unhealthy conditions, will continue to lead an urban existence as long as there are many of them living closely together, because it is people who make the urban experience.

Literary sources suggest the same. They assert that what is essential for the urban experience are the unique human opportunities it offers and the easy access to them which it permits. However much an author may prefer to live secluded out in the country, away from the pressures and the bustle of the large city, the metropolis is the setting which makes high culture and, with it, his literary creations possible, although he may produce them in an isolated place.

Shakespeare wrote his plays not in Stratford but in London, at his time one of the largest cities of the Western world. Only with the creation of a large city and a permanent capital in Kyoto does Japanese literature begin to bloom. At the beginning of the present age of a technological civilization, after having spent most of his long life in a small town, Goethe said that Germany's cultural life was mediocre because men of culture and talent were scattered—rather than living in one big city, such as Paris, "where the highest talents of a great kingdom are all assembled on one spot and, by daily intercourse, strife, and emulation mutually instruct and emulate each other," conditions which permit or at the least greatly facilitate high literature to be created. Goethe himself, and his talent, were not formed in the country town of Weimar where he made this remark, but in Frankfurt, which then was one of the most important cities of Germany.

Nearly two-and-a-half millennia before Goethe's time, Aristides the Just expressed the same idea: "Not houses finely roofed or the stones of walls well built, nor canals or dockyards make the city, but men able to use their opportunity." Thucydides said it more concisely: "It is men who make the city, not walls or ships." Shakespeare, as one might expect, put it most tersely: "The people are the city."

According to Euripides, "The first requisite to happiness is that a man be born in a famous city." Happiness requires an urban existence. All through the Middle Ages, and well into modern times, the conviction was that only city air makes us free. Indeed in many places the law decreed that a serf who reached a city, or managed to live in it for a year, automatically became a free man. Not only did the city free those who dwelt in it, only there did the average man have relatively ample opportunities to develop his mind, some freedom to live according to his beliefs, and with it the occasion to be truly himself. In the past it was felt that only within city walls was there safety—as indeed there was, compared to the arbitrary domination by the lord of the land and the frequent periods of starvation, not to mention destructive wars which ravaged the countryside much more than the cities.

Today many think city air poisonous, that living in cities pollutes our lungs, crowds us so closely together that we have no space to be ourselves, cripples our lives—this, although the cities of the past were incredibly more polluted than those of today, and the inhabitants were crowded into what to us seem unlivably narrow confines. Thus as far as the urban experience is concerned, objective facts count for little when compared to our images of them; and these are largely derived from literary sources.

Life is with people, and nowhere more so than in cities, as the authors I quoted firmly assert. What life is like, what people are like, what life with people is like—this we learn first at our mother's knee. And when she reads to us, from the books she chooses to read. Her views of the city and of life within it depend on how she experiences them, and this is determined to a large degree by what she has read and heard about urban life that she has accepted as her own.

Since we gain our impressions of urban life from our mothers, little wonder that in our unconscious we often experience the city as a mother, that it was Pallas Athena, a female goddess, who was the symbol, the protectress, the embodiment of the spirit of the city in which great literature first flourished. But in real life, and much more in our unconscious, there are also evil mothers, destructive ones. Thus the city can be experienced in the image of a good or of a bad mother.

Mothers are experienced as both, good and bad, although depending on the individual experience, one of these opposite images will dominate, but rarely to the total exclusion of the other. Since we all carry within ourselves these two contrary primordial perceptions— others may call them archetypical images—of the good and of the bad mother, much depends on whether we relate a specific part of our experience—in this context the urban experience—to our image of the good, or of the bad mother.

Here the literary interpretation of the urban experience can make all the difference. Not without reason have I quoted three famous Athenians in praise of city life. Although life was often vile in Athens, as is true for life in any place, the interpretation of the urban existence we owe to these ancient authors spreads a glow over the Athens of their time which still captivates our imagination twenty-five hundred years later.

I could as easily have quoted opposite literary views which depict city life in images of squalor and despair. In regard to the urban experience, it seems that beauty and ugliness reside more often than not in the eye of the beholder, and our perspective on it is conditioned by the writers who influence our views. Much depends then on whether we are guided in forming our views of urban life by its praise by Euripides or, for example, by its vilification by Celine, as embodied in his *Voyage to the End of the Night*—and this although, like Euripides, he speaks of one of the most famous cities, Paris. And this although it is impossible to imagine that Celine could have become a writer of his stature, had his talent not been bred by his living in a city such as Paris.

But the positive images of life in an urban environment, such as those of a Goethe, or the negative ones, such as those of a Celine, if they make an impact at all, are grafted onto much earlier ones formed in childhood. So let us return to considering how a sense of the urban experience is first acquired.

The child who has not yet reached the age when he can independently evaluate his experiences, or who later is not encouraged and helped to speculate about life in the city, tends to think of it along the same terms as do those with whom he lives. On his own, he develops his view of city life on the basis of what he knows about life in the very limited part of the city in which he dwells. A few blocks are all most children know of the city in which they live. The small segment of town the child knows well forms the matrix of his life.

A matrix is a womb, and not only etymologically speaking; it is unconsciously experienced as such. The womb can be experienced as the safest, most comfortable, and satisfying of all dwelling places, where one lived in perfect bliss. But it can also be experienced in the opposite way: as something denying and frustrating, that tried to get rid of one, that nastily pushed one out into an inimical world, there to suffer, if not to perish. In which of these two ways the womb will be experienced depends not on what happened while one grew in it, but is the result of one's early experiences after one left it, which depend on how one was treated by one's mother after birth.

What the child has come to feel about his first dwelling place, he is apt to project into all later ones. His view of the first matrix within which he lived colors his views of all later ones. This is particularly true for the child's experience of the city, the framework within which he now lives and grows, since it has become the matrix of his present existence, as once the womb was.

If all goes well, that is, if the child comes to think that this matrix of his life, like the womb from which he entered it, is protective and offers mainly positive experiences, then he will feel that his neighborhood, his turf, are what permit him to grow up well, provide challenges to enlarge his understanding of the world, a chance to become ever more truly himself. The only vaguely known, or entirely unknown rest-of-the-city is experienced as an extension of what he is familiar with, and hence as essentially friendly and supporting.

When that part of town in which he lives is the safe abode where he finds whatever happiness he knows, then he is convinced that the city in which he lives is the best place in the world, never mind whatever shortcomings it may be saddled with, of which the child can not help becoming aware as he grows up. Such deficiencies of the city of his origin then seem relatively unimportant because of the earlier conviction of the city's perfection which was based on the unconscious identification of this city with the good mother, an identification which continues to color all later, more mature evaluations. Such was true in my case, since my conviction of the desirability of an urban existence was derived from the security I knew in my home, and was reinforced by what my mother told me about it.

My perceptions were derived from various sources, as are those of all children: from what they are told, from what they hear others talk about, from what is read to them, be it stories or even advertisements. If we include as literature oral literature, as we ought to since this is where it had its origin, then these are all literary influences. I owed my image of urban existence to all three of these sources: an impressive story my mother told me, another that she read to me, and a billboard sign. As far as my conscious recollections go, it was the sign which made it most explicitly clear what was good about living in my native city. But the message of this advertisement would not have reached me, or made a strong impression, had it not said in drastic, simple, down-to-earth words what my parents and relatives had already convinced me of.

Vienna, where I was born and grew up, was also where both my parents had been born; to me it seemed part of the heritage I owed to them. My view of urban life was but a reflection of theirs. While other people lived out in the country, or in other cities, such a life was not for us. I took our urban existence for granted; no other was possible, thinkable, desirable. I lived not just in the best possible place; life in any other was out of the question; hence there were no questions to be asked about the nature or merits of the urban environment, nor of the particular one which was ours. I did not reflect on what an urban life offered or demanded, did not wonder what caused Vienna's particular culture or beauty, nor question it—that came only much later.

As the child is convinced that his mother is beautiful, although he does not know why and how, so was I convinced of the unique merits of my hometown. I did not ponder what particular opportunities my urban surroundings provided me with, much as the child does not speculate about what particular chance his home offers him for his growth. Whatever opportunities the city permitted were all the opportunities there were or could be. Nor did I worry about any damage the city might inflict on me—and there were risks and liabilities to life in Vienna then and later, as there are in any environment one lives in. I worried as little as any child does about the damage life within his family may do to him, great as it may be.

The tale my mother told me was a significant part of our family's oral tradition, and I am sure it made such a deep impression on me at an early age because it contained so many elements of another literary tradition with which I was well familiar from many fairy tales. It was the story of an evil stepmother who, to advance her own children, cast out the child of a previous marriage; of an ineffectual father who could not stand up to his second wife, nor protect the child of his first wife who had died; of a boy abused by his stepmother and then pushed out of his home at an early age, forced to seek his fortune in a strange and unknown world, or perish.

Only it was not a fairy tale, but the stories of both of my grandfathers. At the age I was then, it was not their true stories which lent veracity to the many fairy tales I knew, but the other way round; what I had learned from fairy tales convinced me of the truth of my grandfathers' stories. Let me mention only that of my maternal grandfather whom I knew well; my paternal grandfather had died before I was born.

The mother of my maternal grandfather had died in childbirth. His father soon remarried, and there were several more children. They were rather poor, so the second wife resented the oldest son, fearing he would be favored by his father over her own children. She pestered her husband until he agreed that after the son had been "bar mitzvahed"—that is, according to Jewish religion had reached manhood—he would have to leave. Soon after his thirteenth birthday, the oldest son, who had never left the small village in which he was born, was sent out into the world. All he had was the good suit of clothing he had received as his coming-of-age present, and a silver piece of five guilders, worth about two-and-a-half dollars, which his father gave him surreptitiously on his leaving. So as not to ruin his only pair of shoes, he walked barefoot the hundred miles from his village to the big city—Vienna. There, in a very difficult struggle, he eventually managed to make a considerable fortune.

In his mind, in that of his daughter, my mother, and hence in my mind, it was our hometown which had rescued him by giving him his opportunity. It was this city which miraculously changed his life from one of dejection to one of success. Nowhere else but in Vienna, or in a fairy-story place, could a cast-out child make his fortune, or so it seemed to me. Obviously I had not heard that the streets of New York were paved with gold.

The story my mother read to me which made an equally great

impression was part of the autobiography of a then highly esteemed regional writer, titled "When I Was Still a Poor Peasant Boy in the Mountains." The only part I still remember, and the one which was meaningful in shaping my urban experience, was his telling of how, on finishing school when he was about thirteen—like my grandfather—he had walked barefoot to Vienna, attracted by its glamor. Particularly moving was his account of how happiness overwhelmed him when he finally reached the top of a hill from where he could make out Vienna in the distance, a place famous in folklore because according to tradition there the wives of the crusaders had sat spinning while anxiously waiting for the return of their husbands. The hill was marked by an ancient cross with which I was familiar. There, the author tells, he felt anxious about his future, but also extremely lucky that he had gotten to Vienna and would be able to live there. And there he indeed rose to great fame.

In my mind the two stories merged because they seemed incontrovertible proof that my hometown was the place where everybody desired to live, and where it was possible to achieve what one most desired: my grandfather, riches; the poet, fame.

As an adolescent, on excursions into the mountains, I visited the poor village in which this poet had been born and from where he had set out for Vienna. Seeing this place confirmed how lucky he had been to escape to Vienna. I never visited the village where my grandfather was born, but I was convinced it was just like the place in which the poet was born.

Even in those distant days, long before radio or TV, advertising made its impact felt. The messages of advertisements are part of the literature to which the child is exposed; they are usually some of the first printed words he is able to read; hence they form some of his earliest literary experiences. At that time in Vienna the most impressive ads were huge billboard signs proclaiming that those things the Viennese cherish most are Vienna's water—much praised for its purity and freshness since the time it was first piped into the city from far-away mountainous areas—and Anker bread (the product of the largest bread factory in the city, the brand eaten in most homes, including mine). These ads cleverly and effectively created a close association between the city and bread and water, the basic foods which, since most ancient times, are the symbol of sustenance. To me it was a most convincing association: like my mother, like my home, this larger home in which we all lived—the city—nurtured me well, as was only proper, or so it seemed to me.

Like most Viennese children I loved the hot Anker rolls, products of the same bakery as the bread, which I ate for breakfast and many in-between snacks. When many years later Proust's masterwork was published, I was not at all surprised that the taste of the madeleine brought back memories of his childhood, not just of its events, but also the place where they had taken place. I was well familiar with such sensations from my love for the hot Anker rolls. They were delicious, but the intimate connection that had become established through the billboard signs between these rolls and Vienna made them that much more significant as a happy bond that tied hometown and favorite food into an inseparable whole—the city that bred me, and the bread that fed me.

Even at the early age I am talking about, the child does not uncritically accept all literary statements about his urban existence. At that time—and still today—two songs were extremely popular which conveyed a most attractive, although over-sentimental image of Vienna. I heard them sung by people close to me who liked them a lot. One praises the beauty of the blue Danube; the other asserts that Vienna will always be the city of one's dreams. Despite my deep commitment to living in Vienna, I rejected both songs, not so much because I thought them hackneyed—for that, my esthetic sensitivities were not sufficiently developed. I rejected the one extolling the blue Danube, because I knew that its color was a muddy gray. No strong, positive emotions tied me to the river, so there was no reason to see it in a glorified way, contrary to the evidence of my eyes. Literary statements which run counter to the child's experience will be rejected.

Vienna did figure in my dreams; sometimes pleasantly, but often also in nightmares in which I got lost in the streets. This was reason enough to reject a song that asserts that Vienna will always be the city of my dreams. I wanted my hometown not to be the city of dreams, but of their realization. For this, it had to be a real city, not a dream city. Thus there are limitations to literature's shaping the child's conceptions of his urban existence, even at an early age.

As I outgrew a naive acceptance of my city life, it became modified under the impact of more sophisticated literature. For example, the influences of Karl Kraus' extremely critical views of Viennese culture became merged with the sharp but nevertheless loving irony with which Robert Musil described life in Vienna in his *Man without Qualities* and with the romantic nostalgia of Strauss-Hofmannsthal's *Rosenkavalier*. These were but some of my more mature choices from a vast literature devoted to Vienna which I permitted to alter my earlier uncritical images of an urban existence.

However much these literary descriptions altered specific features of my views of Vienna, they never changed my conviction that only an urban setting is the appropriate environment in which to live, or the emotional attachment to my city formed early in life. The same also held true for attitudes to cities which were first formed solely on the basis of literary experiences and only later put to the test of reality. Paris, I knew first through reading. My perspective on it was shaped mainly by Balzac, Zola, and Proust. However much time I spent in a Paris that was very different from the one these and other authors described, I continued to see much of it as I had learned to do from what I had read.

In my thirties I had to adjust to an urban existence very different from that I had known up to then. It is hard to imagine two cities more different than Vienna and Chicago. But based on my attitude that a city environment is what suits best my needs and aspirations, which had become ingrained in childhood, all I needed to do was to free the inner image of the city as the only appropriate matrix for my life from its specific Viennese traits and to modify it in line with my perceptions of the Chicago that was so different externally. This process was greatly facilitated by my being able to draw for help on literary preceptors such as James Farrell. The positive feelings for Chicago and the understanding of the city that I derived from those readings enriched my personal experience. For example, the enjoyable excursions into the Viennese Woods and swimming in the Danube were replaced by the very different but also enjoyable visits to the Lakefront and swimming in Lake Michigan. The specific quality the experience of Vienna owed to the city's ancient history and buildings found its counterpart in the exciting vitality and modern architecture of Chicago.

As I had accepted some images of Vienna gained from the literature and rejected others, the same was true for Chicago. Back in Vienna I had accepted uncritically that Chicago was a city of gangsters and of slaughterhouses, the latter notion due to my reading of Upton Sinclair. As I settled in Chicago I realized that my life there had nothing to do with gangsters or slaughterhouses, nor could the ambiance of the stockyard area become the matrix for my life. So the images of Chicago which I had carried in my mind for years dropped away within weeks under the reality of the city, to be replaced by images owed to a very different literature which was in line with my experience of the city. That I could transfer to Chicago a past commitment to an urban existence as the best setting for my life helped me very much in acquiring an image of Chicago eminently suitable to living happily there. It is one example of the fact that the images of urban life gained in childhood can and do determine one's later attitude to the urban experience.

Having unconscionably taken advantage of your kindness by engaging in an old man's foible to reminisce on times long past and to talk about himself, I shall now try to suggest what are the typical literary images of the urban experience which are forced on our children. My purpose in doing so is to let you judge whether the images of city existence in the literature our children are exposed to at an early age are true to fact, or whether they are conducive to having them gain impressions of city life which will help them to live well in what will have to be the matrix of their lives.

Since children's early, and hence most decisive, experiences within their families are too diverse to permit generalizations, I must restrict myself to those literary sources to which all children are exposed: the textbooks used to teach them reading. Although the vast majority of American children live in cities, one could not guess this fact from the contents of the books they all are made to read during their first three or four years of school, when they are at a most impressionable age, when they learn to read on their own, and when many of them first become acquainted with literature.

The readers designed for kindergarten and the early grades depict life as universally pleasurable. The settings in which this pleasant life unfolds are not citified, but are predominantly rural, or suburban. Consequently it is impressed on the child that he can have an enjoyable life only in a non-urban setting. Even in a book titled *City Days, City Ways*, the children in the stories are shown as living on tree-lined streets in detached, single-family homes. While urban life is not described as undesirable—nothing is in these books—it is denied importance through complete neglect, which suggests to the child that it is not worth being paid attention to.

All the many and various pleasant activities in which the children in the stories in these primers engage take place in settings which convey nothing of urban life, although some of them are located in a playground. When outdoors, the children chase rabbits and squirrels, swim in pools, go on picnics, take motorboat rides on lakes and pony rides; they even travel on trains and airplanes. While a visit to a zoo may suggest a city facility, it indicates a desire to escape its confinements, rather than making a go of an urban existence. When children enter a more urban setting, it is clearly only temporarily to shop in stores. While much is said about the pleasures one can enjoy out in the country, aside from the fact that one can buy things such as jackets or shoes in the city, nothing good is told about urban life.

Titles of stories in first readers of the most widely used series of basic texts may illustrate the emphasis on rural life—"In the Meadow," "Too Much Clover," "In the Green Woods," "Faraway Farm," etc. Not a single one of the story titles suggests a city setting, nor is any of the forty-seven stories in this book placed in an urban environment.

The first and only time in which urban life is directly mentioned in the first five books of this series is in a story in its second-grade reader in which a dog compares his previous life in the country with his present one in the city. Since the dog is the hero of an entire section of this reader, consisting of six stories and filling thirty pages, the child is expected to identify with the animal in a positive way, particularly in his view of the undesirability of city life. (Nothing in the story contradicts this view.) Typical of the underlying attitudes to city life which these readers convey are the following lines:

Before we came here, we lived in a little town called Hillside. We lived at the edge of town. Out there we had space enough to run and play and have fun. It was not my fault that we came to live in the city. Do you know what a city is? A city is houses and garages, cars and people. There is no room for anything else. A city is where everyone keeps on saying "Don't play in the street." "Don't run in front of cars." "Don't ride on a bicycle." "Keep off the grass." "Stop, look, and listen before you cross the street." ... When I first moved to the city, I *hated* it. Do you wonder why?

This series of basic texts is designed for use all over the United States where, after all, quite a few children live in suburban and rural settings. So let us consider the images of an urban existence which are conveyed to the child in readers which were specially designed for use also with minority children who live in metropolitan areas. One of the readers of this series is typically titled *Uptown, Downtown,* promising to reflect urban existences in its stories. One story, "What Do You Think?", is as follows:

The little girl came out of her new house, and what do you think she saw? Just a corner. She went around the corner, and what do you think she saw? Just another corner. She went around that corner, and what do you think she saw? Still another corner. So she went around it, and then what do you think she saw? And what do you think she did?

The emptiness and purposelessness of a city existence projected here is not an isolated instance of what forms the content of this new series of readers designed for city children. The following example from the primer of this series, titled *Around the City*, may further illustrate. Once more the title promises that by reading the stories in this book the child will learn about life in the city. But what do some of the stories tell about it?

All around the city, all around the town, boys and girls run up the street. Boys and girls run down. Boys come out into the sun. Boys come out to play and run. Girls come out to run and play. Around the city, all the day. All around the city, all around the town, boys and girls run up the street, boys and girls run down.

These stories project without relief a depressing image of the emptiness and purposeless nature of an urban existence.

Little wonder that many of those who as children were impressed by what they were made to read (that city life has nothing positive to offer) have little love for an urban existence. Being forced to read that the matrix of their lives is bleak and disappointing—particularly when no suggestions are offered about how things could be improved—tends to discourage both interest in literature and living in cities.

I concentrated on the literary impressions I received in my childhood because these left me with an attitude about living in cities which permitted me—even in difficult moments—to be very satisfied that I could live an urban existence, and encouraged me to engage in efforts to improve those of its aspects I felt it within my power to better. I wish the literary impressions our children gain from their classroom reading would do the same for them. If this were so, maybe the urban existence of the next generation would be a vast improvement over the present one.

Borrowing and Lending:
The Young Reader and the Library

Joan N. Burstyn

I believe that those of us who continue to use public libraries throughout our lives are people who decide for ourselves what is interesting and valuable for us to read. In order to do that, we need confidence in ourselves and skills of discrimination. Library users are also people who share with one another the enterprise of reading. We sometimes create networks to discuss the books we have read, or we meet to listen to authors discuss their craft. We are members of a community. Many of us joined that community as children. Our library cards, issued to us after we had laboriously written out our names, were passports to a new freedom, and to new obligations as members of the library community.

Today, our society contains forces that threaten people's initiative to choose what they read and endanger the belief in community. I want to examine these forces and their relation to young readers in the city.

There has always been a tension in young people's libraries between providing an environment where children, like adults, can learn to find books for themselves, to follow their own bent along paths not foreseen, to explore through fiction the ways people react to disaster or opportunity, and the perceived need to make libraries places where children are taught the characteristics of good citizenship, and ways to use books for research purposes.[1]

The first children's librarians spoke with a fine authority of how to choose good, not trashy books; of how to impose discipline on children in the library.[2] But discipline was different from direction. These librarians of the early twentieth century left the children free to read in the library as they willed; they did not seek to direct their learning. In the years that have intervened, children's librarians have fought hard to keep that freedom for their clientele. But they have fought

© 1981 by Joan Burstyn.

against heavy odds. Many children now, particularly those old enough to have homework from school, use the library as a resource for work assigned to them by teachers. Ivan Illich has observed that once a subject is taught through an official course, be it at school or college, people who obtain the same information on their own feel that it is less valuable, and less valid, than if they had learned it in a course.[3] Children are socialized slowly to that way of thinking; those who learn to use libraries for their own interests as well as for their assignments may even become immunized against it.

The concern for directed learning has manifested itself in school libraries and in those attached to colleges and universities. Teachers consider these libraries as extensions of their classrooms. As a teacher, I have done the same. I have spent much time trying to extend the areas of directed learning, encouraging students to find easily what I stumbled upon by chance. I have "helpfully" suggested books to students.

David Riesman has commented in retrospect that long reading lists serve as dazzling automobile tailfins for faculty; they adorn the body rather than assist the user. I, also, have questioned some of our motives as educators. A student at Rutgers, who had graduated from a high school in Newark, remarked that she had read a great deal on her own while she was in high school, particularly searching out the stories of films before she saw them. Since she had been at college, she had never had time to read more than her assigned work. Her remarks about her use of the library while at college have been reiterated to me by other students at other institutions. Is it our intention as university teachers so to monopolize our students' learning that they have no time to use their own initiative for their reading? Alas, this situation is no Johnny-come-lately to the university scene. Wallace Stevens, at the turn of the century, found his reading more constructive after he had left Harvard and was free to wander through libraries in New York.[4]

I want to turn now to the reasons why both individually initiated use of libraries and the existence of community are threatened in our society. First, there are social pressures on young people to make their learning purposeful. Some people feel that to browse among books, with no purpose but to browse, is to waste time. In Britain as well as in the United States, some librarians report that city children, particularly, use reference and non-fiction books far more than fiction.[5] Some parents feel that reading is for the acquisition of facts, not the indulgence of fancy; they discourage reading for its own sake. Their opinions match those of some teachers who consider libraries only as entensions of the classroom.

I am reminded of two boys in a branch library of the city who were writing papers on famous people. One read me his description of Langston Hughes' life. It was full of elegant phrases lifted from an encyclopedia. I asked the boy whether he himself had ever written a poem. Yes, he said, when he was younger. Had he read any poems by Langston Hughes, I asked. He shook his head. We found an anthology on a shelf, and the boys searched the index for poems by Hughes. The writer read a short poem about the sun and then jumped up to find himself a book about insects. The other boy found another Hughes' poem—a searing comment on teenagers in the city. He nodded approval of that one.

I went back to my table, thinking how strangely we teach; how closely the humanities ape the sciences. Science digests its past; we do not need to read Newton's words to learn about gravitation. We describe Newton's ideas and then send students to find out about his life. But to understand Langston Hughes or Doris Lessing, we have to read their own words, not read about them.[6] Often, we treat writers as though they were scientists, and send young people scurrying to encyclopedias before they have read an author's writing. I would have us reconsider our priorities.

There are technological as well as social pressures against self-initiated learning that is undirected. With new techniques of information retrieval, people have to know what they are looking for in order to conjure up the material from the stacks or on microfilm or microfiche. The possibility of stumbling on new areas of interest is declining. If a person cannot browse, he or she is unable to come by accident upon something to fire the imagination.

While there are both social and technological pressures against individuals choosing to use libraries as they will, there has been a revolution in our attitudes towards possessions that makes lending and borrowing problematic. I am reminded of J.R.R. Tolkien's dragon, Smaug, who craved for jewels and golden goblets, not to savor their beauty, but for the pleasure of possession. He slept with them under his belly in order to protect them from theft.[7] Our consumer society has made dragons of us all. Manufacturers care not whether we use their products; they care only that we buy them, and would have us discard them rapidly so that we may buy another, so-called better, product. We sleep with our tape decks, ten-speed bicycles, and paperback books stuffed under our bellies. Possessions have become our obsession. Because of this, power and authority in all walks of life have become associated with possession.

Let me expand on this idea, because I have not seen its ramifications explored in relation to the concepts of lending and borrowing. In a society where possessions are few, and the opportunity to acquire them is small, power and authority accrue to those who demonstrate that they understand their environment and know how to gain control of it. Thus, it is important for children to learn their neighborhoods, to show their friends how "cool" they can behave in strange places, how well they know the workings of each institution. We think of these as the skills of city dwellers. I think of them as skills valued by those in any place whose status depends on values other than possessions. From the nineteenth century onwards, in our society libraries have been institutions about which it has been important to know, in order to develop a sense of power over the environment.

However, I suggest that the dominant mode of defining power and authority in our society has changed during the last forty years. Possessions have become the key to status. What children want is to possess things. So do their parents. And this dominant mode affects all groups in society, irrespective of their ability to acquire possessions. What this means is that there is no longer as much prestige, as much kudos, attached to knowing one's environment as there used to be, and thus any sense of belonging, as it used to be defined, has been attenuated. (I should add, however, that there is still differential attachment to place among groups in society, and that one of the hidden losses from urban renewal has been the damage to self-esteem among the original inhabitants of renewed areas who have seen destroyed the places from which they gained their sense of self.

What has this to do with borrowing and lending? Borrowing and lending take place within a community. You borrow from those you will see again, and to see them again is to develop a continuity of relationship. Borrowing from a library is different because a borrower may not know personally any other borrowers; the link with the community is weak, but librarians act as surrogates for the readers. They become the people who are known to all borrowers. However, a sense of relationship has to exist for the books to be returned.

There is a poignant story by Kristin Hunter (used as a title for her book of stories by that name) called *Guests in the Promised Land*.[8] In it a group of black city boys go for an outing to a wealthy suburban country club whose members are, according to the story, all white. One of the boys walks, uninvited, into the club house and begins to play, on the Steinway piano at the bar, the gospel music he knows so well. When club members praise his playing but make it clear they have had enough of it, the boy draws a knife and gouges the piano. "You wild animal," the members cry. At which all hell breaks loose as the boy and his companions run amuck through the club house. They vow never to return as guests.

To be a guest is to be an outsider, to have no stake in the community. How many people, I wonder, feel themselves to be guests in public libraries? Libraries sometimes seem part of the "establishment"; they do not belong to us small folk who sense we are continually "ripped off" by the "establishment." If libraries belong to "them," are they not fair game for "ripping off" in return for what they do to us in other ways? Only when we feel that a library belongs to us does our attitude towards it change.

Despite our obsession with possessions, and despite the burgeoning of paperback books which are relatively inexpensive for us to buy, it is still possible for libraries to provide city children (and city adults) with a place of their own. This spring I sat in the young people's room of a library watching it fill up after school. Friends met there, saved chairs for one another, reached for books and sprawled on cushion chairs placed on the carpet. The room, quite obviously, was theirs. Some people were busy on school assignments. One boy spent more than half an hour laboriously copying material from a book about frogs. But another boy was crouched on a seat in front of books about music, browsing through them. He showed me a book of American folk tunes. He was ten and couldn't read music, he said, although his younger sister could. She played the piano, he explained, but he played drums. He came over to me later to talk about another music book he'd found. Another child, of seven or eight, found a story about a raccoon. She mouthed the words as she wriggled on a cushion chair. After a few minutes she gave up. The book seemed too difficult for her. She ran off across the room; the older girl she had come in with was still busy at the card catalog. So the younger one returned to her book. She never finished it, but she persisted for about twenty minutes before she put the book back on the shelf where she had found it.

Another children's room I visited was almost empty. It was still too early for most children to be out of school, but one fourth grader from a private school was working on his homework. One librarian was talking loudly to another across the room about a woman who had been hospitalized for an emotional problem. It was a gruesome story which distracted me as I scanned the shelves. I thought it must have disturbed the boy too. My mind jumped to other occasions when I, the client, had been forced to listen to conversations I had not wanted to: in doctors' offices, motor registration departments, passport offices, registration desks—the times were too numerous to count, but the feeling welling up within me was the same. Resentment. Ah, I thought, guests in the promised land. That's what we were, the boy and I. The room did not belong to us but to the librarians who were not sharing it with us, but were making us feel like outsiders. I left before the after-school rush came in. It may never have come. But the young boy at the table remained.

I would end with a challenge. We should not try to make all learning both directed and intentional. To balance the influence of schools, we need other institutions, such as public libraries, which are primarily dedicated to fostering both individual responsibility for learning and a sense of community among learners. When social and technological pressures force even young children towards directed and intentional learning, and when our hunger for possessions makes even city dwellers into self-sufficient hermits, children's librarians have an awesome but challenging task to make children feel that the library is theirs, and that in it they are free to discover their own interests.

Notes

1. See Sara Innis Fenwick, "Library Service to Children and Young People," Howard W. Winger, issue ed., *Library Trends* 25, no. 1 (July 1976): 329–360.

2. See, for example, Clara Whitehill Hunt, *Library Work with Children* (Chicago: American Library Association, 1924), pp. 2–7, 20–23.

3. Ivan Illich, *Tools for Conviviality* (New York: Harper & Row, 1973), pp. 20–21.

4. Holly Stevens, *Souvenirs and Prophecies: The Young Wallace Stevens* (New York: Alfred A. Knopf, 1977), pp. 217, 219, 238.

5. See Anne Fleet, *Children's Libraries* (London: Andre Deutsch, 1973), pp. 19–21. This book also contains rich material on the physical environment of children's libraries.

6. See Harold L. Burstyn, "Tradition and Understanding: The Sciences and the Humanities," *School and Society* 97 (1969): 419–424, and C. P. Snow, *Public Affairs* (New York: Charles Scribner's Sons, 1971), pp. 93–97.

7. J.R.R. Tolkien, *The Hobbit* (New York: Ballantine Books, 1966), pp. 34–36, 206.

8. Kristin Hunter, *Guests in the Promised Land* (New York: Charles Scribner's Sons, 1968).

Literature for Youth:
The City as Heaven and/or Hell

M. Jerry Weiss

As one who is most interested in the reading needs and interests of children and young adults, I have spent endless hours watching, listening to, and reading to students and teachers. The young and those most concerned with their education are an amazing group of people who are eager to succeed and to bridge the gaps between home and school.

Today's young people, for the most part, are quite capable of articulating their concerns, and the inner-city children express their ideas in a variety of ways, as the sights and sounds of their experiences influence and shape their thoughts.

The city is, indeed, a most provocative environment. A writer who selects the city as a setting often combines the elements of sensitivity, pathos, and violence to develop a "realistic" story which appeals to young readers. Even Charles Dickens, in *Oliver Twist* and *David Copperfield*, created situations and characters, shaped by the London environment, that could cause readers of other times to laugh, hold their breath in anticipation, acquire a sense of the terrible to be found in the city, and find the many good things and people who inhabit the city.

Today's authors and illustrators have learned much from masterly storytellers of the past. They know the ingredients that can hold young readers' interests. They know the pains and problems of the young. Now let's look at a few works to demonstrate the skills they bring to their task.

Fran Arrick's *Steffie Can't Come Out to Play* is both current and controversial. This is the compelling story of a runaway who finds trouble in her dreams of escape, leaving Clairton, Pennsylvania, and becoming a prostitute on Eighth Avenue in New York City. This is a painful story that needs to be read and discussed. This should be

© 1981 by M. Jerry Weiss.

followed by reading Elizabeth Swados' moving musical drama, *Runaways*. Each lyric attempts to explain the conflicts children feel which cause them to run away.

But just as some children see the city as a place of refuge, others see it as a place to leave. Stephen Joseph, a warm and intelligent teacher, edited a collection of poems, essays, and short stories created by his New York City students. The collection, *The Me Nobody Knows: Children's Voices from the Ghetto*, presents a candid series of events and fears that these children have recorded as a result of their living experiences. Winos, drugs, fights dominate the short pieces; but, there is always hope—if only someone would listen and try to do something about the whole mess. Nancy Larrick has edited another similar collection, *I Heard a Scream in the Street: Poems by Young People in the City*. James T. Farrell in *Studs Lonigan*, Louise Meriwether in *Daddy Was a Number Runner*, Piri Thomas in *Stories from El Barrio*, Susan Shreve in *The Nightmares of Geranium Street*, Sharon Bell Mathis in *Teacup Full of Roses*, Alice Childress in *A Hero Ain't Nothin' but a Sandwich*, Kristin Hunter in *The Soul Brothers and Sister Lou*, Frank Bonham in *Durango Street* and *Viva Chicano*, Nicholasa Mohr in *In Nueva York*, and Kin Platt in *Headman* focus on poignant and painful moments while growing up in the cities of this country.

One writer, Walter Dean Myers, stands out with his ability to take the youth of the city, show them laughing, scheming, getting into and out of trouble. His latest book, *The Young Landlords*, shows what happens when Paul Williams and his friends from the Action Group accidentally become landlords and attempt to make their Harlem neighborhood a better place to live.

For the primary grades, many good books are available which are designed to help children understand their environment, stimulate imaginations, arouse curiosity, and provide thrills and fun. Walter Dean Myers is linguistically delightful in his fantasy, *The Dragon Takes a Wife*. His new book, *The Black Pearl and the Ghost, or One Mystery after Another*, shows him to be most capable in creating mirthful mystery stories. Rachel Isadora's beautiful picture book, *My Ballet Class*, shows the stuff that dreams and dancers are made of. What a wonderful preview for Broadway's smash hit *A Chorus Line*. Even the powerful institution, the school, can enchant through the talents of Patricia Reilly Giff in *Today Was a Terrible Day*, Miriam Cohen's *Lost in the Museum*, and Paula Kurzband Feder's *Where Does the Teacher Live?*

The home is that place where so many questions arise, as children learn about others and their own relationships with siblings, parents, and other adults. Marjorie Weinman Sharmat offers much insight in *Sometimes Mama and Papa Fight*. Louise Fitzhugh, in *Nobody's Family Is Going To Change*, introduces young Emma who raises a thought: "Here was a prosecutor in the form of her father, here was a suspect in Willie, her brother, and here was a judge in the shape of her mother, but where was the defense lawyer?"[1] Enter legal-minded Emma who provides humor and intelligence in this delightful story of a Black couple who learn to understand their children and to appreciate each child's dreams and talents.

In literature suitable for young adults, Chaim Potok's *The Chosen* tells the story of two Jewish boys in Brooklyn, one Hasidic and one Orthodox, and how their worlds are so meaningfully different. Barbara Wersba, in *Run Softly, Go Fast*, shows the love-hate relationship between Dave Marks and his father. After Dave's father dies, Dave has to examine his own sense of worth and set of personal values. Paula Danziger shows school can be a source of funny ideas, which might happen to work, in *Can You Sue Your Parents for Malpractice?* Ellease Southerland, in *Let the Lion Eat Straw*, tells the story of Abeba Williams, who is brought from the rural South to Brooklyn by her resentful mother, and who finds in her exceptional musical talent the ability to care and to cope. Love and marriage bring changes in Abeba's life, and then she struggles to provide a decent life for her husband and children.

Ursula K. LeGuin, in *Very Far Away from Anywhere Else*, and John Minahan, in *Jeremy*, speak of young love between very gifted and talented young teenagers. In the latter book, the New York School of Performing Arts provides a very interesting setting for talented youth.

Many important books in the field of biography should be considered for today's young readers. Some of these include James Haskins' *From Lew Alcindor to Kareem Abdul-Jabbar*, Robert Lipsyte's *Free to Be Muhammad Ali*, Alice Walker's *Langston Hughes, American Poet*, Virginia Hamilton's *Paul Robeson: The Life and Times of a Free Black Man*, James Haskins' *The Story of Stevie Wonder*, Jeanne Wakatsuki Houston's and James D. Houston's *Farewell to Manzanar*, and Maya Angelou's excellent autobiography, *I Know Why the Caged Bird Sings*. Dick Gregory, with the help of Robert Lipsyte, has provided many readers with stimulating ideas in his autobiographical work, *Nigger: An Autobiography*.

Poetry can easily be introduced through E. Alma Flagg's *Lines and Colors: Twenty-one Poems*, Stephanie Spinner's edited collection, *Rock Is Beautiful: An Anthology of American Lyrics, 1953–1968*,

Frank Asch's *City Sandwich*, Shel Silverstein's *Where the Sidewalk Ends*, Arnold Adoff's *Eats*, and his edited anthology, *Celebrations: A New Anthology of Black American Poetry*. Young joggers will feel the motion of Adoff's young heroine in his beautiful volume, *I Am the Running Girl*. Eloise Greenfield's collection for younger readers, with illustrations by Diane and Leo Dillon, *Honey, I Love and Other Love Poems*, is pure lyrical magic. And who can overlook the wonderful volume by Nikki Giovanni, *Ego-tripping and Other Poems for Young People?*

Finally, the wonderful world of comedy cuts through all generations and regions of the world. The silly animal nonsense verse of Ogden Nash, the social criticism of Langston Hughes through his marvelous character, Jesse B. Semple, the past and present worlds of Sam Levenson, the awful truths of Mark Twain, the parenting problems of Erma Bombeck and Jean Kerr, and the zany world of Woody Allen are very popular with young students. Selections by these and other famous humorists are available in two recent collections edited by Helen S. Weiss and M. Jerry Weiss, *The American Way of Laughing* and *More Tales Out of School*.

Books, such as those mentioned above, will, indeed, develop a love of reading within our young and help them to see the city as a place of inspiration, of hope, as well as a place whose terrors might some day be tempered.

Note

1. Louise Fitzhugh, *Nobody's Family Is Going to Change* (New York: Dell, 1975), p. 161.

Bibliography

Adoff, Arnold (ed.). *Celebrations: A New Anthology of Black American Poetry*. Chicago: Follett, 1977.
Adoff, Arnold. *Eats*. New York: Lothrop, 1979.
Adoff, Arnold. *I Am the Running Girl*. New York: Harper & Row, 1979.
Angelou, Maya. *I Know Why the Caged Bird Sings*. New York: Bantam, 1971.
Arrick, Fran. *Steffie Can't Come Out to Play*. New York: Dell, 1978.
Asch, Frank. *City Sandwich*. New York: Greenwillow, 1978.
Bonham, Frank. *Durango Street*. New York: Dell, 1972.
Bonham, Frank. *Viva Chicano*. New York: Dell, 1971.
Brodsky, Beverly. *Secret Places*. Philadelphia: Lippincott, 1979.

Brooks, Charlotte (ed.). *The Outnumbered*. New York: Dell, 1967.

Buckley, Peter. *I Am from Puerto Rico*. New York: Simon and Schuster, 1971.

Childress, Alice. *A Hero Ain't Nothin' but a Sandwich*. New York: Avon, 1977.

Cohen, Miriam. *Lost in the Museum*. New York: Greenwillow, 1979.

Danziger, Paula. *Can You Sue Your Parents for Malpractice?* New York: Dell, 1980.

Farrell, James T. *Studs Lonigan*. New York: Avon, 1977.

Feder, Paula Kurzband. *Where Does the Teacher Live?* New York: Dutton, 1979.

Fitzhugh, Louise. *Nobody's Family Is Going to Change*. New York: Dell, 1975.

Flagg, E. Alma. *Lines and Colors: Twenty-one Poems*. Newark: The Branford Press, 1979.

Giff, Patricia Reilly. *Today Was a Terrible Day*. New York: Viking, 1980.

Giovanni, Nikki. *Ego-tripping and Other Poems for Young People*. New York: Lawrence Hill, 1973.

Greenfield, Eloise. *Honey, I Love and Other Love Poems*. New York: Crowell, 1978.

Gregory, Dick, with Robert Lipsyte. *Nigger: An Autobiography*. New York: Pocket Books, 1965.

Guy, Rosa. *The Friends*. New York: Holt, Rinehart and Winston, 1973.

Hamilton, Virginia. *Paul Robeson: The Life and Times of a Free Black Man*. New York: Dell, 1979.

Hansberry, Lorraine. *To Be Young, Gifted, and Black*. New York: New American Library, 1970.

Haskins, James. *From Lew Alcindor to Kareem Abdul-Jabbar*. New York: Lothrop, 1979.

Haskins, James. *The Story of Stevie Wonder*. New York: Dell, 1979.

Houston, Jeanne Wakatsuki, and James D. Houston. *Farewell to Manzanar*. New York: Bantam, 1974.

Hunter, Kristin. *The Soul Brothers and Sister Lou*. New York: Avon, 1976.

Isadora, Rachel. *My Ballet Class*. New York: Greenwillow, 1980.

Jordan, June. *His Own Where*. New York: Dell, 1973.

Joseph, Stephen (ed.). *The Me Nobody Knows: Children's Voices from the Ghetto*. New York: Avon, 1972.

Kaufman, Bel. *Up the Down Staircase*. New York: Avon, 1973.

Larrick, Nancy (ed.). *I Heard a Scream in the Street: Poems by Young People in the City*. New York: Evans, 1970.

LeGuin, Ursula K. *Very Far Away from Anywhere Else*. New York: Bantam, 1977.

Lester, Julius. *Black Folktales*. New York: Grove, 1970.

Lipsyte, Robert. *The Contender*. New York: Bantam, 1969.

Lipsyte, Robert. *Free to Be Muhammad Ali*. New York: Bantam, 1979.

Mathis, Sharon Bell. *Sidewalk Story*. New York: Avon, 1973.

Mathis, Sharon Bell. *Teacup Full of Roses*. New York: Avon, 1973.

Meriwether, Louise. *Daddy Was a Number Runner*. New York: Pyramid, 1976.

Minahan, John. *Jeremy*. New York: Bantam, 1973.

Mohr, Nicholasa. *In Nueva York*. New York: Dell, 1979.

Mohr, Nicholasa. *Nilda*. New York: Harper & Row, 1973.

Myers, Walter Dean. *The Black Pearl and the Ghost or One Mystery after Another*. New York: Viking, 1980.

Myers, Walter Dean. *The Dragon Takes a Wife*. Indianapolis: Bobbs-Merrill, 1972.

Myers, Walter Dean. *The Young Landlords*. New York: Viking, 1979.

Platt, Kin. *Headman*. New York: Dell, 1977.

Potok, Chaim. *The Chosen*. New York: Fawcett, 1978.

Randall, Dudley (ed.). *The Black Poets*. New York: Bantam, 1971.

Roth, Henry. *Call It Sleep*. New York: Avon, 1974.

Sharmat, Marjorie Weinman. *Sometimes Mama and Papa Fight*. New York: Harper & Row, 1980.

Shreve, Susan. *The Nightmares of Geranium Street*. New York: Avon, 1979.

Silverstein, Shel. *Where the Sidewalk Ends*. New York: Harper & Row, 1974.

Soto, Pedro Juan. *Spiks*. New York: Monthly Review Press, 1973.

Southerland, Ellease. *Let the Lion Eat Straw*. New York: Scribner's, 1979.

Spinner, Stephanie. *Rock Is Beautiful: An Anthology of American Lyrics, 1953–1968*. New York: Dell, 1970.

Steptoe, John. *Train Ride*. New York: Harper & Row, 1971.

Swados, Elizabeth. *Runaways*. New York: Bantam, 1980.

Thomas, Ianthe. *Walk Home Tired, Billy Jenkins*. New York: Harper & Row, 1974.

Thomas, Piri. *Stories from El Barrio*. New York: Avon, 1980.

Walker, Alice. *Langston Hughes, American Poet*. New York: Crowell, 1974.

Weiss, Helen S., and M. Jerry Weiss (eds.). *The American Way of Laughing*. New York: Bantam, 1977.

Weiss, Helen S., and M. Jerry Weiss (eds.). *More Tales out of School*. New York: Bantam, 1980.

Wersba, Barbara. *Run Softly, Go Fast*. New York: Bantam, 1972.

Yep, Laurence. *Dragonwings*. New York: Harper Trophy, 1977.

A People's Paper
for the Inner City

John Holt

I would like to begin with a question, which I first asked seven or eight years ago in a letter to a number of reading experts: "Do you know of any research that has been done to find out how many children teach themselves to read?" Of the six or eight persons, all well known in that field, to whom I wrote, only one replied, my friend Daniel Fader, Professor of English at the University of Michigan and author of (among others) *Hooked on Books* and *The Naked Children*. He replied that my question was interesting, that he had never heard it asked before, and that, no, he did not know of any such research.

Some months afterwards, at a three-day conference on reading called by the Governor of North Carolina, I put that same question to the two thousand or so teachers and reading experts attending, asking any who knew of any such research to raise their hands. No hands were raised. I have since asked the same question, in meetings, of perhaps another five thousand teachers, reading teachers, etc. Still no hands. I repeated the question in my book *Instead of Education*, published in the spring of 1976 and since reprinted in paperback, asking any who knew of such research to write me a letter. So far, no letters.[1]

If we ever get around to doing such research, we will probably find that the number of children who teach themselves to read is at least 5 percent, and perhaps much more, that most of these self-taught readers (unless actually forbidden to read in school, which quite often happens) became outstanding readers, and that among the best readers in any sample, many or most were largely or wholly self-taught.

Some of these children sit on the laps of parents who read aloud to them stories they both enjoy, and find to their surprise after a while that the children can read the stories. Some puzzle it out for themselves, from books, or labels, or cereal boxes, or signs in the street. I

© 1981 by John Holt.

began to read at age four. The first word I learned to read was "laundry." The streets in Manhattan where I grew up were full of signs. Most were the names of stores, or things sold there. I had no way to guess what they might mean. But laundries all had "laundry" written over them, and had shirts in the window, and when we went to them, we took laundry to be washed, or picked up laundry that had been washed. One day it came to me in a flash that the letters over the store said, *had* to say, "laundry," and said it so that we would know enough to take our laundry there. In short, I saw all at once not just what the letters said but what they meant and, even more important, what they *signified*, what they were *for*, why they were important. After that, the rest—of which I remember nothing at all—was easy.

I have said all this to make a point. People do not learn to read or to become good readers because they think it will *someday* help them get into college or get a good job. They do it for one reason only— because they get pleasure, satisfaction, and excitement from doing it, *right here and now.* I read a great deal as a child, and so became a good reader, because magazines and books (some good, some "bad") gave me rich material for my private fantasy life, for daydreaming. A child I knew years later learned to read from labels and instruction booklets, so that he could figure out how his father's machines worked. Other children learn to write (and read) so that they can write stories, or letters, and read the letters people send to them. Others may learn to read for still different reasons, or mixtures of reasons. But their reasons are in the present, and are their own.

Of course, children are not going to learn to read unless there is material around *to* read. Of course, they are much more likely to learn to read if they can see that the older people around them read a great deal and like doing it. If reading is not important to the older people, it will probably not seem important to most of the children.

For about two-and-a-half years now, I have edited and published a small bi-monthly newsletter or magazine which is for, and about, and to a large extent by, a group of people who are in a special social situation, usually difficult, often painful, and occasionally dangerous. The magazine is called *Growing Without Schooling.* The people are parents who for different reasons deeply dislike what is happening, or what they fear may happen, to their children in school, and who want to take or keep them out of school and teach them, or help them learn, at home and in any other parts of the world they can make accessible to them. Their situation is difficult, painful, and even dangerous because the schools almost always oppose this effort and threaten them with prosecution in court, fines, even jail, and the loss of their children; and also, because they usually do not know anyone else who is doing or wants to do the same thing, or who understands why they want to do it and therefore supports them.

Of the material in the magazine, some is written by me; some is quoted from other books, magazines, news stories, court decisions, etc.; some is in lists, announcements, etc.; and the largest part is made up of letters from the parents themselves. Topics include: (1) reasons for taking children out of school, perhaps general criticisms of schools and their methods, perhaps simply accounts of bad things that schools have done to children; (2) ways of approaching and dealing with schools and school people; (3) discussions of laws and court decisions, what these are, how to look them up, what they mean, how to use them; (4) legal and other stratagems by which people may get children out of school, such as enrolling them in out-of-state schools, registering one's own home as a school, etc.; (5) alternate educational resources, such as correspondence schools, books, textbooks, teaching materials, etc.; (6) discussions about children, their nature and needs, their relations with adults, their ways of learning things, their reactions to different kinds of teaching, etc.; (7) recommended books about or for children; (8) ways of teaching reading, arithmetic, and other subjects; (9) names and addresses of people (often with names and ages of their children) who want to correspond with others on this subject; and (10) accounts by parents of their actual home-teaching experiences. And so on.

These materials have proved immensely encouraging and helpful to many of our readers. Hundreds have written to say, "I thought no one else felt as I did"; "Without you, we never would have had the courage to do this"; "I no longer feel so alone and helpless"; and so on. Our readers, like people in any new and difficult social situation, are relieved and strengthened to learn that they are not alone, that others have experienced, thought, and felt the same things, have learned things that may be helpful, and are willing to help.

This does not cost much. We type our copy in the office, then send it to a commercial printer to be reduced in size and offset printed. Using a fairly good grade of paper (since we mail copies unwrapped), we are able to send each one of our (as I write) two thousand subscribers information for less than a penny per thousand words. We could do it for even less if we had more subscribers or used cheaper paper (which we will probably do before long), and still more cheaply if we bought a second-hand offset press—I have been told that there are many of these around—and did our own printing.

What has this to do with our city poor? One of the many disadvantages of being poor is that unless you or your friends are the victims of some disaster or accused of some crime, you never see your names in the paper, you can't send out messages, make your words heard or seen by others. Rich people can easily do this. Their voices carry hundreds or thousands of miles. By now, most of us, certainly most poor people, think that *only* rich people can send out messages. The written word, like the law, seems to *belong* to them. If poor people seem to have little interest in reading or writing, it is not because of bad genes or bad character or bad neighborhoods, but in large part because they have no reason to believe that the written word belongs or could belong to them, that they could use it to make known, or get, or do some of the things they want.

This is probably not much changed by the fact that a few non-whites are able to succeed as writers, get published, be famous, nor would it be much changed even if there were many more such writers. At one time, many people thought that once black children knew about books like *The Autobiography of Malcolm X*, etc., they would quickly learn to read so that they could read them. It turned out to be not as easy as that. The odds are good that many more white students, particularly affluent ones, have read about Malcolm than black students. No doubt it would still be helpful if more black children knew of such books and could easily get hold of them. But there must be many black people who know that some blacks are successful and famous writers, but who nonetheless have little interest in reading and writing themselves. Famous writers, after all, are like famous athletes or entertainment stars. They are, in a way, freaks, interesting to look at, but having nothing to do with the lives of ordinary people. What is needed are ways in which the written word may be made more *immediately* interesting and useful to ordinary people. Only if most of the adults that children see around them regularly *make use of* written words will children then be interested in those words.

The paper I publish, and it is only one of the newest and smallest of many special-interest publications, may be a useful rough model for a kind of local community or neighborhood paper that might help to do this. Rich city neighborhoods tend to be rich in information as well as everything else. My home city of Boston, and above all my neighborhoods—Beacon Hill and Back Bay—are very information-rich. Our main daily paper has, along with a large classified ad section, a weekly list of interesting resources and events. Two weekly "radical" newspapers have their own classified sections and calendars, full of the rather different information that interests their readers, mostly people between twenty and forty. Both the Beacon Hill and Back Bay communities have small weekly newspapers, supported by advertising and distributed free in stores, that carry other information of local interest. This part of town is full of health food stores and restaurants, almost all of which have bulletin boards covered with information about apartments, roommates, courses and classes, rides to other places, etc. Two monthly publications exist solely to tell people about second-hand goods of many kinds that other people want to sell. There are, in short, many ways in which people who live in or move into our part of town can find out about the things they want and need to know. But these sources of information are neither particularly useful nor easily available to people in the poorer sections of the city, and there are few if any comparable sources of information for them.

We can make some fair guesses about some of the kinds of information that might be very interesting and useful to poor city people, and that they might be glad to exchange freely with each other if they had a way to do so. Just in living their lives, surviving, getting by, they have to deal with a great many people who, depending on how they feel, can either help them or hinder or hurt them—landlords, repairmen, building inspectors, truant officers, teachers, counselors, school administrators, youth workers, welfare workers, rent control workers, health workers, social workers, doctors, lawyers, police. Probably not many of these people are really helpful, but some may be more helpful than others, and it would help other poor people to know who they were. Also, some of the poor who have to deal with all these officials have probably worked out fairly effective ways to do this, which it would also help others to know.

Poor neighborhoods are much poorer than rich ones in essential services. Where I live, I don't have to go far to get clothes washed, or cleaned, or repaired, or shoes soled, or a car fixed (if I owned one), or to buy food, or medicine, or reading matter, or any of the other things I need. Poor people usually have to go a lot further to find such places and people, and further yet to find good, honest, or reliable ones. These are important things to know—where in a given neighborhood can you get good cheap food, or clothes? Where can you go to get medicine, to get a prescription filled, to see a doctor? What stores will give some credit? Who can fix shoes, or appliances, or radios or TV sets, or cars? What businesses (if any) can you trust?

In addition, since poor people have been pushed out of the money economy, money is no longer for them a useful medium of exchange. They need to find ways to exchange such skills as they have. Many of our *voluntary* poor have learned to do this. The columns of *Mother*

Earth News are full of stories about how people living (by their own choice) in the country with little money have been able to exchange many kinds of goods and skills with others like themselves. They understand very well a basic law of personal economics: if you only get paid two or three dollars an hour (or nothing at all) for your own work, you can't afford to pay other people five or ten dollars an hour to do anything for you that you could learn to do for yourself, or that you can find someone else to do for you, in exchange for something you *can* do. If you can make bread, or something else that other people now have to buy in stores, and if some of these other people can make or fix clothes or other things that you need, it would help you to get together and make a swap, and so bypass the people who, for doing these things, earn much more money than you.

It might be true (or might not) that most poor inner-city neighborhoods are not very rich in skills, compared with country towns or even those same city neighborhoods fifty or a hundred years ago. But there is surely a much bigger pool of skills than anyone in those neighborhoods knows about. And there are many other kinds of acts, not requiring any great skill, that people could do for each other. There might be many old people who would, for example, be willing to take care of other people's children for a while in return, say, for having some meals cooked or an apartment cleaned. There are many mothers who work, and so for whom shopping is a terrible problem. At the same time, there are, and tragically, large numbers of young men and women who have no work at all. Many people desperately short of time, many others with nothing but time on their hands. Some of these could surely make some useful swaps with each other. Young people might do some shopping, older people might watch children, in return for having meals cooked or clothes mended, or other kinds of help.

But I do not mean to suggest that this imaginary neighborhood paper would be only a medium of exchange of technical information. I am thinking about *Growing Without Schooling* as I write this, and while it is true that the people who write the letters we publish exchange much useful information about ways to deal with school people, about the laws and the courts, about good books and teaching materials, about the ways they have helped their children to learn this or that, the most valuable thing they give each other is something quite different. In telling about their experiences they also tell how they felt, and so, say to each other, "I know what you're going through, because I went through it myself. You're not the first or only person to feel this way." As people in many political movements, perhaps most notably the women's movement, have found, it is enormously reassuring and strengthening to know that what you are going through, others have gone through, and have somehow survived it, learned from it, grown from it. Of course, no amount of writing or reading could make the experience of living in a poor city neighborhood in the U.S. in the year 1980 *good* for people. It is not therapeutic. But people would find that experience far more bearable if they had more ways to share it with others.

As I said, one of the things we publish in *Growing Without Schooling* is a directory, a list of the names and addresses of people who choose to list themselves, so that others, if they wish, may get in touch with them. Many people have begun to correspond with others whose names they found in this way. Some have made strong friendships. I know two mothers, living many thousands of miles apart, who have become perhaps each other's best friends, and since they share a great deal of their correspondence with me (so that I can use parts of it in *Growing Without Schooling*), I know how much this friendship means to them in the (in some ways) difficult present circumstances of their lives. How to make such friendships in a city? If you were poor, living in a big city, how, except through blind luck, could you possibly find those few people who most deeply shared your ideas, needs, and concerns?

But is this literature? I don't know why not. I am constantly bowled over by the quality of the *writing* in the letters people send me. They are astonishingly clear, direct, vivid, evocative, personal, and moving, and they make our little magazine one of the most interesting publications I know. I am using many of these letters in the book I am writing about home education. Do letters become literature only when they appear in a book? In any case, if these small, homely, personal exchanges of experience, ideas, and feelings are not literature, they are surely the raw material and seedbed of literature. I have no doubt that the home-schooling movement will produce its share of books over the years—in fact, it has produced some already. In the same way, any community in which more and more people get into the habit of writing to and for each other about their lives will surely before long develop a number of "writers," that is, people who write "all the time," who write for money, who make writing their main work.

One last question. Even if we could solve all the financial and technical problems of getting such papers written, edited, financed, printed, distributed, and used, are there enough people in poor city neighborhoods who *can* write to make such papers possible? What about all this talk about the illiteracy of the poor? I put very little stock in it. I think that most people can quickly learn to speak and write very well when they have something to say and people they want to say it to.

For a while, some friends of mine were corresponding with some men in the Death Row of an Alabama prison. These men could hardly have had more than a few years of schooling, or many occasions to write since they left school. Yet their letters, describing their plight, feelings, and hopes, were not far removed from standard English, and were forceful and eloquent. My office colleague listens regularly to WILD, a black radio station in Boston. The people who call in are ordinary people, yet most of them use language clearly and expressively. In his book, *The Naked Children*, Daniel Fader told of getting to know five children in a Washington, D.C., junior high school. On the basis of its many tests and what it could observe, the school declared that these children could barely read or even speak. After they came to know him well enough so that they were willing to reveal themselves to him, Fader found, not only that these children could read at a good level for their age, but that they could speak about a 95 percent standard English in situations where they felt it would be to their credit or advantage to do so.

Perhaps these examples are not typical. I am not saying that every single person in our inner-city communities is articulate and literate. But I am saying that there is surely a large enough pool of language skill to make possible the kind of small, informal, cheap neighborhood newspapers I have talked about here. When or whether we shall ever see such papers, I have no idea. If and when we do, I think they will prove to be powerful weapons in the struggles of people not just against illiteracy, but against poverty, powerlessness, and despair.

Note

1. At the Conference on Literature and the Urban Experience at Rutgers, April 19, 1980, one person raised her hand, and later told me that such research had been done by Professor Kenneth Goodman at the University of Arizona in Tucson. I wrote to Professor Goodman. His wife, also a professor at the university, very kindly replied, enclosing a paper of her own and telling me of research that both she and her husband, as well as some others, had done. On first glance, it seems to support strongly my views about the ability of children to learn important things without being taught. However, it does seem to be more about *how* children grasp reading without instruction than about how many do. I still have yet to hear of any research of this latter kind.

Notes on the Authors

JAMES BALDWIN is a novelist, essayist, and activist. His works include *Go Tell It On the Mountain* (1953), *Notes of a Native Son* (1955), *Another Country* (1962), *The Fire Next Time* (1963), *No Name in the Street* (1972), *If Beale Street Could Talk* (1975), *The Devil Finds Work* (1976), and *Just Above My Head* (1979).

AMIRI BARAKA, poet, playwright, and political activist, is the author of such plays as *Dutchman* (1964), *The Slave* (1964), *Black Mass* (1966), *The Toilet* (1967), and *Slave Ship* (1969). In addition, he has published several volumes of stories, poems, and essays. His most recent works are *Selected Poems* and *Selected Prose and Drama* (1979).

BRUNO BETTELHEIM is a psychologist and educator who has written extensively on perception and the environment. His many writings include *Love is Not Enough—The Treatment of Emotionally Disturbed Children* (1950), *The Informed Heart* (1960), *The Children of the Dream* (1969), *The Uses of Enchantment* (1976), and *Surviving, and Other Essays* (1979).

JOAN N. BURSTYN, Professor and Chairperson of the Education Department at Douglass College of Rutgers University, and Associate Editor of *Signs: Journal of Women in Culture and Society*, has written numerous articles and has lectured on education throughout the country. She is the author of *Victorian Education and the Idea of Womanhood* (1980).

RICHARD EDER, following a career as foreign correspondent, Washington Bureau correspondent, and film critic for the *New York Times*, served for three years as drama critic and writer on intellectual and cultural subjects for the *New York Times*. He is currently head of the Paris Bureau of the *Times*.

LAWRENCE FERLINGHETTI—poet, novelist, playwright, translator, and publisher—is part of the continuing San Francisco poetry movement. His work, from *Pictures of the Gone World* (1955) and *A Coney Island of the Mind* (1958), through *Landscapes of Living and Dying* (1979), has continually drawn upon his urban background and experience.

LESLIE FIEDLER is a professor at the State University of New York at Buffalo. His works include *The Image of the Jew in American Fiction* (1959), *Love and Death in the American Novel* (1960), *The Return of the Vanishing American* (1967), *Freaks* (1977), and *A Fiedler Reader* (1979).

IHAB HASSAN, born in Egypt and a naturalized American citizen since 1956, is a professor at the University of Wisconsin and the author of the following books on modern literature: *Radical Innocence: Studies in the Contemporary American Novel* (1961), *The Literature of Silence* (1967), *The Dismemberment of Orpheus: Toward a Postmodern Literature* (1971), *Paracriticisms* (1975), and *The Right Promethean Fire* (1980).

JOHN HOLT, since the publication in the mid 1960s of his two works on American education, *How Children Fail* and *How Children Learn*, has been a writer and speaker on educational theory and practice. His more recent work, emphasizing adult education and the teaching of children at home, includes books—*Escape from Childhood* (1974), *Instead of Education* (1976), and *Never Too Late: A Musical Autobiography* (1978)—lectures, and the publication of a bi-monthly magazine, *Growing Without Schooling*.

DAVID IGNATOW teaches at York College in the City University of New York. He is poet and author of *Figures of the Human* (1964), *Facing the Tree* (1964), *Rescue the Dead* (1968), and more recently, *Tread the Dark* (1978).

ALFRED KAZIN, currently a professor at City University of New York Graduate School, is an author, critic, editor, and lecturer. His writings include *On Native Grounds* (1942), *A Walker in the City* (1951), *The Inmost Leaf* (1955), *Contemporaries* (1962), *Starting Out in the Thirties* (1965), *Bright Book of Life* (1973), and *New York Jew* (1978).

JERRE MANGIONE, currently Professor Emeritus of American Literature at the University of Pennsylvania and Visiting Professor at Queens College, has written extensively on the experience of the ethnic immigrant in American cities, especially in the 1930s and 1940s. His recent writings include *The Dream and the Deal: The Federal Writers' Project, 1935–1943* (1972), and *An Ethnic at Large: A Memoir of America in the Thirties and Forties* (1978), as well as numerous articles, short stories, and book reviews in journals and periodicals. One of his best-known books is *Mount Allegro* (1943).

LEO MARX, William R. Kenan, Jr., Professor of American Cultural History at M.I.T., is a lecturer, editor of Thoreau and Whitman, and author of *The Machine in the Garden* (1964) and articles on American cultural history.

TONI MORRISON'S novels include *The Bluest Eye* (1969), *Sula* (1974), *Song of Solomon* (1977), and *Tar Baby* (1981). In addition, she is a senior editor for Random House and is a member of the Authors Guild Council and the New York State Council on the Humanities.

JOYCE CAROL OATES' work includes novels, short stories, poetry, drama, and criticism—both literary and cultural. Her recent books are *The Assassins* (1975), *Crossing the Border* (1976), *Childwold* (1977), *Night-Side* (1977), *Son of the Morning* (1978), *Unholy Loves* (1979), *Bellefleur* (1980), *A Sentimental Education* (1980), *Three Plays* (1980), and *Angel of Light* (1981). She is Visiting Professor at Princeton in the Creative Writing Program, a co-editor of the *Ontario Review*, and a member of the American Academy and Institute of Arts and Letters.

MARGE PIERCY is a novelist, poet, lecturer, and author of several volumes of poetry including *Breaking Camp* (1968), *Hard Loving* (1969), and *To Be of Use* (1973). She has written a number of novels which deal with the contemporary American scene, including *Small Changes* (1973), and more recently, *Woman on the Edge of Time* (1976) and *The High Cost of Living* (1978). She has also published *Living in the Open* (poetry, 1976), *The Twelve-Spoked Wheel Flashing* (poetry, 1978), *Vida* (1980), and *The Moon is Always Female* (poetry, 1980).

CHAIM POTOK is the author of the novels *The Chosen* (1967), *The Promise* (1969), *My Name is Asher Lev* (1972), and *In the Beginning* (1975). Most recently, he has published *Wanderings* (1978), a history of the Jewish people.

PEDRO JUAN SOTO, Professor of Spanish and Spanish-American literature at the University of Puerto Rico, is a journalist, short-story writer, dramatist, and novelist. His works include *Ardiente suelo, fría estación* (1961), *El francotirador* (1969), and *Temporada de duendes* (1970).

STEPHEN SPENDER is a British poet, critic, and essayist. His many works include *The Still Center* (1936), *World Within World* (1951), *Selected Poems* (1964), *Love-Hate Relations: English vs. American Sensibilities* (1974), and *The Thirties & After* (1979). In addition, he has written biographies of T. S. Eliot, D. H. Lawrence, Henry Moore, and a soon-to-be published biography of W. H. Auden.

HELEN VENDLER is a critic, lecturer, and, currently, Poetry Reviewer for *The New Yorker*. She has written *Yeats's Vision and the Later Plays* (1963), *On Extended Wings: Wallace Stevens' Later Poetry* (1969), and *The Poetry of George Herbert* (1975). Some of her numerous essays are collected in *Part of Nature, Part of Us* (1980).

M. JERRY WEISS, Distinguished Service Professor of Communications at Jersey City State College, is a contributor to a number of journals specializing in education and communications. He has edited collections of plays, humor, and essays on education.